LAW SCHOOL SCHOOL LABYRINTH

SECOND EDITION

A GUIDE TO MAKING
THE MOST OF YOUR
LEGAL EDUCATION

STEVEN R. SEDBERRY

KAPLAN PUBLISHING

New York

This publication is designed to provide accurate and authoritative information in regard to the subject matter covered. It is sold with the understanding that the publisher is not engaged in rendering legal, accounting, or other professional service. If legal advice or other expert assistance is required, the services of a competent professional should be sought.

Published by Kaplan Publishing, a division of Kaplan, Inc.
395 Hudson Street
New York, NY 10014

Printed in the United States of America

Library of Congress Cataloging-in-Publication Data

Sedberry, Steven R.
   Law school labyrinth : a guide to making the most of your legal education / by Steven R. Sedberry.
      p. cm.
   Includes index.
   ISBN 978-1-60714-861-6
   1. Law students—United States—Handbooks, manuals, etc.   2. Law—Study and teaching—United States.   I. Title.
   KF283.S43 2009
   340.071'173—dc22   2008048725

10 9 8 7 6 5 4 3 2 1

Kaplan Publishing books are available at special quantity discounts to use for sales promotions, employee premiums, or educational purposes. Please email our Special Sales Department to order or for more information at *kaplanpublishing@kaplan.com*, or write to Kaplan Publishing, 395 Hudson Street, New York, NY 10014.

Again, for the girls—Beth, Meredith, and Lauren.

Contents

Preface to the Second Edition

When *Law School Labyrinth* was published in 2009, the economy was cruising along and all of us passengers were largely oblivious to what lay just around the corner. People were buying houses with nothing down and spending money like there was no tomorrow. The legal economy was no different. Law firms were hiring like crazy, offering huge salaries to new graduates who probably never earned much more than minimum wage. Law students with huge debts were confident that a big six-figure paycheck would make quick work of any outstanding loans. Life was good.

And then the bottom fell out.

The stock market began its herky-jerky spasm that resulted in an almost 2,000 point decline. We began to read terms in the papers like "subprime mortgage" and "synthetic collateralized debt obligation" that described, at least in part, the faulty premise upon which much of the red-hot economy had been based. Almost overnight, the global economy teetered on the verge of collapse. Employers stopped hiring and laid workers off.

The legal economy was even worse. Law school graduates, formerly courted in summer-long recruiting extravaganzas, were unable to find employment. Big law firms rescinded job offers. At the same time, social media sites began to gain incredible traction. People from disparate backgrounds were suddenly bonding in a way our world has never before experienced, sharing everything from our greatest fears to what we had for breakfast that day. Anyone who could type had a blog. Some were articulate, informative, and amusing. Others were simply the new millennium version of a primal scream—anger-filled, profanity-laced rantings. But everyone was having their 15 minutes of fame.

My first tweet about two years ago was hesitant and banal, something along the lines of, "Hello, this is my first tweet." I wondered whether it would simply end up in a void somewhere. To my surprise, I gained a new follower within seconds. I began to hear from people, and in particular law students and students contemplating law school. Emboldened, I expanded my horizons. The *Law School Labyrinth* fan page has become a fun, engaging forum for prelaws, law students, and lawyers.

After the economic collapse, many predicted that law school enrollment would dry up. The big law firm model no longer worked, they announced. Books and blogs were dedicated to eviscerating legal education and the profession. Suddenly the "disaffected lawyer" was in vogue. People who loved to hate lawyers loved the fact that big firms had stopped hiring. "See? We told you," they crowed.

And yet, ironically, law school has become an even more likely destination for students. Perhaps it's the "hide in grad school until the economy recovers" phenomenon. But as I became more imbedded into social media, I was amazed at the similarities among these students, especially in terms of their worries and hopes about law school. Despite the economy, they were determined to graduate from law school. The economy will change; it always has and always will.

The real question to anyone facing the law school decision is simple: "Do I really want to be a lawyer?" Prospective law school students should ask this introspective question regardless of the state of the economy. The law school labyrinth has always been a crucible of sorts. It's tough, demanding, and it will probably change you in a profound way. And anyone who isn't committed to the process and ultimate outcome will likely find dissatisfaction.

Why would anyone want to become a lawyer? My own opinion is that lawyers are in one of the best positions in our society to help people. And any first-year law student approached by someone during Christmas break with a problem can recognize the power of the profession to help others.

Sure, some law students are more concerned with getting accepted into top tier schools, making Law Review, and choosing between several big prestigious firms. But many care more about passing the bar exam, choosing a practice area, career satisfaction, and finding a job. And there are jobs out there. You just have to be a bit more creative to find them. Marketable skills, which will translate well into the job market, are critical.

We have updated this book in the hopes of making it even more useful to law school students and those considering a career in the law. The first edition of *Law School Labyrinth* provided an overview of the law school experience, insight into various law student activities, and most importantly, a methodology that law students can use in order to be prepared for the onslaught long before they set foot in the classroom.

This edition is supplemented with new ideas on law school success. In addition, we discuss areas relevant to recent law graduates and new lawyers not covered in the first edition, including ethics and what the "character and fitness" to practice law means. We include information on how to use the Internet to your advantage in law school and law practice.

After the first edition of *Law School Labyrinth* was released, I realized to my chagrin that I had not acknowledged the massive help and support I received from people in the writing of the book. I shall hereby attempt to rectify that mistake. First of all, I would like to thank the entire Kaplan Publishing team for their confidence in me as a new author and for their incredible professionalism in developing, editing, publishing, and marketing the book. I could not have asked for a more supportive publisher. Second, I thank my wife Beth, whose patience and support during the writing of the first edition, as well as this one, were invaluable to this author. She is my biggest fan and critic; both contributed to making this book what it is.

Finally, I thank the readers (and my social media buddies) who have reached out and asked questions and made observations about the subject matter of this book. I am flattered and thankful that you took the time to read and comment on *Law School Labyrinth*. This edition was written with you in mind.

—Steven R. Sedberry

Introduction

JAMES[1] **SAT IN AN** uncomfortable chair in the large, stark law school auditorium looking around the room. The institutional fluorescent lighting harshly illuminated the room. His chair had a revolving base that was bolted to the floor in front of a shabby table, alongside six other equally uncomfortable chairs. There was a dull din created by the tittering of fellow neophytes scattered around the auditorium and an electricity of sorts in the air on that early morning of the first semester. Today was the first day of class.

Although other first-year law students, or "1Ls," were seated throughout the auditorium, the first three or four rows of seating were empty. Clearly, no one wanted to sit at the front. Some 1Ls sat in clusters of

---

[1] All references to professors, people, law schools, and events herein are fictitious and are instead based upon an amalgamation of my law school experience, both real and imagined, and those of various law students with whom I am acquainted. Accordingly, any resemblance to existing people is purely coincidental.

two or three students, chatting nervously. Other 1Ls sat alone, looking as if they were waiting to be summoned for some serious medical procedure. Still others laughed and talked somehow too loudly, their false bravado betraying the reality of their stomach-churning panic, boiling just beneath those facades of confidence.

Now that he was actually in law school, the reality of it all had begun to settle in. The night before, James had read dozens of pages of the most dense and difficult material he had ever encountered. Most of it made little sense. The assignment was to read several judicial appellate opinions contained in the new casebooks, referred to by law students and lawyers as *cases*. The various class reading assignments had been mysteriously posted on the student bulletin board the day before. No one told James to check the board. He had simply overheard a couple of students talking about it. If that hadn't happened, he would have shown up for class that first day completely unprepared.

So the first thing James learned about law school was assume nothing; question everything. James silently thanked those two students yet again and wondered how many other lessons lurked somewhere in this labyrinth. *Labyrinth,* James thought, and he vaguely remembered something about a raging Minotaur, half man and half beast, waiting to destroy the unwary. He ruefully congratulated himself on this apt metaphor; however, the thought of his own cleverness brought little comfort as he waited for the professor to arrive.

The night before class, James had feebly attempted to brief the cases. Regardless, all of the reading was now a veritable jurisprudential jambalaya. He did these briefs because he was terrified of the infamous Socratic method. James had seen all the movies about law school in which the curmudgeonly professor eviscerates student after student in the Socratic dialogue with a series of relentless questions which did not seem to have any point or conclusion, leaving the students red-faced and humiliated. And as he sat there, he seriously doubted that he would even be able to remember the names of the various parties to the lawsuit, who had sued whom, or even what had started the lawsuit in the first place.

James was startled from this classroom reverie when the professor suddenly entered the room. Professor Davis wore a well-tailored suit with a crisp, wing-collared starched shirt and a very stylish silk tie. He was a respected and esteemed professor, scholar, and the author of a number of casebooks and treatises. He had a youthful maturity, an incredibly polished appearance, and somehow looked substantially more intimidating than a crusty old movie professor. In the movies, the crusty old professor had a heart. Whether the same was true of Professor Davis remained to be seen.

The auditorium stage lights gave Professor Davis an almost theatrical appearance. His meticulous grooming suggested a meticulous mind. And yet, as he looked about the auditorium, he had the detached, primal air of a tiger surveying his prey on the Nepalese grasslands. At that moment, Davis seemed larger than life, almost superhuman. He opened a notebook, which contained a classroom seating chart of students (including a photograph of each taken at orientation, just in case someone were to try and hide) and stared intently for what seemed like a very long time.

He peered over the seating chart through half-rimmed spectacles at the class of about a hundred students and smiled. Although Davis's smile was well constructed of perfect teeth, accentuated by a mouth upturned at each corner, this was not a smile that said "nice to meet you." Davis's eyes betrayed the fact that the tiger hadn't made a kill yet that morning. And this tiger knew he would eat soon.

The apprehension, which was so perceptible in the auditorium only moments before, now turned to a collective mood of abject terror. The silence of the 1Ls, who had been tittering only moments before, was now deafening. Davis looked to stage left of the auditorium, paused for what seemed like at least a minute, closed the notebook, and asked detachedly, "Mr. Brown, should a five-year-old child be held liable for battery?"

The assigned reading was *Garratt v. Dailey*, an arcane case about a little boy who had moved a lawn chair, causing an elderly arthritic woman to fall and be injured as she attempted to sit down. *Garratt* is a classic case, often the first case read by neophyte law students. The issue presented in the case was whether little Dailey possessed the intent necessary for old Mrs. Garratt to sustain a lawsuit for battery.

James breathed a deep and audible sigh of relief. The entire class looked around the room to see who the lucky Mr. Brown was.

A lanky jurist-in-waiting, wearing a tattered ball cap embroidered with the phrase "Rock On!" looked up from his notepad, where he had been doodling only moments before, obviously startled. "Deer in the headlights" would be a gross understatement. One of the zombie extras from a late night fright classic movie was more apt. The poor fellow was absolutely apoplectic.

It seemed that the entire class turned in unison to look at Mr. Brown, who now, with mouth agape and eyes resembling ping-pong balls with pupils, appeared to be completely paralyzed. Mr. Brown came to eventually, quickly closing his mouth and looking intently into his casebook. He looked at his notes, then up at Professor Davis, and then back down at the book. He responded to Professor Davis's question.

"Uh . . . no," he stammered, again looking up at the professor and down frantically, as if the answer to the question had somehow evaporated. The look on Mr. Brown's face said, *I know it's here somewhere.* He added, "Uh . . . sir," almost apologetically.

Davis was no longer smiling. The silence in the large auditorium was deafening. He asked, "And why not, Mr. Brown?"

Faced with this unexpected second wave of attack, Mr. Brown visibly attempted to defend himself. He sat up a bit straighter. He cleared his throat. He looked directly at Professor Davis, down at his casebook, and back at Professor Davis. *Maybe he was going to actually do this, he was going to go mano a mano with Professor Davis in the Socratic dialogue!* James became almost giddy in anticipation. *Go for it, Mr. Brown,* he thought. And yet, deep down inside, a part of James knew that somehow a snare had been set, and the truth was that there was no way out for Mr. Brown.

Mr. Brown looked at Professor Davis and stammered out his reply, "Uh, because he was too young to be held legally responsible." *Good for him,* James thought. "Legally responsible" at least sounded like something a lawyer would say. Maybe Mr. Brown was going to get a reprieve after all.

Davis paused for what seemed like at least five minutes. He stared intently at Mr. Brown. Finally, he turned from him, looked at his watch, and sighed. "Thank you for that deep and cogent analysis, Mr. Brown," he said almost as an afterthought. Had Professor Davis been a spitting man, it is almost certain that he would have expectorated in punctuation.

As the irony of Professor Davis's "compliment" sunk in, several students laughed, then a few more. Within seconds, half of the auditorium was laughing uproariously.

It was then that James learned another key truth about law school. Here, we quickly learn to feed upon our own. We will also do just about anything to avoid becoming dinner. Survival of the fittest and all that.

Davis very dramatically reopened and studied his seating chart. Mr. Brown flushed a deep and glowing red, waiting for the next question with which he would redeem himself. It never came. He gave a slow and almost pleading look around the room. Davis called on his next prey, er, student.

Welcome to law school, James thought.

Chapter 1

Lessons from the Labyrinth, or How I Learned to Stop Worrying and Start Booking Classes

A LABYRINTH IS A MAZE of confusing and seemingly endless passages, often circular and filled with dead ends and wrong turns. According to Greek myth, Daedalus created the first labyrinth. He used it to imprison the Minotaur, a fearsome beast, half man and half bull. Woe to those hapless and unsuspecting souls who found themselves in this labyrinth. Generally, no one made it out alive. One day, an unfortunate fellow by the name of Theseus found himself entrapped in the labyrinth. However, by following a magical golden thread back to the entrance, Theseus was able to find his way out.

The road to success in law school and law practice is an emotional and intellectual labyrinth, which continues throughout your professional career. You may find yourself traveling down winding paths and rabbit trails that don't appear to lead anywhere. On occasion, you may face an apparent dead end, which turns out to be merely a detour. As you traverse the labyrinth, doors to intellectual "Eurekas!" may open suddenly, only to quickly close again. The journey is winding and circuitous, and the law school portion may lead you to believe that there is no end in sight. The labyrinth is demanding, at times fickle, and always unrelenting.

Think of this book as your personal golden thread to guide you through the law school labyrinth.

I began my own journey into the law school labyrinth with literally no idea or thought as to how to make my way through it. Law school was a lifelong goal for me and I was just glad to be there. I had dreams of changing the world and helping to fight injustice. Like many of you, I longed to become involved in causes about which I could become passionate in a collegial environment. Prior to law school, I had anticipated intellectually stimulating discussions and debates with colleagues regarding the history and principles of law. I imagined that these discussions would be gently guided by dedicated professors who had mastered their craft. I believed that law schools had evolved beyond the crusty old professor humiliating students during the Socratic dialogue. Instead, I found law school to pretty much be what most law students claim it is. In law school, I found confusion, fear, excessive competitiveness, and chaos all around me.

Having spent a number of years in the business world prior to law school, I understood that the key to solving any problem is to understand the discrete processes that influence it. I refused to accept the mystique surrounding law school. Instead, I began to identify and analyze the variables that contributed to a law student's success or failure. Using myself as a guinea pig, I experimented with my study approach. I realized that law school presents a paradox to the neophyte law student. On the one hand, law school appears to be all about the process—the analysis, logic, and debate that students of all types love. The Socratic method, for example, can facilitate an endless debate on a particular point of law. Students can argue minutiae and factual details ad nauseam. Because there is so much ego and insecurity involved, the Socratic Method can deceive students into thinking that it is law school. As a result, new law students mistakenly immerse themselves in the classroom to the exclusion of everything else.

It's only when their first-semester grades come in that they realize there is much more to being a successful law student than free-flowing analysis. It's also about knowing the law and being able to solve legal problems, and doing so when it counts—at exam time.

I began to do less of what most law students think they should do, i.e., mindlessly reading and briefing cases. Lawyers typically refer to the recorded judicial opinions as *cases*; cases are written by the judge and explain what the law is and the rationale for it, as authored by the deciding judge. This book uses the terms *judicial* and *appellate opinions*, *decisions*, and *cases* interchangeably; they mean the same thing. *Cases* are the currency by which a judge conveys the law. I began to spend more time trying to understand the big picture of the law. To my surprise, my grades began to improve dramatically. My new study approach required less time, and I found that I actually developed a better understanding of the material.

This book will provide you with that strategic approach to law study, through the Pyramid Outline™ method described later in this book. The purpose of this approach is to help you invest your precious study time in such a way as to yield the greatest return on your investment and specifically to help you optimize your chances of making good grades. A repeated theme throughout this book is that law school is the first step in your development as a lawyer. And in my opinion, grades are a good predictor of your success as a lawyer. Simply put, doing well in law school means that you are on your way to developing the skills necessary for a successful legal career.

In addition, this book discusses the various career paths and options for lawyers. Many students make the law school decision naively, frequently based upon an unrealistic idea of what lawyers actually do. This book will give you a realistic perspective of what being a lawyer is like, which will help you to make an informed career decision. A lot of social media gurus would have you believe that all new lawyers are miserable. I believe that the practice of law is one of the most rewarding careers imaginable. But as with any career, there are pluses and minuses. Understanding both will go a long way toward avoiding unexpected career dissatisfaction.

Since graduating from law school and passing two bar exams, I have spoken with literally hundreds of law school graduates about their experiences. Most people are very willing to talk about law school—the stress and difficulty of it all are emblazoned forever into one's memory. Like survivors of a war, there is a common thread among all law students that creates a solidarity, regardless of their law school. And this common experience is the canvas upon which the suggestions, techniques, and methodologies are applied in this book.

Law school will, if you let it, teach you an entirely new way of thinking. Unlike professionals in many other disciplines, lawyers must consistently think and reason analytically and logically, communicate clearly with assertions always factually supported, and do all of this in an efficient and effective manner.

But in law school, the professor can make you feel stupid. Smart people who feel stupid are usually more willing to learn. And for the first time in your academic career, things may not come so easily to you. You have to work through dense passages of indecipherable reading material. You take notes and even your own notes don't make sense. The ever-present threat of exams looms in the not-too-distant future. Coupled with the headlines about lawyer layoffs and law student debt, you may find yourself discouraged and questioning your own capabilities.

My message to you is this: enjoy the experience. Think of law school the way you think of any other necessary but painful activity, like training for a competition. The pain is worth the gain. In law school, I assure you that you will learn more than at any other time in your life. You are only a few short years away from a law license and a legal career and the ability to have a hugely positive effect on people and our society as a whole.

You may be asking yourself, "But how do I deal with the immediate threats? The Socratic method, exams, and the like?" This book will help you deal with those threats and traverse the labyrinth. It will provide you with a solid study methodology, which will help you reduce the flailing about that many 1Ls (and some 2Ls) do. Adopt the methodology, or adapt it to your own style. But above all else, have a plan of attack for law school. It will ultimately enable you to enjoy the law school experience that much more.

There truly is light at the end of the tunnel. Law school is difficult, but you will survive it. If you stick with it, you will graduate and obtain your license to practice law. You will become a lawyer. You just will.

MY LAW SCHOOL ORIENTATION

I will never forget the crisp September morning of my law school orientation. It was one of those sneak peek days into the beautiful fall season to come. The temperature was about 50 degrees. The aroma of a fireplace burning wafted past me as I pulled into campus. The sun was rising as I made my way from the campus parking garage to 1L Orientation. I was finally fulfilling a dream I had harbored for the past 20 years. I was actually going to law school. In life, fulfilled dreams are so rare. I wanted to relish this one for as long as I could.

A million things were running through my mind. Every Hollywood stereotype in recent memory seemed to come back to me. I kept thinking about the curmudgeonly law professor's disgust with the hapless 1L in the early scenes of a movie I had seen years earlier. I wondered if I would end up like the character I remembered from another movie from the mid-1990s. The lawyer won the case, but looked more like a disreputable used car salesman than a lawyer. I certainly hoped I would turn out more like the archetypal 1950s lawyer fighting for truth, justice, and the American way.

I found my way to the foyer of a large auditorium with what appeared to be several hundred other nervous 1Ls. The registrar had set up check-in tables, and I took my place in the line marked by a placard that said: "Welcome to Vanderbilt Law School." As I advanced through the line, I noted that little student cliques had already begun to form around me. Groups of students, who I knew had just met a few minutes ago, laughed jovially as people do when greeting old friends. In a setting as intimidating as law school, it seems that students become so insecure that they are drawn to each other immediately, in an almost defensive circling of the wagons. This almost instinctive behavior of huddling in cliques continues throughout law school and, to a lesser extent, in law practice.

As I made my way through the line, I was greeted by a smiling administrative assistant with a badge that said: "Hi! My Name Is Sara!" Sara directed me to the "Qs–Ts," where I was given a name tag. I then made small talk with a couple of other students I had seen in the line.

Shortly before orientation was scheduled to begin, students began to herd themselves into the auditorium. I took a seat in the front row, next to a guy who appeared to be preparing to take notes (I learned later that sitting in the front row is indicative of a "gunner" and a sure way to alienate yourself from your peers). He began to write and I nervously tried to read what in the world could possibly be so important to merit note taking at this preliminary stage in the process. It was indecipherable but already voluminous. My stomach knotted.

At precisely 8:30 A.M., the dean of the law school stepped to the podium and introduced himself, noting wryly that this year was also the first year that he was debt-free from law school loans. Some of the students around me groaned. The dean talked about law school and introduced some of the faculty and administrators.

Afterward, people just hung around the auditorium as if they were afraid they would miss something. I wondered what was going on in other students' minds. I looked around and noticed a group of six or seven students clustered together, as a well-dressed 1L spoke animatedly. He was describing a summer program he had taken in Chicago, sort of a law school prep program. Immediately, my stomach tightened. Had I already missed out on something important before law school had even begun? I listened as he continued his soliloquy.

"All the top professors were there," he said. "They told us what law school exams were like and we actually took some practice exams," he continued. "They graded the exams and gave us feedback on our answers," he said. "They say that statistically, many of their students graduate at the top of the class." He was now positively beaming. My stomach churning began to turn into raw, unadulterated fear. This law school prep program appeared to provide its fortunate participants with a recipe for surefire law school success. I was suddenly convinced that I was doomed to fail.

In reality, I had just fallen for the first trap in the labyrinth.

LESSON #1: YOU MUST TRAVERSE THE LABYRINTH IN ORDER TO MASTER IT

The first trap in the labyrinth is that there are simply no shortcuts involved in learning to "think like a lawyer." You simply must do the work in order to develop the skills. There are numerous gimmicks out there—like the prep programs—that purport to give students a leg up on the competition. There are law student self-help books that will supposedly help you do just that. A particularly popular approach taken by writers and a lot of social commentators is that of the cynic. Law school is a game and the game is rigged. Law professors are arrogant idiots. Law firms and law practice will ultimately lead to career dissatisfaction. The appeal of this approach is understandable. Law school is stressful and difficult. Many students, for the first time in their academic careers, find themselves somewhere other than at the top of their classes. Life makes more sense to these students if they accept the view that there is some inherent flaw in the system or that the game is rigged. Unfortunately, the law school phenomenon is not that simple. There are good reasons for the law school pedagogy. As I will explain, the study of law is the way it is because it imitates the practice of law.

There are other books written by law professors who, it seems, should be able to give you an inside view into law school. These books appeal to Type-A law students who just know that there are inside information, shortcuts, and "holy grail" outlines out there that will help them to graduate at the top of their classes. And they believe that these professor/authors will give it to them. However, these students have fallen for the second trap in the labyrinth (and in the interest of full disclosure, I fell for it myself). These students waste so much time and energy searching that it distracts them from doing the real work involved in learning to think, reason, and write like a lawyer. The truth is that there are no short-cuts, and most of these books were written primarily to provide templates and checklists for the various tasks typically associated with law school and the study of law. Further, in my opinion, many law professors are so removed from the law student's struggle that they really can't offer solid practical advice. Simply, most law professors attended law school a long time ago. And although most professors were very successful in law school, most cannot articulate why they were successful.

As you will learn, there really are no shortcuts through the law school labyrinth. Law school is all about the journey itself.

You learn to practice law by the lessons imparted along the journey, and you develop your legal skills as a result of that journey. You will learn to think like a lawyer through your intellectual bumps and bruises, a veritable trial-and-error cornucopia. You will invest a huge number of hours in reading cases, often for the meager return of a kernel of knowledge about the law.

However, at times, you will have astounding revelations and all of that reading suddenly seems to come together.

From the day that you register for the LSAT until the day you pass the bar and beyond, you will be faced with circuitous path upon circuitous path through the labyrinth. You will receive confusing instructions regarding procedures and deadlines that don't make sense. At every turn, a new gate appears and you have to break some sort of a code to pass through it.

However, as the old saying goes, "That which does not kill you makes you stronger." The ultimate result of the journey through the labyrinth is that you will grow more analytical skills than you ever could have imagined. You will learn to process and retain more information than you would have before thought possible. You will learn to anticipate problems and question everything. You will be able to think your way through almost any type of problem. But you learn all this in the labyrinth by doing, rather than by studying abstract theory.

There are things you can do to make your learning process more efficient. And that is the point of this book. To provide you not only with the "whys" behind all of it, but to also give you tips and suggestions to help you avoid a great deal of wheel-spinning and instead focus on high-return activities.

LESSON #2: YOU ARE ON YOUR OWN IN THE LABYRINTH

Unlike your undergraduate studies, no one will guide you through the labyrinth. First-year law students are especially left to their own devices to figure out what is happening and why. Some 1Ls rely on the advice of their peers, upperclassmen, or friends who have graduated from law school.

However, reliance on such advice assumes that the advisor has broken the operating code of the labyrinth. This is a risky assumption, which may result in the blind leading the blind.

Fatal False Turn 1: Assuming That Your Classmates Are There to Help

Given the fact that law school is graded on a curve, it is highly unlikely that a classmate who has broken the labyrinthian code will reveal his or her secrets. Cordial study groups in which everyone shares what he or she knows are a relic of your college days. 2L and 3Ls may be of greater help your first year; however, after the first year of law school, they will likely be in many of the same classes as you. As a result, the grading curve is in play within these classes, and competition is fierce there as well.

Because of the grading curve, you will rarely, if ever, hear other students talking about an actual study methodology, assuming they have one. Instead, you will hear a lot of posturing comments that range from "I study until 4:00 A.M." to the diametric opposite, "I never read the cases. I never even bought the casebook." Both of these types of comments are, in reality, designed to mislead the competition—either to engender fear or to lull it into a false sense of security.

Fatal False Turn 2: Assuming That Your Professors Are There to Help

To be clear, I do not believe that law school professors deliberately "hide the ball." Instead, I believe that law professors are simply so removed from the process that it is difficult for them to identify with the struggle. It's sort of like teaching a child basic math. To an adult, it is so automatic and so instinctive, that we have forgotten how difficult it can be, at first, to master a simple calculation. And to law professors, legal analysis is so basic and fundamental that it is difficult for them to identify the discrete steps involved.

A colleague of mine, whom I will call Maggie Smith, relayed the story of an eagerly anticipated meeting with one of her professors after a disappointing first semester at an Ivy League law school. Maggie had really enjoyed the professor's class. The professor, whom I will call Professor Jones, had clerked for one of the justices of the U.S. Supreme Court and spoke with authority regarding the operation of the Court. Professor Jones had what I will call a consultative Socratic style. According to Maggie, in Professor Jones's classes, no one was ever really wrong, even if they obviously hadn't prepared adequately for class. He was Maggie's favorite first-semester teacher. Maggie told me that when she had finished the constitutional law exam, she actually felt pretty good about her performance. And the fact that Professor Jones was such a nice guy cinched it for Maggie; she just knew that most of the class would get an A. Imagine her disappointment when she learned later that she had received a C+ on her exam. Maggie scheduled a meeting with Professor Jones because she really wanted to understand what went wrong.

As Maggie entered Professor Jones's office, she was struck by how small it was. Maggie had imagined that his office would truly be a sort of ivory tower, complete with volumes of treatises on the nuances of the Constitution. Instead, the plainness of Jones's office appeared to be more suited to a bookkeeper or an administrative assistant. Seeing this sparse little office was good for Maggie in that it demystified, at least to some extent, the whole law school professor invulnerability notion of which she had convinced herself. Professor Jones seemed definitely human, sitting there in that cramped little office. Regardless, he had decorated his office with very interesting and comfort-inducing accessories. There was an afghan on his credenza and several interesting but unidentifiable objets d'art on his filing cabinets and coffee table. There were also several artifacts which clearly established his credentials, including a signed photograph of a deceased Supreme Court justice.

As Maggie tentatively walked in, Professor Jones looked up at her from his desk. It seemed from the look on his face that he didn't do many of these types of meetings and that he anticipated that Maggie was there only to gripe. He was drinking a Starbucks latte or mocha; needless to say, he did not bring one for Maggie. He gestured for Maggie to sit down in front of his desk. She took a seat in the small, overstuffed chair facing Professor Jones that put her about a foot below his eye level. Although Maggie was 5'10" tall and Professor Jones was perhaps slightly over five feet, he loomed above Maggie in this somewhat ergonomically contrived arrangement. Maggie almost apologetically began the meeting by saying, "Thank you for meeting with me, Professor Jones."

Without smiling, Jones abruptly folded the newspaper he had been reading, tossed it into the waste can next to his desk and asked, "I take it, Ms. Smith, that you were unhappy with your grade?" Somehow, this person wasn't the nice Professor Jones Maggie had known during the semester. This was Jones's testier doppelganger.

Maggie tensed almost instinctively and quickly replied, "I'm not really here to challenge my grade, Professor. The reason I am here is to try and understand what I need to do to improve my studies."

Professor Jones seemed to loosen up. Perhaps this was the kindly Professor Jones after all. Maggie relaxed a bit in the small chair and continued, "I would really appreciate any feedback or guidance you can give me." Jones paused and looked away for a few seconds as he began to answer. The depth of concentration was evident, as was his somewhat bemused, scholarly expression. Had this been 20 years earlier, Maggie was convinced Professor Jones would have tamped and lit a pipe at this point. Jones began to speak.

Maggie eagerly awaited what she anticipated would be an epiphany, a law student's Rosetta stone that would unlock the secrets of law school. She was confident that the net result of this meeting would be worth the temporary discomfort. Maggie just knew that the next words out of Jones's mouth would propel her on her way to success.

"Well," Jones said, "your analysis was a bit thin."

"Thin," Maggie responded, her chest deflating as the words left her lips.

"Yes," Jones reiterated, "your answers were a bit thin."

Somehow, one would have expected something more from a law professor and former United States Supreme Court clerk.

Nonetheless, Maggie decided to plunge in. "By thin, do you mean that my answers were too short?"

Professor Jones looked at her and said, "No, your answers weren't developed enough. You didn't appear to have thought through the issues such that your exam would merit an A."

In other words, Professor Jones was telling Maggie that she didn't get an A because her paper wasn't A material, and her paper wasn't A material because she didn't get an A (in logic circles, this is known as circular logic).

By the time Maggie left Professor Jones's office, she was more confused than ever. Jones was one of the nicest professors in the law school, who genuinely seemed to care about the needs of students, but even he could not articulate with any precision exactly what an A answer looked like. Maggie had wanted him to tell her, to show her, what a top-grade exam might look like. Instead, Jones simply and cryptically indicated that Maggie's analysis was insufficient. Maggie's first thought was that Jones must somehow be "hiding the ball" (a term used by law students to refer to the intentional obfuscation and omission of information by law professors, for the purpose of creating confusion and chaos).

In retrospect, however, Maggie now believes that Jones wasn't obfuscating deliberately, but instead was simply incapable of answering the question. I share Maggie's belief. In my own quest through the labyrinth, most of the professors I spoke with, although they could recognize good legal work when they saw it on an exam answer, could not or would not articulate the individual components of such work and their relative importance. During a casual discussion with an adjunct professor in which I lamented about the mystery of law school exam grading, he related that he had booked his Business Entities class during his second year of law school (as you will learn, *booking* means receiving the highest grade in the class). He said, "I have no idea of what I did differently for that particular exam. I worked as hard as I always did. My writing skills were the same. Perhaps it was just that the law school gods were smiling on me that day." I found it amazing that he had scored so well on a law school exam and had absolutely no idea why.

He was like a pro golfer trying to explain to a beginner how to hit the ball.

Most law professors can't tell you what it takes to succeed because to them, legal reasoning and analysis is almost intuitive.

The reason Professor Jones could not describe an A exam to Maggie was simply this: he was too close to the situation to be able to objectively identify the variables in the process. Professor Jones had been studying the law and performing legal analysis for most of his adult life. The elements of a good golf swing are difficult to break down, and the pro has played for so long that these elements are intuitive. He or she isn't even aware that they are occurring. They simply can't step back and break the process down into simpler components. As a result, they can't describe what an A answer should look like.

One professor told me, "An A exam is sort of like Justice Potter Stewart's definition of pornography." *Jacobellis v. Ohio*, 378 U.S. 184, 197 (1964) was a landmark case concerning the Ohio ban of a movie directed by French director Louis Malle, on the basis that it was obscene. Justice Stewart, in an effort to craft a legal definition of pornography (extreme pornography had been previously held to be unprotected under the First Amendment), said, "I shall not today attempt further to define the kinds of material I understand to be embraced . . . but I know it when I see it. . . ."

As another professor said, "It's all about arguments. Make the arguments and you will do well in law school." As is discussed later in this book, that suggestion may very well have been among the best pieces of advice ever offered by a law professor.

LESSON # 3: DON'T OVERESTIMATE THE EFFECT OF CLASS PREPARATION AND PARTICIPATION ON YOUR GRADES

Before I started law school, I had not given much thought to grades and certainly not to what it would take to get all A's. That said, somewhere in my inner psyche lurked the fear that I would not be able to cut the intellectual mustard. In addition, I didn't really have much of a clue about the basics of law school. I didn't really understand the pedagogy. I knew little about the subject matter. And I was haunted by my less-than-stellar undergraduate performance. It seemed to me that there were numerous uncontrollable variables involved, which naturally resulted in anxiety as the semester began.

I decided that I would focus my energy on the one primary variable that I could control. I decided that I would work harder than anyone else.

Fatal False Turn 3: Using Undergraduate School Methods

One of my false turns was mistakenly relying on my old undergraduate methods for class preparation, class participation, course work completion, and exam preparation.

It seemed logical that good old-fashioned hard work would mitigate my risk of failure. I also assumed that the undergraduate student model would work in law school—go to class, engage in the discussion (even volunteer if necessary so you can get extra credit), follow the professor's instructions, take copious notes (actually write down everything said in class by anyone, but especially the professor), read the material, work the problems, review notes. In short, I thought I should lose myself in a forest of activity. That first year of law school, my typical day began at 6:00 A.M. I would get up, take a quick shower, eat a light breakfast, and

then begin reading, or more accurately, reading and rereading. I read
for a couple of hours before class. Next, I would make the 20-minute
drive to school and attend class for three or four hours. Any breaks
between classes were spent rereading the cases. I would have a quick
lunch and again read the cases. Generally, my class schedule was such
that I would have perhaps one more class that afternoon. I would drive
home and then hit the books again until 10:00 P.M. or so. My reading in the evenings focused on the assigned reading for the next day's
classes. This process started all over again the next day. My reading in
the morning focused on rereading the material I had read the evening
before. On the weekends, I might sleep in until 7:00 A.M. and read all
day and well into the evening. I didn't exercise because I believed that
I didn't have time for it. I rarely, if ever, indulged in any recreation or
downtime.

Having successfully climbed the corporate ladder, I was no stranger
to, and unafraid of, hard work. Based on everything I had read about
law school and law practice, I assumed that a 14- or 16-hour day was
mandatory for the students who wanted to succeed. As my first semester
progressed, I became increasingly optimistic that I actually had a shot
at success. I looked around and saw students that did not appear to be
innately brighter than I was. In class, I felt like I was getting it and following the case reasoning and Socratic dialogue. And I was investing
plenty of time in the process. More importantly, I knew no one who was
working as hard as I was. As I looked around me, I noticed that not
everyone shared my work ethic. I saw students frequently congregating
around Blackacre (a weekly on-campus happy hour for law students)
with what appeared to be all of the time in the world on their hands. The
Bar Review (a weekly off-campus happy hour for law students) was always
a sold-out event. I would hear students talk about day trips, such as the
one-hour drive from Nashville to the Jack Daniels distillery in Lynch-
burg, Tennessee. At times, I felt that I was the only 1L putting in the kind
of hours that I assumed the effective study of law deserved.

After first semester grades came out, I was disappointed with my
performance (a B+ average), even though it placed me in the top third
of my class. Although I had been out of school for a number of years,
I knew that I could do better. I looked around and saw students that I
knew were no smarter and certainly worked no harder than I did but

who seemed to have done better that first semester. Having been at the top of the career heap for so many years, to find myself now merely near the top was indeed humbling. If I considered my grades as a return on the total amount of investment in my studies, the ROI (return on investment) was extremely low!

The problem was that I had operated under the misconception that there was only one investment option (spending hour upon hour reading and summarizing cases and doing nothing else). The reality is that these activities have a minor effect on law school grades, unless they assist in the development of your understanding of the subject. However, understanding a subject and how to work within it requires a more strategic approach. Although you should certainly be prepared for class, the majority of your time should be invested in truly understanding the subject.

Another misconception that many students bring with them from undergraduate school is that their professors will tell them exactly what information they should know for exams. If the professor does not spend time on a subject in class, you do not need to spend much study time on it. Not so in law school! Although the professor may spend a great deal of time in your contracts class on the subject of damages because it happens to be a personal area of interest, at exam time you absolutely must know the entire body of contract law. This is true whether or not the information is covered in class. Professors are looking for you to spot legal issues and resolve them, just as a practicing lawyer would.

LESSON #4: LAW SCHOOL CAN ACTUALLY HELP YOU TO BECOME AN EFFECTIVE LAWYER

You may be asking yourself at this point, "Why do law schools teach law this way? Why is law school made more difficult than it has to be? Why don't professors just give students the so-called black letter law instead of making things so confusing? After all, isn't that why I am in law school—to learn the law?"

A cynical response to these questions would be that law schools care about your tuition dollars and not much else. In other words, once they have your commitment and money, you are on your own. Professors don't really care about students because they are not accountable to them. Law school rankings determine the market demand for a law school, rather than its effectiveness. Most books written on the subject agree that the study of law is confusing, intimidating, and frustrating. Many books have asserted that the Socratic method is an outdated relic of the past. These authors argue that law has been taught the same way for too long and the time has come for a change. Certain members of academia have also joined in this editorial fray, arguing that the length of study should be reduced to two years instead of three, in a similar format to business school. They argue that everything you need to know from the study of law occurs during the first two years.

However, I believe that when understood in its proper context, the current law school pedagogy, including the Socratic method, is quite effective. A law professor would probably argue that the Socratic method isn't all bad. The reason law schools operate the way they do is because much of law practice operates this way. As a lawyer, you are paid to figure things out for yourself. The reality is that you will spend your entire professional career learning the law. The law is constantly changing and evolving. The fact that this pedagogy has essentially remained unchanged for over a hundred years is a testament to its effectiveness and ultimate approval by practitioners. Further, the threat of a Socratic beating will ensure that every student thoroughly reads the assigned cases. And eventually, with enough time, the Socratic method will teach a student legal reasoning.

No doubt you have heard the old adage "Give a man a fish and he eats for a day; teach a man to fish and he eats for a lifetime." Similarly, the process of traversing the labyrinth has numerous intrinsic benefits. The skills you gain will serve you throughout your career. Reading cases and engaging in the Socratic dialogue (or following along with it if you are not actually in the hot seat) will enable you to learn to start with very little information and weave these threads into meaningful legal advice. And ultimately, in law practice, there will be many times when the only place to turn for an answer is to your own skill, knowledge, and experience.

When you are a lawyer, clients will seek your professional advice. The client may not even know whether their particular situation creates a legal problem. They may be so caught up in the moment that they cannot even clearly identify and articulate the relevant facts. They may not want to admit certain facts. Instead, they come to you with a bundle of disjointed information. They need you to help them determine which facts are relevant and how the law applies to these facts. You may actually know very little about the nuances involved in the substantive law affecting the issue or issues. Your job is to identify the problem or issue, analyze it, and provide advice to the client. You conduct exhaustive research. You figure it out, using the skills you developed while in law school and experiences gained in practice.

Early in my first semester of law school, as I made my way out of the classroom after class one day, I overheard a professor talking to a group of students. One wide-eyed 1L asked the professor whether a particular area of the law would be tested on the bar exam. The professor looked sternly at the student and responded, "We don't worry about your passing the bar. You take BARBRI for that." (BARBRI is a company that provides preparation courses and materials for the bar exam.) He paused for effect, peered intently over his half-rim glasses and continued haughtily before his minions, "We teach you to think," which sounded vaguely like a line from a curmudgeonly movie professor. Somehow, it struck me as silly that this 40-something law professor thought he was curmudgeonly.

This "we teach you to think" attitude is prevalent among the top law schools. I would argue that law schools, especially the top schools, are overplaying their role in the development of students' thinking processes. Certainly, while in school, you will hone your deductive and analytical reasoning skills. You will learn how to sift through facts, apply those facts to legal principles, and develop analyses to predict how a rationally thinking judge will rule on an issue. But your core thinking skills were developed a long time before you entered law school. So I would further argue that the "we teach you to think" mind-set takes credit for the intelligence of a group of incredibly bright people who were that way long before they ever thought about law school.

LESSON # 5: LAW SCHOOL IS A PROCESS THAT CAN BE MANAGED AND OPTIMIZED

After receiving my first semester grades, I simply couldn't accept the objective measure of my performance as a student or as a future lawyer, for that matter. I had had a prior career and long history of success. I knew that I had somehow missed the point, whatever it was. As a result, I began to do my own research into the law school process and to develop my own theories regarding successful law school methods. I retraced my steps from that first semester. I became obsessed with trying to figure out what differentiated performance among students. Because of my prior business experience, I knew how to establish goals and plans to meet those goals. I also understood how to identify processes, break them down into their simplest components, and develop measures to monitor the process and ultimately improve it. In business, this process is frequently referred to as continuous improvement. In addition to my business career, I had also taught as an adjunct professor at a private university. This experience gave me some insight into how professors think, the issues they face, the grading process, and how they interact with students.

I approached my grades dilemma with a mind-set of continuous improvement. I read everything I could find on succeeding in law school. However, most of the books offered advice that was not helpful and in some cases, even counterproductive. Most dealt with IRAC, the classic law school analysis model: Issue (identify the issue presented by the facts provided), Rule (identify the applicable rule of law), Analysis (apply the law to the facts), and Conclusion. Most provided mock outlines but did not explain *why* students should create outlines. They focused on formulaic approaches to the study of law and exam writing. The reality is that the process of law school is complicated and very personal; many students don't understand it until long after they graduate, if ever. This is because they become so caught up in the mechanics of law study and practice that they are unable to see the bigger picture of what is actually going on.

However, because I had thought about law school for so long and had brought with me to law school a very atypical perspective—an objective viewpoint based upon my business turnaround experience—I was able to objectively observe the study and later, the practice, of law. Here is the good news: the labyrinth can be beaten. The starting point in successfully traversing the law school labyrinth is to focus your energy on study activities that will yield the highest return on your investment.

My hypotheses were proven in my second and third years of law school. As it turned out, I ended up booking two classes while in law school. My grades improved dramatically and I began to earn A's and even A+'s. More importantly, I improved my grades substantially without working any harder than I did that first year, although there was no way I could have worked any harder than I did during that year!

And that is the central theme of this book—law school is about working smarter, not harder.

Obviously, there aren't really any magic golden threads to take you through the labyrinth like the one that Theseus used. But if I could successfully make it through the labyrinth, then I am confident that you can too. I stepped into the labyrinth with no prior knowledge, no insight, and no real understanding of the law school process. Over time and through much trial and error, I began to understand the labyrinth. This book will help you to traverse the labyrinth and avoid the snares and pitfalls that trapped me that first year. It will enable you to view law school for what it really is: a process. Using the methods and study techniques contained in this book, you will develop a plan and a road map to enable you to succeed. And ultimately, you will find law school to be an incredibly enriching and rewarding experience. You will learn much and develop your intellect and knowledge, as well as hone your reasoning skills to a razor-sharp edge. And best of all, once your traverse the law school labyrinth, you will apply those skills to your own practice of law.

Join me now as we begin your journey into the labyrinth . . .

> **Law school is about working smarter, not harder.**

Chapter 2

The Money Minotaur: Keeping Law School Costs at Bay

ONE OF THE VERY first fatal snares in the law school labyrinth is figuring out how to pay for the journey. In the 20 years I spent in the business world, I was dreaming about law school. Luckily for me, I was able to build up my savings during that time, so once I actually realized my dream, I was able to pay for it. Many of you will not be that lucky. In fact, for most of you, the money Minotaur will loom over you before you've stepped foot in the labyrinth.

So I have recruited the help of Eileen Crane, one of Kaplan Test Prep and Admission's leading experts in law school financial aid, in order to provide the most effective advice and up-to-date info on financing a law degree. This

> **Remember, law school is a three-year financial commitment.**

chapter will outline all the right turns to take in the labyrinth so you can know the facts and plan your finances effectively. That way, you can focus on what matters most—your law school studies—not trying to figure out how you're going to pay the bills. Unfortunately, many applicants ignore common sense when planning for law school and delay thinking about the financing part until late in the process. Some applicants don't even think about it until after they've received their first acceptance letter. Others only plan ahead for the first year or even just the first semester. It's like starting a long trip with just enough money for the first week of expenses.

When you're thinking about applying to law school—optimally, 18 to 24 months before you plan to enroll—you should also be planning how you're going to pay for your education.

PLANNING AHEAD FOR LAW SCHOOL EXPENSES

You are going to have to make tuition payments on top of what you owe for your current living expenses (rent/mortgage, car payments, food, gas, electricity, phone, cable, etc.). You may find that you will need financial assistance such as loans or government financial aid in order to make your law school dreams come true.

Therefore, plan ahead, be honest with yourself about your costs and resources, and make certain you don't find yourself in a tight situation.

Average Law School Tuition Costs

To get a sense of what law school tuition may add to your bottom line, here's a list of full-time tuition costs for some well-known public and private schools, both large and small:

- Large state school
  - UC Berkeley:
    - Resident: $26,896
    - Nonresident: $39,141
- Large private school
  - Duke: $42,160
- Small public school
  - University of Indiana:
    - Resident: $19,125

- Nonresident: $36,510
- Small private school
  - Boston College: $38,340

Of course, this is just a small sampling. But as you can see, it doesn't much matter if the school is large or small, public or private. Any way you slice it, the tuition costs alone are going to be a big investment.

Assess Your Money Situation

Here's a brief quiz to assess your financial health in preparation for enrolling in law school. Remember, no one will grade this exam but you, so be honest.

FINANCIAL HEALTH QUIZ

1. I am living within my means. For example, I do not finance essential living expenses with credit cards or cash advances.
   ☐ Yes   ☐ No
2. I am able to pay much more than the minimum payments on my credit cards (or even in full) at the end of each month.
   ☐ Yes   ☐ No
3. I have not made any major purchases (such as a car, furniture, wedding, vacation, etc.) that will not be paid in full before I start law school.
   ☐ Yes   ☐ No
4. I am up-to-date on payments for all my other financial obligations (undergraduate student loans, mortgage payments, etc.).
   ☐ Yes   ☐ No
5. No matter how tight my finances are, I manage to have discretionary income at the end of each month.
   ☐ Yes   ☐ No

If you answered yes to fewer than three questions, this may indicate that you need to work on effective financial planning and practices.

Of course, this five-question quiz won't tell you everything you need to know about your financial health. But the bottom line is that if you enroll in law school with monthly obligations that are beyond the costs of your current living expenses, you will quickly find yourself in a tight spot!

If you don't have the skills necessary to manage your finances, you'll need to develop them. Don't use the excuse that "you're not good with money" or "you don't have a head for finances." The habits you have now will affect your financial future. One major responsibility lawyers have is to manage money and the value of investments for others. If you do not take care of our own finances responsibly, some state bars will not believe that you can take care of others' money either. Responsible financial planning guarantees that you will not be kept from taking a state bar.

Helpful Tips for Keeping on Top of Your Finances

Here are some quick suggestions to help you start getting a grip on your personal expenses.

Live Conservatively. Now is not the time to incur major expenses or make any major purchases. Don't quit your job early and take a tour of Europe or participate in some other high-priced adventure. You likely can only afford one dream at a time.

Instead, save your available resources for future law school expenses, or at the very least, don't run up debt beyond what you can pay off. You may be able to afford law school payments by a combination of savings and keeping your living costs lower than your current expenses. Plus, if you are receiving financial aid—be it through the government or your own private resources—you must live within the school's cost of attendance budget (see page 32 for more on what this is all about).

Also, be honest with yourself in terms of your living expenses. Don't spend money where you don't have to. For example, are you going to a metropolitan area where parking costs are high? Or are you going to a school in an area where cars are necessary, but parking is cheap and easily available?

Obtain a Copy of Your Credit Report. How good or bad is your credit? What is your credit score? Most lenders of credit-based alternative loans require a minimum score of about 630 out of a possible 900.

There are three national credit agencies, all with websites that contain helpful information about credit and finance. They also describe the process of requesting a report. The three credit bureaus' websites are:

- *www.experian.com*
- *www.transunion.com*
- *www.equifax.com*

However, you don't have to pay extra to receive a credit report. You can get reports from all three bureaus for free from websites such as:

- *www.annualcreditreport.com*
- *www.freecreditreport.com*
- *www.myfico.com*
- *www.consumerinfo.com*
- *www.ftc.gov*

Avoid surprises by getting a copy of your report at least six months before you apply for law school loans. Credit errors may take up to six months to correct. If you've missed payments, it takes time to get your payment history back on track.

Ask for Help If You Need It. If you need help developing a manageable budget and assistance with creditors, contact the Consumer Credit Counseling Service, a free nationwide service, by calling 800-388-2227 to learn the location of the office nearest you. The agency works with people whose bills exceed their resources, to develop spending plans and negotiate repayment terms with creditors. However, be aware that adjusting your debt may affect your creditworthiness and credit score.

Another source of information is the Debt Counselors of America website: *www.dca.org*. If you are having difficulty with a creditor who you believe is acting improperly or illegally, review the fair debt collection practices at *www.ftc.gov*.

Pay Off Your Consumer Debt. Financial advisors warn that credit card debt should not exceed 10 percent of a person's monthly pay. To extrapolate that to most students' situations, the cost should not exceed 10 percent of the amount that the school budgets for your monthly living expenses. If it exceeds that amount, how are you planning to manage the payments? You can't just ignore your debts. Imagine completing three or four years of hard work in law school, only to be prevented from sitting for the bar exam because the bar examiners have noted your poor credit record?

Remember, lawyers are supposed to exhibit a responsible financial attitude. How people handle their own finances says something about how they'd manage funds entrusted to their care.

Create a Separate Savings Account. Set aside the amount needed for your payments in a separate savings account. This is one way of making sure you always have the money for these mandatory expenses.

Additional Reading on Finances

Here is some suggested reading to help you get a better handle on your finances.

Books. Buy these books or borrow them from your local library:
- Morris, Kenneth M., and Alan M. Siegel. *The Wall Street Journal Guide to Understanding Personal Finance.* New York: Simon & Schuster, 2004.
- Kobliner, Beth. *Get a Financial Life: Personal Finance in your Twenties and Thirties.* New York: Fireside, 2000.
- Sander, Peter J., and Jennifer Basye Sander. *The Pocket Idiot's Guide to Living on a Budget.* New York: Alpha Books, 2005.
- Tyson, Eric. *Personal Finance for Dummies.* Hoboken: Wiley Publishing, Inc., 2006.

Websites. Check out these websites for free financial information:
- *www.fool.com*
- *www.efmoody.com*
- *www.accessgroup.org/students/index.htm*

FINANCING OPTIONS

Few people can simply write a check to pay for law school in full. If you fall into that category, congratulations! If not, you'll join many of your future classmates who use financial aid in some form or another. If you plan on applying for financial aid, it is critical that you are as thorough as when you apply for admission. Complete your financial aid application on time or early, make copies, and keep records of everything you send. Read all the information you receive in the mail and ask questions when you don't understand something.

Financing Options Basics

Financial aid is part of a successful financial plan for most students. The aid itself can take many forms. Options include scholarships or grants, usually funded by the law school, federal and privately funded loans, and work programs.

These terms can sometimes be confusing, especially if you have never applied for financial aid before. The table on page 29 will help you keep track of the various financial aid options you may choose to utilize. Let's take a look at each of these financial aid options.

Grants and Scholarships. A grant or scholarship is free money that does not have to be repaid. The primary sources are law schools and private foundations. The schools create their own criteria for awarding funds in order to accomplish the institutional goals that attract the kinds of students that they want in their student body. The schools also establish their own application processes and set their own deadlines. Carefully read the application for each school to which you are applying. Learn about the policies and procedures they use to award scholarships.

Federal Aid. The federal government provides aid to students in the form of loan programs. Stafford subsidized and unsubsidized student loan programs are the largest sources of funds for law students nationwide. Perkins loans are also available at some law schools.

Loans. Some law schools have loan programs for their students. Check with the school's financial aid office to see if this type of loan is available.

> **Research all of the possibilities carefully and apply early. The schools to which you are applying are usually the best source for assistance. Make sure you know their deadlines and application procedures.**

In addition to private loans you can take out on your own, there are several private organizations which also lend funds specifically to law students as a supplement to the federal programs. Two private loans used by many law students are the Law Access loan and the Total Higher Education loan program (T.H.E.).

Work-Study Programs. The federal work-study program funds the majority of jobs for law students. Federal work-study allows students to work part-time during the school year. Participants are paid an hourly wage and receive a paycheck for the hours worked. Schools differ in the amount of funding they have available for work-study. Schools participating in the federal work-study program are now required by law to provide off-campus employment opportunities which meet community service guidelines.

Usually, you'll need to have completed a year of course work to be eligible for one of these off-campus positions. These jobs can be used to gain valuable legal experience. Your eligibility for a federal work-study job is based on financial need. Not all law schools participate in the federal work-study program, though. And funds are limited at the schools that offer the program.

GRANTS AND SCHOLARSHIPS

With the Internet making information so readily accessible, it is well worth your time to do extensive research into grants and scholarships. There are many small grants and scholarships that individuals, families, and charitable foundations have created, but it takes patience to find them. Also, if you are awarded a grant or scholarship from an individual, family, or some charitable foundation, you must report it to the law

TYPES OF LOANS	STAFFORD SUBSIDIZED	STAFFORD UNSUBSIDIZED	PERKINS PROGRAM	SCHOOL FUNDS	PRIVATE LOANS	WORK-STUDY	GRANTS AND SCHOLARSHIPS
Amount							
Interest Rate							
Grace Period							
Repayment Schedule							
Forbearance							
Credit Limit							
Fees							

school financial aid office. It will impact the financial aid package you can receive at your school. But it is always better to receive free money than to have to pay back loans with interest over 10 to 20 years.

Grants and Scholarships from Law Schools

Institutional aid at law schools breaks down into two areas: need and merit. Historically, most high-cost private schools gave need-based grants because they had a mission to expand the opportunity to all students, regardless of wealth, to attend. Over time, schools decided to grant merit scholarships to reward those who had performed well. Hybrid grants then evolved with schools offering a mixture of each kind of grant. As law school applicant pools rise and fall, different approaches are used with institutional funds to attract the kind of students a school wants in their student body.

In the official guide to ABA-approved law schools, the amount of grants that are awarded to students is provided on the ABA data pages for each law school.

If You Miss the School's Application Deadline

All law schools have a finite amount of money to award. A late financial aid application is a late application, and it really doesn't matter why, as painful as that might be for the applicant. If you apply after the deadline, you lose the sympathy and maybe the respect of the admissions officers. When all the funds have been given out, there is little, if anything, an admissions officer can do.

Avoid this problem by applying on time. If you do apply late, for whatever reason, take the following steps AND contact the school to explain your tardiness:

- Follow the application procedures.
- Make an appointment with a financial aid counselor at the school after the school has received your results, and ask for suggestions about how to supplement the loans you will be eligible to receive.
- If you meet the law school's eligibility for grants but the school ran out of funds before you completed your application, see if the aid office maintains a wait list.

Try to make certain your name is on that list so that you can be considered for any funds that are returned or deobligated by another applicant.

Grants and Scholarships from Other Aid Sources

If you belonged to a local chapter of any national social or service organization in college, this is one of the first places you should look for scholarship assistance. Often, these organizations will offer small ($500–$2,000) one-time awards to former members who plan to pursue graduate study.

If you've lost track of the address of your group's national organization, contact your undergraduate school. Most deadlines for any scholarships offered by these organizations are in January or February of the year before you plan to enroll.

> **Remember that there are lots of law students, just as eager as you, who are scouring the same places to find free funds.**

If you do find some scholarships you think you qualify for, think of them as bonuses rather than as sure things. Most organizations receive a large number of applications each year. The competition is tough, and the more general the eligibility criteria, the larger the number of people applying.

Don't Pay to Find Free Money!

There is a myth that has helped make small fortunes for people who are clever enough to prey on hopeful students. The myth is that there is some astronomically high number of unclaimed scholarships each year. Sometimes the myth comes with an exact figure, $6.6 billion. The source of the $6.6 billion number was testimony at a U.S. Congressional hearing in 1983. However, it refers to an estimated number of unused employee education benefits offered by companies. To locate these unclaimed billions, the myth says that you should peruse books on the best companies to work for in the United States. Most will offer employee educational benefits. Then you have to get a job at one of these companies or be the son or daughter of an employee whose company offers benefits to employee's children. Not a very likely path to a full scholarship, is it?

Also, you don't need to pay $50, $100, or more for a computer search, as many people are conned into doing. Some states, such as New York, have closed down a number of these computerized search services for fraudulent business practices.

If you receive mail offering to search for free money for you, save your money and do your own search. And if you receive a solicitation from a scholarship organization which sounds too good to be true, it probably is. Your time is better spent making certain you meet the application deadlines for the law school to which you're applying. Here are some websites for free scholarship searches:

- *www.finaid.org/scholarships*
- *http://scholarships.salliemae.com*

FEDERAL AID

Federal aid for law students takes the form of loans and work-study. To be eligible for federal financial aid, you must:

- Be a U.S. citizen or permanent resident
- Not be in default on any federal student loans borrowed previously
- Not owe a refund on prior federal grants you may have received
- Be registered for the selective service (men only)

These criteria are not just relevant to federal loans and work-study. Many law schools also restrict their own institutional funding to students who meet the above criteria. If you don't meet all of the criteria, don't panic. There may be time to address these problems—assuming that you're reading this at least 18 months in advance of when you plan to enroll in law schools!

If you're in default on a previous student loan or owe the government a refund, you should correct this situation as soon as possible. You must correct these deficiencies before you enroll, or your access to funding sources will be severely limited. Also, you should be aware that any existing loan defaults or debts owed to the federal government could disqualify you from sitting for the bar examination in the state in which you would like to practice law—an obvious hindrance to the aspiring attorney!

FAFSA: The Federal Aid Application Form

In order to get loans from the federal government to go to law school, your eligibility for federal aid must be determined. That requires you to file a Free Application for Federal Student Aid (FAFSA) application. It collects information about:

- Your income and assets
- Your spouse's income and assets
- Your family size
- Your marital status

This and other information is used to calculate how much money you can get toward law school tuition. A need analysis is the official term for the process of determining the amount of money you qualify for. The department of education sets federally determined formulas to determine how much money a student qualifies for. Law schools and financial aid administrators do not set formulas. In addition to the FAFSA, some schools require students to complete a second need analysis form. Often, this is a financial aid profile administered by the college scholarship service or a need access, which is administered by the access group.

How to Get a Pin Number and Fill Out Your FAFSA. Prior to electronically filling out the FAFSA, you must apply for a pin number. This pin number will be your ID number for the rest of your student life, and it is critical that you save it in a safe place. You can apply for a pin number at: *www.pin.ed.gov*. Within a short period of time, you will receive a pin number by email.

The FAFSA can be filled out online or can be mailed on or after January 1 of each year. You should fill it out in January in the year in which you plan to enroll in law school. The forms are usually available by December 1 each year.

The best place to fill out the FAFSA is online at *www.fafsa.ed.gov*. By filling out the FAFSA online, it is highly likely that there will be fewer mistakes made in the processing of your application. It is also much faster than paper processing of FAFSA applications. Approximately three to six weeks after you submit the FAFSA online, you will receive an email confirming that your FAFSA was received. You will be sent a student aid report, which lists all the information that you have supplied to the government. It is critical that you review all the information to confirm that all the data is correct. If it is not correct, follow the instructions for how to correct the mistakes. This should be done immediately, as it can impact the level of aid you qualify for and will be awarded.

The free application for federal student aid (FAFSA) form is always required to apply for any federal financial aid.

Paper versions of the FAFSA forms are also available at some public libraries and all college and university financial aid offices. You can also visit the U.S. Department of Education website (*www.ed.gov*) or call the hotline at 800-4FED-AID.

Renewal FAFSA. If you completed a FAFSA form for the prior academic year, whether or not you enrolled in school or received aid, renewal FAFSA information will be emailed to you (if you applied online) or mailed to your permanent address (if you applied on paper) each December. The renewal FAFSA will contain data about you that you provided previously which saves you time when completing the application. Either a FAFSA or a renewal FAFSA is acceptable when applying for federal financial aid for your first year of law school.

Calculating Your Need
The calculation of how much you and your family can contribute toward your legal education always seems the most incomprehensible part of the financial aid process. It's actually quite straightforward once you know the guidelines and rules.

Cost of Attendance. The first concept to understand is financial need. Think of it as simple subtraction:

cost of attendance − expected family contribution = financial need

Your cost of attendance (or COA) includes the following:

- Tuition
- Books
- Fees
- Room and board
- Food
- Transportation needs
- Insurance

These COA expenses are set by the law schools after surveying current students to ascertain their current cost of rent, transportation, etc. Sometimes the COA includes money for dependents; sometimes it does not. It is critical that you research that before you apply to a specific school so that you are not surprised when you get your financial aid award.

Assets are financial holdings, such as checking and savings accounts, stocks, bonds, trusts and other securities, loan receivables, home and other real estate equity, business equipment, and business inventory.

Components of Your Expected Family Contribution. Many graduate students are not supported by their parents once they have graduated from college. If you received federal money as an undergraduate student, remember that your parents' assets and income were part of the equation to determine how much money you were granted or loaned.

As a graduate student, you're automatically considered independent of your parents, even if you live with them! For federal aid eligibility (federal Stafford, federal Perkins, and federal work-study), the income and assets of your parents will not be included in the equation. Therefore, your expected family contribution (EFC) as an individual will mean an assessment of your personal assets and income.

What are some of the components reviewed in assessing family contribution? They include:

- Number of family members
- Number of family members in college at least part-time
- Costs associated with two people working
- Taxes paid (federal, state, and local)

- Total family income from the previous calendar year (base year income)
- Income protection allowance (IPA) for basic living expenses
- Asset protection allowance for retirement
- Net value of any assets (value minus debt)

If you're married, your spouse's income and assets will be assessed in the calculation of your family contribution. If you have children, your expected family contribution will be reduced.

Base Year Income. If you enroll in fall 2010, you'll be asked to provide your income for the calendar year 2009. This is because, for most people, the best predictor of what their income will be in any given year is their income from the year before. In spite of the fact that most law students will be completely unemployed when they enter law school, assets from previous years are used to determine future need.

Income Protection Allowance (IPA). Income protection allowance provides for basic living expenses not included in the standard student expense budget. This allowance will vary according to the cost of living in the place where you attend law school, the number of family members, and the number in college at least half-time. For a single student or married student with no dependents, the IPA is $5,300; for students with dependent children, the amount varies depending on the number of family members.

Asset Protection Allowance. The asset protection allowance depends on your age. A portion of your assets will not be considered in the calculation because they're protected for your retirement. If you are older, more of your assets are protected.

Employment Allowance. The concept of an employment allowance grows from the realization that it costs to have both members of a married couple work outside the home. The formula allows 35 percent of the lower income, up to $2,800, to be deducted as an allowance against total income.

The Federal Methodology (FM): How the EFC Components Are Evaluated. The Federal Methodology, or the formula used in need analysis to determine eligibility for most federal financial aid programs, has been written into law by the U.S. Congress. Congress reviews this formula every several years and recommends changes to it. The federal formula was established to set objective standards that would be uniformly applied to all applicants.

Broadly, FM follows this procedure:

- Your household income is looked at.
- Taxes that you've paid are subtracted.
- The cost of maintaining your other family members is subtracted.
- A portion of your household's assets is added.
- A percentage of the result is calculated, and this is the expected family contribution.

Although this formula may not take into account all the vagaries of an individual student's situation, it produces generally comparable data on all students applying for financial aid. The financial aid officer at the school then has the option of adjusting data elements (through professional judgment) to make the contribution realistic for the individual student.

Many high-cost, private law schools require students to submit parental information when applying for institutional grants or scholarships. Generally, if your parental information is required, and the analysis shows that your parents have the ability to contribute, a parental contribution will be factored into the assessment of your eligibility for school-based aid, whether your parents plan or are able to assist you or not.

Stafford Student Loans

The two U.S. federal loan programs available to law school students are generally considered the core loan programs, since they carry certain attractive features defined by law. The two programs are the Federal Stafford Student Loan Program and the William D. Ford Federal Direct Student Loan Program. However, few law schools participate in the Ford Direct program; most schools participate in the Stafford program.

Student eligibility for either of these programs is the same. You must:

- Be a citizen, a permanent resident, or an eligible noncitizen of the United States
- Be enrolled at least half-time (usually six credits per term)
- Be in good academic standing, making satisfactory progress toward the degree (as defined by the school)
- Not be in default of any previous loans without being in an approved repayment program
- Have progressed a class year since receiving your last Federal Stafford Loan
- Show financial need based on the information provided on your FAFSA in order to qualify for the interest subsidy

The eligibility criteria, interest rates, fees, grace period, deferment and cancellation provisions, and other terms are all basically the same for both programs. The key difference lies in who provides the loan funds. The Federal Stafford Student Loan is part of the Federal Family Education Loan Program (FFELP); loans are made by a private lender such as a bank, a savings and loan association, a credit union, or an insurance company, and are insured by a state or private guarantee agency sponsored by the U.S. federal government. Under the William D. Ford Federal Direct Student Loan Program, the U.S. federal government is the lender.

The Federal Subsidized Stafford Loan Program provides two types of loans: subsidized and unsubsidized. Subsidized loans are loans for which U.S. taxpayers pay the interest while you are in school. Based on your need analysis, you could be offered subsidized loans which are a better deal, but you have to meet the government's financial need criteria. For either type of loan, you may defer payments of principal and interest until you graduate or drop below half-time enrollment. There's a grace period of six months before you'll have to start repayment.

Most schools participate in the Stafford program.

Unsubsidized loans are loans on which the interest is building while you are in school. The policy behind this is that the student needs a loan, but the need analysis shows that the student has sufficient assets to pay the interest and the taxpayer does not need to assume that responsibility. Many students are awarded a mixture of subsidized and unsubsidized loan money.

Borrowing Limits. Graduate students may borrow up to their demonstrated need with a maximum of $8,500 per year in the Federal Subsidized Stafford Loan Program. The total borrowing limit, including undergraduate Federal Stafford Loans, is $65,500.

The Federal Unsubsidized Stafford Loan Program allows an eligible student to borrow up to $18,500 per year, minus any Federal Subsidized Stafford Loan approved. The total cumulative maximum is $138,500 (including the Federal Subsidized Stafford Loan).

Interest Rate. As the program's name indicates, the U.S. federal government subsidizes the interest on the Federal Subsidized Stafford Loan. You're not required to pay interest on these loans until after you leave school.

If you have a Federal Unsubsidized Stafford Loan, you're responsible for the interest while you're in school, but most lenders will allow you to capitalize the interest and not pay it until you leave school. Capitalization means that the interest accrues while you're still in school and is added to the principal at a predetermined time (often at the point of repayment). The interest rate on these loans has a cap of 8.25 percent. The current rate is very competitive—around 4 percent. Applications and information about current interest rates and repayment schedules are available at participating lending institutions.

Application Procedures. To apply for a Federal Stafford Student Loan, you must first complete the FAFSA. You'll receive a Student Aid Report (SAR) in three to four weeks. It'll give you the results of your application and your eligibility. The schools that you originally listed on the FAFSA will receive your eligibility information electronically.

Tips for Completing Your Aid Applications

Applicants often want to know how to position themselves for the best financial aid. Financial aid officers will tell you that honesty is the best policy. Be very careful as you collect the needed documents before you fill out the FAFSA and any institutional financial aid applications. Make sure you can document your income and assets. Applications are audited by schools, and schools will demand refunds if discrepancies in your FAFSA or aid applications are found. Read the directions that accompany the application forms very, very carefully. If you have any questions about how to answer a particular question, after you have read the instructions carefully, contact a financial aid administrator or the law schools to which you are applying.

Don't Spend Down Your Assets. Let's assume that your resources (whether it is your income, family contribution, or some combination of these) disqualify you from receiving aid from the school. Or perhaps you don't receive any funding based on merit. Sometimes students will ask whether they should spend down their assets to make themselves more eligible for financial aid. This may not be the best strategy.

In general, you should always apply for financial aid before deciding whether to spend down your assets. But you can learn what impact your assets have on your eligibility for aid. Go to *www.finaid.org*, and use several "what if" scenarios to see what impact your assets would have on your eligibility.

Depending upon your age and whether you are single and/or have dependents, a portion of your assets may be sheltered from any contribution for school expenses. For federal purposes, any asset that you are living in—whether a condominium or house—is ignored when determining your eligibility for federal aid. (Note, however, that institutional policies concerning home equity vary widely and may be viewed as a resource for determination of school-funded assistance.) Other assets—whether invested in a CD with a future expiration date, a mutual fund, or in stocks—must be reported at the current market value when you complete the financial aid application.

Consider Your Salary from Last Year. Since your eligibility for some types of federal financial aid, namely Federal Stafford Loans, federal work-study, and Perkins loans, is based on your prior year taxable income, you may initially have difficulty qualifying for these funds if you were employed full-time last year.

However, in all cases you would still be eligible for the Unsubsidized Federal Stafford Loan for up to $18,500 per year or up to the annual cost of attendance, whichever is less.

Keep Detailed Records of Your Applications. The federal government requires you to honestly and accurately report your assets when you are applying for financial aid. During the process of evaluating your FAFSA, the federal processor may identify your application as one that the school is required to follow up on. During this process, you'll be asked to document your taxable income from the prior year and your assets as they existed at the time you filed your application. In other instances, school procedures may require that you document the data provided on the form. The normal documentation is a signed copy of the prior year's federal tax return. You might also be required to provide proof of the value of assets such as bank accounts and investments. This verification process could also require you to provide documentation of your marital status and the size of your household. If your income was so low that you didn't file a return, you will be asked to provide a written statement outlining your sources of income for the previous year.

William D. Ford Federal Direct Loan Program

The Ford Direct Loan Program involves individual schools originating the loans, rather than banks or other financial institutions. This program is the same as the previously discussed program; it only varies in the source and disbursement procedures of the money. And remember, only very few law schools accept this program.

If you accept the loan, your school will electronically request approval from the federal servicer. Once it receives approval, the school can disburse the first semester portion of your loan (minus fees) to your student account. The entire process—from loan certification to disbursement of the check—can take less than a week.

Case Study: She Could Have Planned Her Federal Aid Differently

Let's say that Serena Student does not qualify for grant assistance, so she will be paying the costs through her savings and student loans. She has savings of about $35,000 and plans to attend a state school with $20,000 in annual tuition costs. She decides to pay the entire cost for the first year from savings, leaving $15,000 for her last two years. She spends the remaining $15,000 in year two and borrows the other $30,000 from the Stafford Loan Program. She takes an $8,500 subsidized Stafford loan (the annual maximum available) and a $21,500 unsubsidized Stafford, where interest has accrued from the date the funds were disbursed.

There were several ways of arranging her finances that might have been less costly, and Serena would have had more alternatives *after* law school if she'd thought ahead. For example, she could have prorated her $35,000 in savings over the three years (about $11,000 per year), borrowing a $9,000 unsubsidized Stafford loan each year to supplement her savings.

Or she could have borrowed an $8,500 subsidized Stafford loan each year, a $5,000 unsubsidized Stafford loan each year, spent $6,500 each year from her savings, and kept the rest to meet current and "life after law school" expenses.

Many students fail to plan ahead to bridge the gap between law school graduation and when their first job begins. During the summer following graduation, students are feverishly studying for the bar exams, held in the later part of July. It is difficult to both work and adequately prepare for the bar exam; students want to pass the exam on the first try. Keeping some of your savings for this purpose is good long-range planning and keeps you from spending on items that have fleeting value.

In the worst of all worlds, Serena borrows the full cost of education each year, uses her assets to supplement the loans, lives the good life while in law school, and ends up with thousands of dollars in student loans and no savings to cover living expenses during the bar.

LOANS FROM LAW SCHOOLS

Along with grants and scholarships, some schools offer loans to their students through their own resources. Don't wait until you have been accepted by a law school to begin applying for these loans. If you delay, you may miss the opportunity to qualify for these internal funds that may not be available later in the applicant year.

You can learn what a school's procedures are for applying for institutional funds by reading the admissions application booklet or website. Read through the application materials at the same time as you prepare your applications. Deadlines and application guidelines are usually quite specific and rigid. Follow these procedures and deadlines; schools rarely make exceptions.

Institutional Fund Applications

Often a school will have an institutional application that is completed and returned directly to the school. Sometimes the application is in the admissions booklet or can be downloaded from the school's website, and it should be completed by all applicants for admission. Other schools provide the application only to accepted prospective students. In either case, follow the process outlined for the particular school you're interested in.

Some private schools with large endowments base their awards on information collected on the FAFSA. Sometimes they require that parental information be included on the FAFSA. They use it to help them identify students who are truly in need of institutional funding, who otherwise would be highly unlikely to be able to attend that school.

If a school does not use the FAFSA to award their institutional aid, they often require one of two applications currently in use. One is the financial aid PROFILE sponsored by the College Board (the same people who administer the SAT; see *www.collegeboard.org*) and the other is the Need Access Application, processed by the Access Group (*www. accessgroup.org*). The law school application booklet should specify which applications are required and deadlines for filing the forms.

PROFILE and Need Access Application procedures are similar. Both allow you to complete a standardized application and pay to have it sent to the schools from which you hope to receive aid. The deadlines for these applications are determined by each school. Generally, the deadlines are in February or March. But the sooner you complete your financial aid file, the sooner you will learn the results of your request, assuming you're accepted for admission.

At peak processing times, allow four to six weeks for the schools to receive the results of your application. Once your results arrive at the school, it may take another one to four weeks to have your financial aid file reviewed, depending upon the volume of applications received at the same time. You see why it's important that you don't wait until the due date to submit your application. Also, before mailing off any financial aid applications, make a copy for your personal financial aid file. The severe winter storms during the winter of 1996 caused applications to be lost. It could happen again. So be prepared. A copy will help you complete the next year's form, too, so keep that in mind.

ASSESSING YOUR FINANCIAL AID PACKAGE

Sometime after you complete the application process for financial aid, you will receive an official notice from the schools that have admitted you. This notice is called an award letter in financial aid language. It will list the funds that the law school has awarded you from their own resources (if any), along with federal aid for which you qualify. The award letter also lists the student expense budget used to determine your award (COA) and your expected contribution (EFC).

Although a decision to choose one law school over another should never be based solely on financial reasons, they will obviously play a role in your decision. Use the Financial Aid Package Comparison worksheet provided in this chapter to compare your net expenses at each school.

Ask the Right Questions

While many of these questions are not strictly financial aid questions, they have a potential bearing on your financial future during and after law school. Get your answers before you decide to commit to a law school—not halfway through or afterwards.

If the law school does not have its own financial aid office, contact the admissions office. They may refer you to the main campus financial aid office, where someone specializes in financial aid for that school's graduate students. Some of these questions can also be referred to the office of career services. Here are some important questions to ask:

- What are the terms for renewing my grant/scholarship from the law school? Does aid policy change for upperclassmen?
- What has the average annual tuition increase been over the last couple of years?
- What is it likely to be in the future?
- What is the average indebtedness of students who graduated last spring? What is the typical monthly payment necessary to pay the average debt off within ten years?
- What is the default rate for graduates? Are there any loans your students cannot obtain because of problems with repayment of the school's graduates?
- What percentage of graduates have legal employment by graduation? How many have legal employment within six months of graduation?
- What is the most common type of legal employment graduates obtain right after law school?
- What is the typical starting salary for those graduates?
- I am interested in public interest/government employment/ teaching/corporate work/_____ (you fill in the blank). What percentage of graduates typically enter this field?
- What services does the school provide for students who are unemployed after graduation?
- Does the school have a loan repayment assistance program to assist graduates in low paying and/or public interest jobs?
- What is the eligibility criterion for receiving benefits?
- What are the benefits?
- How many graduates participate in the program annually?

Comparing Financial Aid Awards

Suppose you got a better aid offer from your third- or fourth-choice school. What should you do?

Contact your first- or second-choice school, and ask them if they have already awarded all the scholarships they intend to award. At that point, an admissions officer may ask you what other offers you are considering. You should be honest but very, very polite. Some applicants believe that making demands to a first- or second-choice school will cause them to offer money not originally offered in the acceptance letter. That is rarely true. But most students recognize that any offer from their top schools means greater opportunities in some aspect of their future career; that is why they applied there.

Different schools will have different responses to your inquiry. Their responses are largely governed by how they award aid. Is financial need a factor or the only criterion? Does parental ability to help enter the equation? Is the money awarded solely based upon merit? Are your credentials above the median at one school but average for another?

The general information on scholarship and grant policies is discussed in every law school's admissions brochure. Read this information before you decide to make a phone call. Schools have a variety of methods for making sure they know who is on the phone prior to giving out any financial aid or scholarship information. They make a note of your name, and your inquiry goes into your permanent record. Make sure that you are mature and polite when speaking to anyone at the school. Deans report absolute horror when a candidate is rude or dismissive of office staff and then ingratiating to the director or dean of admissions.

If you call a school to make an inquiry into your award, and School Y awards its aid solely on financial need, its staff will review your file to make certain no errors were made when your award was determined. They will also ask if any changes have occurred since you provided the information which would increase your eligibility for aid.

But they usually do not enter into bidding wars with other schools. Because each school determines its own criteria for awarding institutional aid, each school's response is likely to be different.

A student who is offered merit funds might have very competitive credentials for the school that is recruiting him or her, and this student would have a high probability of doing well there academically. Since good grades are important for law graduates, a stellar academic record is an invaluable asset. There are widely differing opinions about whether excellent grades at a lower ranked school are more valuable than lower grades at a school with a better academic reputation. That's a personal decision each prospective student must make. Obviously, you want to look at whether you received grant or scholarship aid and in what amounts. Some other things you should consider when comparing award offers:

- In each case, what is your student contribution?
- If a parent contribution is listed, how much is it?
- How much are you expecting to borrow in one year? In total?
- What are the terms of the loans? Does interest accrue while you are enrolled?
- What are the requirements for the grant aid to be renewed, or is it a multiyear award commitment?
- What percentage of initial grants are renewed in the second and third years? (Many schools offer only a one-year grant, renewable based on grades, which is extremely difficult to predict.)

More Than Tuition

When you're looking at aid packages and making your decision, remember to look beyond the cost of tuition. First, your living costs can vary significantly depending upon whether you choose an urban environment—usually more expensive than a rural setting—or if the law school offers subsidized student housing.

Also, consider whether transportation to and from law school and your permanent residence is reasonable. If you have to pay for plane tickets to return home, you need to add that cost to your expenses. Are you going to have to buy additional clothes for a different climate? If you have lots of belongings, moving them can be very expensive unless you do it yourself.

Location, Location, Location. If you plan to practice in the region where the school is located and it has a good reputation locally and many job opportunities for its graduates, then going to that school could be an excellent choice, regardless of whether or not it was your first choice. Attending the school and doing well, making job contacts through part-time academic year employment, and building relationships with professors and local employers will help to ensure your successful career path.

Financial Aid Package Comparison

Step 1: Estimate Your Resources

Contribution from Assets	$ _____
Contribution from Summer Savings	$ _____
Parental Contribution	$ _____
Spouse/Partner Contribution	$ _____

Your Estimated Total Resources: $ _____

Step 2: Compare School Expenses and Financial Aid Awards

Schools:	A.	B.	C.
1. Tuition and Fees	$ _____	$ _____	$ _____
2. Living Costs	_____	_____	_____
3. Long-Distance Travel	_____	_____	_____
4. Total School Expenses (Add 1–3)	_____	_____	_____
5. Your Estimated Total Resources (From Step 1)	_____	_____	_____
6. School Estimate of Your Total Contribution	_____	_____	_____
7. Difference (Subtract 6 from 5)	_____	_____	_____
8. School Analysis of Your Financial Need	_____	_____	_____
9. School-Based Grant/Scholarship	_____	_____	_____
10. Other Grants	_____	_____	_____
11. Other Grants	_____	_____	_____
12. Total Gift Aid (Add 9–11)	_____	_____	_____
13. Federal Perkins Loan	_____	_____	_____
14. Federal Stafford/Federal Direct Loan	_____	_____	_____
15. Federal Unsubsidized Stafford/Direct Loan	_____	_____	_____
16. Private Educational Loans	_____	_____	_____
17. Total Loans per Year (Add 13–16)	_____	_____	_____
18. Federal Work-Study	_____	_____	_____
19. Total Financial Aid (Add 12, 17, 18)	_____	_____	_____
20. Total Unmet Need (Subtract 19 from 4)	_____	_____	_____

Step 3: Calculate Your Total Loan Debt and Monthly Payments

Schools:	A.	B.	C.
21. Your Estimated Total Debt per Year (Item 17)	$ _____	$ _____	$ _____
22. Total Estimated Debt* Multiply yearly debt by number of years in program (Item 21 x 3 or 4)	_____	_____	_____
23. Total Estimated Monthly Payment Multiply total debt (Item 22) by $.0122	_____	_____	_____

*If you will take out loans that have interest accruing while you are in school, add approximately $800 per year for each $10,000 borrowed. (This assumes an 8% interest rate.)

However, if you have no interest in living in the region where the school is located and choose it primarily because of the financial incentives, it is critical that you spend summers working in the region where you would like to practice, making contacts with attorneys in that region. If you know attorneys who live in your preferred region already, contact them to let them know that you will be entering law school and ask about potential summer employment in their firms or referrals to their colleagues who may be interested in hiring a law student for the summer.

If you plan to relocate to a city, you should know that most major metropolitan areas are attractive to a large number of hopeful law graduates. This is especially true if any law schools are located there. It is very difficult to break into that kind of market with few job contacts and a law degree from a nonlocal school.

Loans Are Always Available! Under current federal programs, the Stafford and unsubsidized Stafford loans are available even to late applicants. Assuming your credit record is not a barrier, you are also eligible to borrow supplemental funds through private commercial programs up to the cost of education.

Try to pare down what you'll take with you to law school. It'll cost you less to move and keep your life less complicated.

HOW FEDERAL LOAN PAYMENTS WORK

Once you know how to apply for federal Stafford loans and decide which school you will be attending, you will probably want to know more about how to actually get the loans, how the schools receive that money, and what your payment responsibilities will be.

How Your Federal Loan Money Gets to Your School

Because Stafford loans (the primary program accepted by law schools) are made by a private lender such as a bank, a savings and loan association, a credit union, or an insurance company, check with your school to see if they have a lender they recommend. Compare fees. Some lenders reduce or eliminate some of the optional fees lenders can charge. Your school should have this information. Once you indicate who you intend your lender to be, the lender will send you a master promissory note (MPN). You will then return the promissory note to the lender or submit the completed MPN to the financial aid office at the school that you plan to attend.

You will be asked on the MPN if you want to capitalize the interest on your student loans. Consider not capitalizing the interest on your loan, if possible. This means that if you are given unsubsidized money, you can pay-as-you-go to deal with the interest that is accruing on your loan. It may not be that your parents or spouse can pay for all of your costs, but they may be able to help decrease your future debt by paying the interest each month. If you find this to be possible, when you graduate and go into repayment, your loan amounts will be much lower.

Once you've submitted any additional required documentation, the school calculates your eligibility for the subsidized and/or unsubsidized portion of the loan, certifies your loan, and forwards the MPN directly to the lender.

Once the loan is approved, the lender transmits the funds to the school via electronic funds transfer (EFT), then the school financial aid office will disburse the funds, after tuition and fees have been subtracted, to you. The amount you are given in this disbursement is to support you until the next semester or disbursement of money. There are no other ways to get more money until the next school disbursement. You should not consider this money only for the 14 to 16 weeks of school, as it may be 20 to 22 weeks before you get the next disbursement of money. You will need to plan ahead to make sure your money lasts that long.

Take this timetable into account when applying for a federal Stafford loan:

- It takes three to four weeks for the federal processor to process your FAFSA.
- Depending on the lender and the time of the year, you may not receive any money until 8 to 12 weeks after completing the loan application.

Your Monthly Payments

The amount of your monthly payment will depend on the total amount you borrowed, the number of months in the repayment schedule you chose, and whether you elected to pay interest on any unsubsidized loans while in school (capitalizing).

Usually a student will have a repayment schedule of ten years; however, borrowers can choose repayment schedules of up to 25 years. Prior borrowers can opt for federal loan consolidation, which is described in more detail in the section called Loan Repayment Options later in this chapter.

If you don't meet the repayment terms of the loan, you will be considered in default, and the entire balance of the loan becomes due. If your loan goes into default, you must rehabilitate the debt before you'll be eligible for additional federal aid, including loans. See the section called Help for Loan Defaulters later in this chapter.

Deferments

Under certain circumstances you may be able to defer, or postpone, the payments of your Federal Stafford Loan. For example, you may qualify for a deferment of principal and/or interest on your federal loan if you are:

The Federal Stafford Loan Program and the Ford Federal Direct Loan Program share a standard repayment plan: equal monthly installments over a maximum of ten years, with a minimum monthly installment of $50.

- Studying at least half-time at a postsecondary school
- Studying in an approved graduate or postgraduate fellowship-supported program or in an approved rehabilitation program for the disabled
- Unable to find full-time employment
- Experiencing economic hardship

Deferments aren't automatic. You must apply for a deferment according to the procedures established by your lender.

Forbearance

Forbearance means the lender agrees to grant you a temporary suspension of payments, reduced payments, or an extension of the time for your payments. You can request forbearance in situations that aren't covered by normal deferments, such as those listed previously.

HELPFUL ADVICE ON PRIVATE LOANS

Private, commercial loans can make up the difference between what the federal loan programs offer in aid and what the individual school costs of attendance are. Usually, there's no requirement for a cosigner or collateral, depending on your credit history. The lenders assume that you'll be able to repay in the future. However, the loan terms are different from federal financial aid programs. For example, interest accrues from the time the funds are disbursed. In most cases, the fees charged to originate and guarantee are higher, but not always. The interest rate charged does not have the same cap as federal loans.

Your Ability to Get a Loan Depends on Your Credit!

When students first start using credit cards, they are often inexperienced at managing money and do it badly. Missed payments or bank checks written with insufficient funds create credit problems for students who are not careful about handling finances. Because private loans are credit-based, a clean credit file is an important asset.

Treat your credit history as carefully as you treat your grade point average. Just as a poor GPA in one semester takes several semesters to recover from, it takes quite a while to restore your credit rating again after a missed payment. The negative score remains on your credit report, just as the grades from one bad semester are always part of your academic record.

Before you apply to law school, it is critical that you check to see what your credit score is, what credit history the main credit bureaus have for you, and that all the information is correct. If there are errors in your credit history, it can take up to six months to correct them. Lenders use a minimum credit score requirement to determine the interest rate that a student will be charged. Items included in determining a person's credit score are the number of late payments, the total owed on credit cards, and the number of cards the person has.

In addition, any bankruptcy proceedings within the last seven years or outstanding liens or charge-offs reported to the credit bureau will affect your credit history and the rate at which you will be charged for student loans. Remember: student loans are not dischargeable through bankruptcy.

Every year when you apply for a private student loan, your credit history will be reviewed. Don't miss credit card payments while you are in school, thinking they won't matter. You could be denied loans for your second or third years if you skip credit card payments while in school.

Don't Take on More Than You Need!

Recent default data shows that graduates who default are those who overborrowed as law students. The difference between income-producing debt and non-income-producing debt is important for you to understand. It's like the difference between borrowing for a house and borrowing for a vacation.

One type of borrowing provides for an essential (like housing), the other is for things it would be nice to have. Borrowing for tuition, which will allow you to complete your legal education, is income-generating debt. Borrowing for living expenses should be done very carefully, as you will be paying those debts off in the future without a similar income-producing return. The loans you take today obligate future income and take away from the options you might like to have later.

Servicing future debt means less money for things like saving for retirement. If a student overborrows by just $1,000 during her law school career, she could reduce her potential resources for retirement by $67,303. The $12.43 per month she needs to service a $1,000

Every $10,000 borrowed may equal payments of approximately as much as $110 per month, assuming a standard ten-year repayment.

loan debt for 20 years, if invested in a tax-deferred annuity yielding the historical annual average return of 12 percent (based on the S&P 500), results in an estimated $67,000 more for retirement. Suddenly, cutting back your expenses by $30 a week to reduce your expenses by $1,000 a year has greater significance. If a student were able to reduce expenses by $1,000 per year for three years, the $37.29 that does not have to go toward servicing that debt could yield triple the funds available to invest in retirement. This would result in as much as $201,909 more for retirement under the scenario described above.

Because many students assume that they will be rich as lawyers, they do not worry about their debt. But the current average salary for graduating, first year attorneys is only in the $40,000 to $50,000 range. It's not that much money after taxes. The big firms still have starting salaries in the six figures ($135,000 to $145,000 is the current average), but fewer than 20 percent of law school graduates get those coveted, high-paying jobs. Check out the average salaries of lawyers at *www.nalp.org* and for more info and stats.

To calculate the loan payments you'll have, check out these calculators:

- *www.accessgroup.org/software/Access_Advisor/index.htm*
- *www.salliemae.com*
- *www.findaid.org*

Private Loan Programs for Law School Students

As mentioned earlier, there are loan programs out there specifically for law school students. Here are some of the most common programs:

- Law Access Loan Program—sponsored by the Access Group
- T.H.E. Loan Program—sponsored by Northstar
- GradEXCEL/EXCEL—sponsored by Nellie Mae, a private loan agency
- CitiAssist—contact Citibank for more information

As the economic environment changes, new private loan programs are added and other programs are discontinued. Check with the individual programs for their current provisions. For another source of current loans available to law students, along with a comparison of similar programs, visit *www.estudentloans.com*.

LOAN REPAYMENT OPTIONS

In this age of much higher loan debt, the amount that students borrow for college is equivalent to what students used to owe for college and law school combined. It's a relief to learn that there are a number of strategies available to help make the payments more manageable. Make no mistake: a loan is a loan. Even if you're able to stretch the payments out to make them easier to afford, a loan is still an encumbrance to future income. The payments might have an effect on the career decisions you make and the jobs you pursue, as well as other life choices.

The obvious way to reduce the loan payments you'll have to make after you graduate is to borrow less while you're in law school. In addition, the following options are available to make loan payments more affordable:

- Federal loan consolidation
- Income contingent loan repayment

Federal Loan Consolidation

Federal loan consolidation programs allow students with substantial debt to combine several federal loans into one larger loan with a longer repayment schedule, which means that the total cost of the student's law school education becomes much higher. They also help resolve the problem of having multiple lenders. One key restriction, however, is that these programs apply only to federal loan programs. Private loans are not always eligible for consolidation. It is not always wise, depending on the market, to consolidate your loans. Confer with your school financial aid administrator to ascertain if consolidation of your loans is a wise choice at the time you are considering consolidation.

When you consolidate your loans, you will execute a new promissory note with your consolidating lender, who will pay off your earlier loans. You may have the option of deciding which loans to consolidate. Often, students consolidate their higher interest loans but keep their Federal Perkins Loans separate since the interest rate is so low. The new loan has an interest rate based on the weighted average of the rates of the consolidated loans.

Normally, to qualify for federal loan consolidation, you must be in your grace period or in repayment. If in repayment, you should be no more than 90 days delinquent in making your payments (under the Federal Direct Loan Consolidation Program, you may be in default status, provided you have made satisfactory arrangements for repayment). There are differences in consolidation loan programs. But the principle is the same: to help students repay their educational loans. You should check out the details of the consolidation loan programs as you approach graduation or the beginning of the repayment period. Find out if your student loan lender participates in the consolidation program. If your lender doesn't participate, you can shop around and arrange a consolidation loan through a lender that does.

Income Contingent Loan Repayment

Since January 1995, the William D. Ford Federal Direct Loan Program, through its Individual Education Account (IEA), has allowed graduates to have federal Stafford and unsubsidized Stafford loan payments based on after-graduation earnings. There are three other repayment options offered as well, and graduates can choose to move between the programs as their financial circumstances change.

In addition to the standard ten-year repayment plan for federal loans, borrowers have the following options:

- Option 1: Extended repayment. Similar to the standard repayment plan, it allows the student to repay a fixed amount over a period longer than ten years.
- Option 2: Income contingent repayment. You pay a percentage of your salary no matter how much you've borrowed. If you have high debt, this option could require many more years of repayment than the standard ten years. As your salary increases, so would your loan repayments. The drawback to this option is that the longer you take to repay, the more interest you pay on the loan. Indeed, if your payment doesn't cover the current interest due, unpaid interest will be capitalized, increasing the amount of principal you owe. If you are married, your spouse's income is included

in the calculation used to determine your monthly payment.

- Option 3: Graduated repayment. This allows you to opt for lower payments at the beginning of the repayment cycle when your salary is lower. The payments automatically increase as the number of years you have been in repayment increase. The repayment term remains ten years, but the payments are more manageable in the beginning when you will probably make a lower salary.

The Ford program offers a free service to project loan payments under the various direct loan consolidation options at no obligation to the borrower.

The government may help you when you repay your loans. The Taxpayer Relief Act of 1997 provides assistance to borrowers in repayment during the first 60 months of payment. If your adjusted gross income is less than $55,000 (single) or up to $75,000 for married borrowers, up to $2,500 of the interest paid on student loans, including private and federal loans, can be used to reduce your federal taxes. See the IRS website: *www.irs.ustreas.gov.*

Help for Loan Defaulters

One additional aspect of the Federal Income Contingent Loan Program is that it offers previous loan defaulters a way to bring their loans into current status so that the borrower is eligible for federal aid to fund future education.

A borrower with a defaulted loan can enter into an income contingent repayment agreement and have his or her aid eligibility restored as a result. Prior to this program, loan defaulters were required to make monthly payments for at least six months before they could apply for additional federal aid.

Once in the income contingent repayment program, the student must continue making payments on the loan even while enrolled in law school. The process requires at least 90 days to arrange. If you are in default on a prior federal loan and hope to enroll in law school at the beginning of fall term and receive federal aid, you should begin making arrangements to participate in the income contingent loan program at least six months before in order to allow sufficient time for your defaulted loan to be brought current and your new application to be processed.

Loan Repayment Assistance Programs (LRAPs)

For graduates interested in pursuing a career in public service, a number of law schools and a few states offer loan repayment assistance programs, called LRAPs. Approximately 84 law schools offer some form of LRAP assistance to their graduates. See Equal Justice Works at *www.equaljustice works.org* for a complete list and links to each school and program.

There are many variations in the way that LRAPs are created. Each law school that has a program has created it based on the individual needs and goals of the school, so if this type of program piques your interest, get the details on the program offered by each school you are planning to attend. Each has its own definition of public interest and its own formula for determining benefits. Equal Justice Works periodically surveys law schools to find out which additional schools have added LRAPs and tracks the changes schools make in their programs. They periodically publish a manual on LRAPs, available online at the above website.

SUMMING UP

I hope that this chapter on financing law school has made you realize that there's a lot more to getting into law school than just taking the LSAT. A successful start to your journey through the labyrinth requires substantial financial planning and a great deal of time and effort on your part, in order to survive the threat of the money minotaur.

But if you make a concerted effort to follow the advice in this chapter, you will be well prepared and will put forward the best possible case for yourself. Three years of law school and a lifetime as a lawyer will be your reward.

Chapter 3

How to Hit the Ground Running Your First Day as a 1L

"**L**OOK AT THE STUDENT** to your left; look at the student to your right. One of you won't be here next year."

Most 1Ls have heard or will soon hear this unsettling quote. The reality is that, barring some cataclysmic event, all of you will actually graduate. Law student lore regarding failure rates is a holdover from the law school experience of years ago. Schools today are more selective on the front end in accepting and rejecting applicants, and as a result the need to arbitrarily weed out students has been reduced (with the caveat that lower-tier schools maintain an accreditation formula which may necessitate a higher percentage of student failures). If you work hard and smart, you will graduate and likely do quite well.

The law school process is designed to encourage you to think, prepare, speak, write, and even begin to act like a lawyer. The core components of the process are the Socratic dialogue, which emulates many functions of law practice (such as analysis, client consultation, negotiation, and the various components of litigation), and the cases themselves, which are essentially the state of the law at the time the opinion was written and as articulated by the appellate justice. Make no mistake, your first-year grades generally determine your law firm and other clerkship opportunities. This chapter will reduce some of the mystery behind the law school process and explain some of the basic components that you can expect, especially during your first year, as well as ways to deal effectively with the labyrinth. In addition, at the end of this chapter is a checklist of things you can do before school begins, which will enable you to hit the ground running.

UNDERSTAND THAT YOUR FIRST-YEAR GRADES ARE OF CRITICAL IMPORTANCE

There is absolutely no way around it—grades are simply the most important thing that you will take with you when you graduate from law school. And because recruiting by law firms is almost entirely based upon first-year grades, your academic success in school will likely have a lasting effect on your career. Like a military paratrooper in battle, you must hit the ground running and take command of your study plan as quickly as possible.

First-year grades determine which students are selected for law review and moot court, which are surefire tickets to an incomparable clerkship or other exceptional opportunities during your second and third years in law school—and beyond! Clerkships often determine your employment opportunities following graduation. So if one of your objectives is a good job after graduation, then you should plan on doing well that critical first year. You will be competing against every other student in your class for grades and class ranking, in most cases. Some of the top law schools have done away with rankings—certainly a hotly debated topic and the bane of law firm recruiters who seek the top 15 percent of a class.

Here's the bad news. Your entire grade for any 1L class will likely be based upon one exam, which is generally graded anonymously and based upon the grading curve. How you spend your time preparing for that exam is left entirely up to you. Further, you should understand that your exam will probably not even be marked or returned to you, and your professor will not give you any feedback. In fact, during your entire time in law school, you will most likely receive no feedback or direction from anyone as to how to improve your performance. Whether this is fair or not is irrelevant; it's just the way things have always been and probably always will be in law school. I would argue that one reason this system has prevailed is that it makes the professors' job that much easier; it virtually eliminates all accountability as far as grading exams fairly and thoroughly and, for that matter, professors' effectiveness as teachers. If you don't receive back a graded exam, you cannot easily challenge your grade.

The good news is that if you follow the techniques recommended in this book, you will increase your chances of mastering the subjects and writing exams so you can stand out on the grading curve. This book provides the guidance and techniques to help you learn to read the law and write effectively about it, spot issues, and develop cogent and organized arguments. The result will be that you will maximize your exam performance and achieve better grades.

Not too long ago, I caused a minor stir when I tweeted, "Anyone who tells you to take the summer off before law school instead of preparing either made Bs or has a very short memory." My post resulted in a host of angry responses, especially from folks who advise 1Ls to take the summer off before law school. Could it be that I was creating a panic in order to sell books? These folks were outraged that anyone could suggest that students actually prepare for law school.

I wrote this book because the entire time I was in law school I suspected that some students had an advantage. They just seemed to understand what was going on and what they needed to do to graduate on top. These students weren't more intelligent than anyone else. But they understood the game. Perhaps mom was a lawyer or they were dating a 3L. I didn't know. But they appeared to hit the ground running from the day they set foot in law school. While the uninformed 1Ls were re-reading cases, the savvy soon-to-be law reviewers were investing their time in money activities—creating meaningful outlines that helped them to assimilate the law and spot key issues, and writing practice exams.

This book is my attempt to level the playing field a bit. It describes at least one method, the Pyramid Outline, to help you focus your studies, and gives you an orientation to the entire law school process so you can avoid the kind of stuff that will suck up a huge amount of time with little payback where it counts—exam time.

The bottom line is that you are investing a huge sum of money and three years of your life in your legal education. Merely showing up for law school on your first day in the hopes that someone will tell you what to do is yet another false turn in the labyrinth.

If you are starting law school this fall, get busy. Begin to understand the law school process. Whatever you do, don't walk into your law school expecting it to be like college. There may or may not be a syllabus. There are no pop quizzes, and there is no warm-up.

As a result, here are some tasks that I recommend completing before orientation day. In other words, these are the first turns to take in the law school labyrinth:

- Do some on-campus reconnaissance.
- Accept the Socratic method for what it is—a pedagogical tool that will have virtually no effect on your grades.
- Understand the role of your professors.
- Be familiar with the United States legal system.
- Know what to expect in your 1L classes.

Let's look at these tasks in more depth.

DO SOME ON-CAMPUS RECONNAISSANCE

A visit to your law school the summer before the onslaught of new, nervous 1Ls will likely yield a gold mine of information. Talk with the administrative personnel at your school and get to know them; they will become invaluable resources to you later. A little kindness with these people will go a very long way. Learn as much as you can about the details of your school: the classrooms, the professors, the library and study facilities, food services, student organizations (both honorary and otherwise), student mailboxes, and the like.

In particular, the law library will be the center of your universe your first year. This is because, despite the innovations of the electronic age, law schools still teach legal research the old-fashioned way—through the use of reporters. Legal reporters are the books that report judicial opinions (also referred to by law students and lawyers as cases) and are organized by geographic jurisdiction. Most lawyers today use electronic research to determine the status of a particular law or element of the law;

you will also learn how to conduct electronic research. But you first must go through the ritual that all law students experience, that is learning how to conduct paper research.

Additionally, you will probably spend a great deal of time studying in the library. 1Ls tend to congregate in the library and it also functions as a social venue. Further, law libraries have numerous treatises and hornbooks, which are analyses of particular areas of the law. I recommend that you spend some quality time with some of these books before you begin school. Pick up a few and thumb through the pages. In particular, look for treatises on your first-year subjects—torts, criminal law, real property, civil procedure, contracts, real property, and the like. You will begin to get a sense of what the study of law is all about.

ACCEPT THE SOCRATIC METHOD FOR WHAT IT IS

I'll never forget the first time I was called on in class.

"Mr. Sedberry, do you think that a party who has sent a purchase order for goods to another party should be required to purchase those goods under the following circumstances?"

I was startled from my brief pre-class notes review to realize that class had begun and Professor Reed had called upon me. It was late in my first semester of law school, and I had begun to think that I had somehow avoided the professor's seating chart and his scrutiny.

Professor Reed finished his now indecipherable question, " . . . which was responded to with a form acknowledgement with different terms should be bound to the terms of the purchase order or the form acknowledgement?"

Struggling to recall the facts of the three cases which were assigned for reading, and then to decide which case he was talking about, I sputtered out: "Well, uh, the court held that, uh . . ."

Certainly, this was not one of my more articulate moments.

Professor Reed responded (actually, in a rather compassionate way): "Not what the court held, Mr. Sedberry, what *you* think?"

"Uh . . . uh . . ." I parried skillfully. The classroom had become so quiet that I thought I actually heard the proverbial pin dropping. My mind went completely and utterly blank.

"Uh . . . well . . . er . . ." I continued, driving home my point and proving to everyone within earshot that I was brilliant. Professor Reed looked genuinely concerned that I might pass out. Students on either side of me stared intently down at their casebooks, clearly not wanting to get drawn in to what was quickly becoming an irreversibly humiliating situation.

The year before I started law school, I had given an address to a state legislature at the invitation of the governor of that state. I had made presentations to dozens of business groups and industry associations, involving thousands of people. I had been interviewed by television and newspaper journalists. I had conversed with senators, former United States vice presidents, CEOs, prominent sports figures, celebrities, and other extremely intimidating people. At that point in my life, I was rarely intimidated or speechless.

And yet, as Professor Reed asked me a couple of simple questions, in what was pretty much a nonconfrontational and conversational way, I babbled as if I were under a powerful anesthetic. My face flushed a deep red. I began to perspire and my breathing became shallow. I reverted to that scared ten-year-old inside all of us who becomes speechless when asked to explain the homework problem to the class.

Simply put, the Socratic method does something to your head.

Nonetheless, in order to succeed in your journey through the labyrinth, you absolutely must be able step back and look at the Socratic method for what it is. At its core, the Socratic method is simply a pedagogical tool. It's kind of like using a student as a sparring dummy in a karate class or as resuscitation dummy in a CPR class. Not that I'm calling you a dummy.

The Origins of the Socratic Dialogue

Socrates of ancient Athens fame is commonly credited as the father of philosophy and philosophical dialogue. Socrates would meet with a group of protégés and quiz them with a series of increasingly pointed questions. Each of these dialogues, as guided by Socrates, ultimately led to a lightbulb moment for his protégés, as they realized the point of the discussion. Plato, a student of Socrates, immortalized this didactic process through his writings, in which various characters debate a topic through questions. At its core, the method was used to challenge hypotheses commonly held by students. Almost every thought that can be articulated rests upon assumptions. The Socratic method is also a way to identify and dissect those assumptions.

The Socratic dialogue begins when the professor asks a student a simple question, or one that appears to be simple on its surface. The student will typically answer the question quickly. Most likely, implicit in the student's answer are a variety of assumptions, both large and small. The teacher then asks another question, which points out the assumptions and most likely cannot be answered in a manner that is consistent with the student's prior answer. In other words, the professor begins with a general question that elicits a generalization from the student. The professor then poses questions that pin the student's assumptions down and ultimately illustrate the logical fallacy of the student's answer. Although not always the outcome, this is the point of the dialogue. Candidly, it's largely a no-win situation, which is something that is very difficult for the typical type A, overachieving law student to grasp. Of course, the Socratic method is only as effective as the professor that is administering it.

The stress and fear created by the Socratic method has been described in numerous books and movies. But I believe that if you place the Socratic experience in the proper perspective, it can actually be an extremely useful tool in your development as a lawyer.

The Socratic Method: A Sink or Swim Pedagogy

Ever since it was first used in law school by Harvard's Christopher Columbus Langdell, the Socratic method has been the bane of law students everywhere. This teaching method is somewhat analogous to learning to ride a bicycle or to swim. Assuming that you learned these skills as a child, it is likely that your mom or dad taught you by placing you on the seat of the bicycle or in the water. They did not sit you down and explain to you the physics involved. They probably did not try to help you understand concepts such as balance, motion and inertia, gravity, or buoyancy. Instead, they put you on the bicycle, gave you a push, and told you to start pedaling. You almost certainly fell down numerous times, got back up, and started pedaling again. Similarly, when teaching you to swim, they put you in the pool with floaties or the like and told you to start kicking. You probably sunk, took in some water, sputtered a bit, and got pulled out. Regardless, you went at it again and again. And eventually, you learned how to ride the bike and/or swim.

The reason your parents taught you this way is that it is ultimately the most efficient teaching method. The various elements involved in learning to ride a bike are hugely complicated. Trying to explain the principles of buoyancy to someone who has never swum is difficult and unproductive. It is simply easier to show someone how to do something than it is to explain it. In order to maintain your balance on a bicycle and propel yourself forward, all of the elements must come together at the same time. If your parents tried to break these elements down for you before you ever got on the bike, you would probably eventually learn to ride. However, just putting you on the beast and giving you a push in the right direction works much faster. You intuitively teach yourself how to ride. Likewise, you learn to swim by kicking and sputtering in the water until it becomes intuitive. The Socratic method works in much the same way. To break down the skills that a lawyer uses instinctively would be hugely complicated, confusing, and likely counterproductive.

The Socratic method also resembles athletic training. A coach typically prescribes training exercises designed to simulate the sport and to develop the agility, coordination, and strength to optimize an athlete's performance. A law professor skilled in the Socratic method will continually challenge the student's assertion until a working hypothesis is established. The hypothesis is usually an elaboration of a particular element of the cause of action you are covering. For example, it may deal with the intent element of battery in torts or the definiteness requirement in contracts (which is necessary in order to create an offer capable of being legally accepted, thus forming a legally enforceable agreement). By engaging in this dialogue, you will learn to prepare carefully, think and react quickly, and anticipate the moves of your opponent.

Law professors assign cases for reading and then interrogate students exhaustively regarding the issues, legal principles, and analysis contained therein. The students justify their assertions with facts or law. The professor, through Socratic dialogue, encourages students to extend the assertions through the labyrinth.

In the worst-case scenario, the assertion is no longer supportable. You come to a dead end in the labyrinth and look around. The professor is no longer there guiding you but is instead challenging your apparently silly assertion. Your classmates gleefully enjoy your predicament. The benefit of this process is that law students who have been led down this segment of the labyrinth are determined to never to let it happen again. You realize that you must have facts and not mere speculation to support your assertions. You intuitively learn that any underlying assumptions in an argument must be clearly identified, articulated, and challenged in order to prove their validity. You learn to avoid jumping to conclusions and instead carefully analyze all assumptions made in your arguments.

The Socratic method yields exactly the right result. Fearful students scrutinize each case thoroughly, in an effort to anticipate what issues the professor might raise in class. Fear also motivates the students to engage, listen carefully, and take copious notes.

Keep in mind, however, that this fear simply makes the professor's job easier. The more prepared the student is, the more easily the Socratic dialogue will flow because the professor is able to anticipate the student's responses and adapt the dialogue accordingly based upon experience with earlier students. Regardless, a central theme of this book is that you should do as little class preparation as possible (so long as you are comfortable in the event that you are called upon) and instead spend more time actually learning the body of law, developing your legal reasoning skills, and writing practice exams. Focusing your energy solely on the cases or the Socratic method out of fear of being called upon is like focusing on pedaling without learning balance and how to turn the bike. You need all of these elements in order to propel yourself forward.

Dealing with the Socratic Threat

I found that for a while at least, the Socratic method actually impeded my ability to understand the law. During that first year, I dedicated an inordinate amount of time to reading cases in an attempt to memorize them. Rather than trying to understand where the case I was reading fit into the overall body of law before me, I read with a mind-set of trying to anticipate questions the professor would ask. In business lingo, I was entirely tactical in my focus. I had no strategic perspective whatsoever. Instead, I focused on the potential embarrassment of being called upon by a professor. My ego and pride drove my study methodology.

What I didn't know then (but should have) is that the game is rigged. The professor knows the questions and the answers. This means that any time a student is called upon, it is likely that they are going to look pretty foolish, even on their best day. This is because if the dialogue goes in one direction, the professor can take it in an entirely different direction with one well-placed question, leaving the student completely stumped. That's the point of the Socratic dialogue: to force the student to identify unstated assumptions and reconsider anything previously thought to be well settled.

Students mistakenly believe that if they memorize the case and understand the rules and all of that, they will be well prepared for the Socratic onslaught. However, they come prepared for a polka and the professor turns the dance into a bossa nova. This creates fear and motivates students to read and reread the cases in the vain hope that they won't get fooled again. Instead of focusing on the minutiae of the cases, they should focus on the process: what is happening during the Socratic dialogue and why. This will help the student to learn to analyze, reason, and think like a lawyer.

You will probably find that not all professors are skilled in the Socratic method, and my experience in law school was that there was no typical Socratic experience. There was simply too much variation in terms of professors' effectiveness and preparation, as well as the variation in students' responses. As with the students, some came prepared for class; others appeared to be completely unprepared. I had one professor who viewed class as his personal stand-up comedy act; he used the class to try out new material. Interestingly, at exam time, this professor also authored one of the most difficult exams I experienced during my three years of law school.

Students come to the Socratic method thinking that it is a test, a wits match with the professor. It is more akin to a martial arts demonstration, in which the grasshopper is obliterated by the sensei. Therefore, you learn from the Socratic method by observing. You follow where the professor is leading. You may eventually even be able to anticipate the professor's next move. But the Socratic method, at its core, is a demonstration designed to teach you how lawyers think.

An example of a typical and proper Socratic dialogue should go something like this:

> Professor: Mr. Sedberry, should striking a person's face be the basis for a legal cause of action and from which damages can be recovered?
> Student: Yes, because if you touch someone who doesn't want to be touched, they should be able to recover from you monetarily, as payment for their injuries and as a deterrent.
> Professor: So all unwanted touching should be against the law?
> Student: No, only touching that causes pain or is offensive.
> Professor: And so, Mr. Sedberry, you are asserting that when a doctor administers a shot of penicillin to you in order to cure an infection, you should be able to sue him?
> Student: No . . .

The best way to defend against the Socratic attack is to develop a framework upon which to hang these Socratic dialogues, in order to make sense of them and understand the key principles your professor is trying to impart.

Your Socratic Method Framework. My first piece of advice to you is to simply relax. Take a deep breath. Accept the fact that you are likely going to be embarrassed for a few minutes, and move on.

You must overcome any fear. Fear will simply get in the way of your progress. You must accept that the Socratic dialogue is a totally unfair proposition: the professor knows the questions and the answers and is likely going to try and trap you. It's inevitable. Further, your Socratic performance will have absolutely no effect on your grade. It is also highly unlikely that you will be called upon more than a few times during your law school career, in total. And however you perform, it will all be soon forgotten anyway!

Certainly, you should prepare adequately for class. You should read and brief the case, or summarize it in such a fashion that you will be able to quickly recall its important components. But do not let your fear of embarrassment dictate how you prioritize your precious study time. Instead, focus most of your energy and time on your study process.

It is so much more important to focus your time on learning the subject and how to reason within it analytically and with justifiable positions and arguments. Reading a case will teach you a rule, an element of a rule, or an alternative interpretation of a rule. So read the case in order to understand the rule. Read the case in order to understand the logic underlying the rule. Read the case in order to understand the various arguments made in support of or against the rule. Read the case in order to understand where the rule fits into the entire body of law. Read the case in order to understand the evolution of the law. *Do not* read the case solely to avoid embarrassment in class.

Go into each class forearmed with two key pieces of information:

1. An understanding of the topic at hand
2. Where that topic fits into the overall outline of the course

Carefully note where the case is placed in the casebook's table of contents or outline in order to determine the relevance of the assigned reading. Allocate a substantial portion of your study time to understanding where the case fits into the overall subject and why. Read the case carefully, brief it using the methods contained in this book, and insert it into your Pyramid Outline which is explained on page 133. The type of time allocation I am advocating will, in all likelihood, enable you to deal more effectively with the Socratic dragon as well. You will be better prepared by understanding where the assigned cases fit into the overall legal scheme, and as a result you will be more confident. Instead of worrying about whether you will be called upon by the professor, actively engage yourself in the Socratic dialogue, regardless of whether you are the designated punching bag that day. Ask yourself where the professor is leading the student and why.

Take comfort in the fact that after your first year of law school, the use of the Socratic method by your professors will decline dramatically.

Some professors in second- and third-year classes do not call on students at all. In effect, these classes are more akin to traditional postgraduate seminars. There are lectures, an exchange of ideas, and perhaps a paper to write in these classes. Most likely, your risk of exposure to a Socratic grilling will be small, or if you are called upon, the pain will be brief.

Here's a recap of how to deal with the stress of the Socratic dialogue:

- Don't forget to breathe! It will help you to relax and keep oxygen heading in your brain's direction.
- Focus on the question that is being asked. Try and anticipate where the professor is heading, but don't get too far ahead of the professor. Listen carefully and do not read too much into the question, which may or may not even be related to the assigned reading.
- If you do not understand the question, ask for clarification. You are much better off admitting that you aren't following. It is entirely possible that the problem rests with the professor's communication skills, not your analytical skills.
- Try and recall the big themes presented by the case. The professor is likely asking for your synthesis of some issue that is raised by the case. This is where reading the LexisNexis or Westlaw unedited versions of the case will come in handy. The headnotes will give you a good road map of what the case is about.
- When it's all over, forget about it. Your performance or lack thereof will have no effect on your grade, and by next class no one will remember a thing you said or that you were nervous. Further, it is no indication of your future potential as a lawyer. The only thing you should do is ensure that you have captured the essence of what the class was about in your class notes and outlines.

Again, don't take the Socratic threat too seriously. Simply understand that the Socratic method is a small disturbance in your overall journey through the labyrinth. In spite of the way it may seem (especially if you are in the hot seat), the net result of a major failure under Socratic scrutiny is a big fat zero where things really count in law school—your grade point average.

UNDERSTAND THE ROLE OF YOUR PROFESSORS

There are professors who are absolutely committed to helping students in any way that they can. That said, you will also probably encounter professors who are difficult and apparently completely lacking in compassion for the law student. The purpose of this section is to help you begin to think about how you will personally deal with the variety of professors you will encounter in the labyrinth and the politics of dealing with them.

Although your exams will likely be graded anonymously, your professors will nonetheless have a tremendous impact on your grades and to a great extent, your attitude toward law school. As a result, you should develop a plan as early as possible concerning your interaction with professors.

The interpersonal dynamics in law school are incredibly complex. Students, in a pressure cooker of intelligentsia, combined with the Socratic threat, are competing in a game of extremely high stakes (arguably, the game has an impact for the remainder of the students' working lives). Students are frequently the most impressed with the professors who exhibit the most sadistic tendencies in class; that is almost a Stockholm Syndrome phenomenon. These professors earn the admiration of these impressionable students, which in turn legitimizes and probably increases Socratic sadism. In addition, most law schools engage in annual student voting for selection of the best professors, which is essentially a "most popular professor" contest. These teaching awards tend to foster the mind-set among some professors that they need to be accepted by students, and these professors go to great lengths to distinguish themselves. The professors who win these contests may not be the best teachers, but they generally distinguish themselves in some fashion with impressionable law students. Typically, these are the professors who are viewed as "hip" and try to cultivate an image among law students as "the cool professor" or perhaps as a system rebel. Although most professors typically do not get caught up in these rankings, you may occasionally run across one who does.

A friend of mine from my bar review class, I'll call him Scott, graduated from an Ivy League institution near the top of his class. He had a first-year Property professor who was in has late 40s and referred constantly in class to Treasury bills, racing yachts, and fine art in his hypotheticals. (Hypotheticals or "hypos" refer to hypothetical factual situations which the professor creates, typically extending the reach of principles discussed in the case reading and used in the Socratic dialogue to illustrate the effect of that extension.) On the first day, this professor also invited students to refer to him by his first name, which I will say is Dave. Dave was also a Socratic Sadaam Hussein who absolutely bullied the more timid 1Ls. Dave would begin his Socratic dialogue at times with, "I want you to think very carefully before you answer, Mr._____." When the student would begin to answer, Dave would invariably interrupt with, "C-a-r-e-f-u-l-l-y, Mr._____, not carelessly." Or he might use the classic, "I said 'think hard,' Ms._____; it appears instead that you 'hardly think.'" Even for a law professor, this was pretty condescending stuff.

Most of the class, composed of young, impressionable Gen Xers, absolutely ate this stuff up. After all, how cool is a professor who dabbles in the money markets, races in the America's Cup, owns a Van Gogh, and can beat the intellectual tar out of people—sort of a geeky Bruce Wayne?

According to Scott, who has an incredibly dry sense of humor, it was more likely that Dave had been divorced at least once, had four angry teenagers at home who hated him, had a big mortgage and credit card debt, and drove a six-year-old American minivan with a bumper sticker on the back proudly declaring that "My Child Made Straight A's at Walker Middle School." Nonetheless, Dave was a perennial contender in the most popular professor contest. I would imagine Dave rationalized all of it by viewing it as toughening up the students and preparing them for battle.

I heard about another professor from a prestigious Southern school who was a legal prodigy in his 20s and law professor in his 30s. This professor had all the credentials: top school, law review, Order of the Coif[2], federal district court clerkship, and a top firm job. This professor also sported a pageboy-style haircut, always spoke very fast, and referred

---

[2] No, this is not a reference to his hairstyle. Order of the Coif is an honorary organization for law students who graduate in the top 10 percent of their class. The term *coif* refers to the headgear worn by certain old English barristers. Not all law schools have chapters of the Order of the Coif.

constantly in his hypotheticals to Britney Spears and Christina Aguilera. This professor was also a pretty relentless Socratic aggressor, which was perceived as very cool by many 1Ls. To me, it was more likely that this professor probably considered his pocket protector as a fashion necessity and admired Spock's haircut and Vulcan attitude. Regardless, it seems fairly obvious to me that more than a few professors consciously or unconsciously seek the approval of the students they teach. They are, after all, only human.

The point of all this is to hopefully help you to view your professors for what they are: facilitators in your law school education, with strengths and weaknesses just like you. Don't be intimidated, but instead see them as hopefully and legitimately earning your tuition dollars. Professors are people too. As a consumer paying substantial tuition dollars each semester, you have the right to expect a minimum level of competence and courtesy in exchange.

You will most likely meet professors you like, some you don't like, and some who terrify you. The first two responses are reasonable; the last one is not. Fear of a professor will impede your ability to learn. If you find yourself intimidated, then you must do all you can to overcome this fear.

You have the right to expect a minimum level of competence and courtesy in exchange for your substantial tuition expenditure.

Get to know the professor. Make appointments to see the professor during her office hours. You should, however, have a legitimate reason for the meeting. Don't simply drop by to chat or in an effort to earn brownie points. After you have scrutinized the assigned reading, prepared for class, and thought about the issues, there will likely remain legal concepts that puzzle you. These make for good reasons to meet with your professor. However, you need to wrestle with the concepts before you meet with the professor. Make notes of your questions and prepare for the meeting as you would for any other important meeting. Let them help you see the big picture.

I suggest you avoid the after-class bull session ritual that many law professors host. In fairness, these sessions more likely occur because of the sycophantic law students who fawn over the professor in the hopes of earning brownie points. You will probably observe that after class the same four or five students will typically trot up to the professor, pepper him or her with questions, and monopolize the professor's time. As a result, it becomes difficult to get any legitimate questions you might have answered. If you are really struggling with a subject, you would be better served to think about your questions and schedule some time with the professor individually. Professors will be much more candid with you in one-on-one sessions and appreciate your genuine interest. In my own opinion, most professors are pretty intelligent people who can see through the bull session charade.

The bottom line to your professors is this: they, and their employers, view their role as largely to teach students through the Socratic method pedagogy with the casebook and cases as the educational platform.

Further, your interaction, if any, with many of your professors will be largely limited to the classroom experience. They will grade your exams anonymously. Unlike in undergraduate school, what they think about you personally will have little effect on your grade. Consequently, and unlike your undergraduate professors, they will not be the central point in your development as a lawyer. Instead, you will teach yourself through your study methods, case reading, and working with the materials to think like a lawyer. Essentially, your professors will function as facilitators of your learning experience. But with respect to Professor Kingsfield, they cannot teach you to think. You are going to have to do that for yourself.

BECOME FAMILIAR WITH THE UNITED STATES LEGAL SYSTEM

In order to understand how the law is created and administered, it would probably help most students to understand something about the various branches of government, administrative agencies, and the judicial system. Unfortunately, as with much else, law schools assume that you already have this knowledge or that you can quickly develop it. As a result, most schools do not offer a Law 101 class. No one in law school will explain to you the history and structure of the legal system of the United States. No one will tell you how the various lawmaking bodies interact with each other. You will never be tested on your knowledge of the United States legal system. However, this knowledge will greatly enhance your overall understanding of the law and thus, your ability to write an effective exam answer.

In order to make sense of the concept of legal precedent, you need to have a basic understanding of the processes by which the law develops. This knowledge is critical as you begin your law studies and the practice of law.

American Law

American law has developed primarily from five sources:

1. English common law
2. United States common law
3. The United States Constitution
4. Federal and state statutes
5. Governmental administrative agencies

What Is Common Law?

Common law is Anglo-Saxon in origin and refers to laws that are derived from rulings made in court rooms (judicial decision-making), as opposed to laws that are passed (legislative statutes). In other words, common law or case law is derived from studying precedents—previous decisions in similar cases.

The United States common law system is based on legal precedent, which is sometimes referred to as *stare decisis*, (pronounced STA-ray DE-ci-sis), meaning "to stand by things decided" in Latin. (You will find that lawyers frequently like to sprinkle Latin phrases here and there; it makes their work that much more mysterious. I view it as a somewhat charming relic of the past and enjoy doing it myself now and again.) Stare decisis simply means that the decisions of a higher court or its own prior decisions obligate a court to rule consistently with those decisions. The notion of stare decisis brings predictability and legitimacy to the law.

The Rules and Elements of the Law. The law consists of rules, and rules consist of elements. As in the field of chemistry, the term *element* refers to the simplest components of a rule, which can be broken down no further. Elements are important in legal analysis because if one is missing, then a plaintiff or prosecutor will be unable to support a cause of action. For example, the tort (torts are civil lawsuits between a plaintiff and a defendant, as opposed to criminal actions) of battery requires: (1) an act by the defendant, (2) harmful or offensive contact, and (3) the intention by the defendant to cause such contact.

The rule of battery is numbers 1–3 read together. Each of numbers 1–3 represents an element of the rule. Another example is the crime (crimes, in contrast to torts, are legal actions brought by governmental authorities involving criminal penalties such as incarceration, instead of mere monetary damages) of burglary which requires: (1) the breaking and entering, of (2) the dwelling house of another, (3) at nighttime, (4) with the intent to commit a felony.

In this example, a defendant would be liable for burglary if all elements of this crime were fulfilled. Much of the legal analysis you will learn will be to determine the elements of a rule, how they work together, and the logical limits of the rule and its elements.

Common Law versus Civil Law. Civil law is Roman in origin. It was originally developed from Justinian's *Corpus Juris Civilis,* a set of pronouncements by the Byzantine emperor which had the effect of law and evolved from there into a system based on civil code. A civil code is a comprehensive series of enacted and recorded laws that form the basis for a system of government. A civil code typically contains a great amount of detail as to what constitutes compliance with, or conversely, disobedience to the code or law. Therefore, the principle difference between common law and civil code is that common law relies on precedent from judicial court rulings and interpretations that continue to evolve over time, while civil law relies on more static laws that are codified, or published, by the government. At least in theory, a civil code is self-executing, which means that it provides enough detail so that the citizenry knows what it can and cannot do, and there is consequently no need for judicial interpretation.

Given the Anglo-Saxon origins of common law, it won't surprise you that the United States and the United Kingdom are two of the few governmental systems operating under common law. In fact, only Louisiana's state law is derived from the civil law system because it was originally a French colony. France was conquered by Rome, as was Spain, and therefore they have civil law systems, as do their former colonies like Quebec and most of Latin America.

The Study of Cases in Law School. In law school, you will frequently study cases—also called judicial decisions or opinions—made at the appeals or appellate court level. The format of a typical case is explained in greater detail in chapter 4, but in essence, these are the documents a judge uses to convey the law. Cases are excellent teaching tools for three reasons:

1. They convey the facts of the case. The appeals court must clearly explain the facts in order to uphold or deny a lower court decision. Obviously, the facts of a case play a very important role in determining whether a crime has been committed and if so, how that crime should be prosecuted.

   All laws have elements or criteria that must be met in order for liability or guilt to be established. For example, in criminal law, there are generally these requirements (in Latin, of course!): (1) *actus reus* (pronounced ACT-oos RAY-oos), the actual act of committing the crime; and (2) *mens rea* (pronounced MENS RAY-ah), the mental intent to commit the crime.

   Now, suppose you are presented with a case where Bart is accused of murdering Barry. To be convicted, the prosecutor must prove, beyond a reasonable doubt, that Barry died because of Bart's actions (*actus reus*) and that Bart intended to end Barry's life (*mens rea*); in other words, Barry's death was not accidental. If the prosecutor can't prove *both*, Bart can't be convicted of murdering Barry.

   Therefore, being able to identify whether the facts of the case meet these elements of the law is necessary for success in the practice of law and on law school exams. For example, if the fact pattern of an exam question also states that "Bart was living at Sleepytown Institution for the Insane at the time he killed Barry," you would discuss in your answer whether or not Bart was indeed insane, *and* if he was, whether such insanity would mean that he wasn't capable of intending to kill Barry.

2. They describe the current law. The appellate court explains the current state of the law in a jurisdiction, based upon prior judicial decisions or precedent. This is just as important as the facts. Again, our common law system depends on the decisions of a higher court or a court's own prior decisions, which obligate the court to rule consistently and predictably.

3. They show the judge's legal reasoning process. These cases showcase how judges (who are also lawyers) think, reason, and write. By reading the case, the law student gains insight into the judge's reasoning and analytical process. A well-written judicial opinion is one in which the judge shows her work and explains how she got to the decision at hand. This enables you to begin to understand the legal reasoning process and emulate it. Again, this is an excellent teaching tool. Showing one's work is critical to law school exam success. Jumping to legal conclusions without showing your work is a recipe for a C grade.

The United States Constitution

From the very beginning, the United States Constitution, itself a fairly simple document, has been the subject of interpretation by the United States Supreme Court. Ever since the landmark case (which you will study in your first constitutional law course) *Marbury v. Madison*, 5 U.S. 137 (Cranch), the Supreme Court declared that, under Article 3, it possessed the sole power to interpret the Constitution. As a result, the Supreme Court has decided upon numerous issues regarding the division of power in the government (Articles 1–3), individual rights (various amendments), and the roles of state and federal government.

Federal and State Statutes

A statute is a law written by a governing body, such as a state or federal legislature. As you probably know, federal statutes are enacted by a collaborative effort of the United States Senate, House of Representatives, and the Executive Office (the president). Similarly, state statutes are enacted by the various state legislatures.

Both federal and state legislatures are advised by numerous lawyers who are government employees and who often explain to nonlawyer legislators the effect and legality of proposed legislation. Additionally, municipal governments also enact statutes of sorts, usually called ordinances.

Governmental Administrative Agencies

We know that the United States Congress and the various state legislatures enact laws. These laws often delegate authority to various federal and state agencies—created under constitutional authority—to implement these laws. These agencies in turn promulgate laws, such as tax regulations and commerce regulations.

Agencies such as the Internal Revenue Service (IRS), the Equal Employment Opportunity Commission (EEOC), the Environmental Protection Agency (EPA), the Federal Trade Commission (FTC), the Food and Drug Administration (FDA), the Fair Housing Commission (FHC), the Federal Communications Commission (FCC), and countless others arguably create and interpret law every day.

America's Hybrid Legal System. Technically, the United States system of government has become a hybrid of sorts, somewhere between the common law and civil law systems. This is because most laws contain inherent ambiguity, and courts are often called upon to interpret these laws and regulations, thus acting as the ultimate arbiters of these laws. This can be problematic if a judge goes beyond simply interpreting a law. She is said to be legislating from the bench, which is considered beyond the scope of the judge's authority. However, the line of exactly where a law ends and judicial decision-making begins is often quite blurred.

Regardless, and despite the fact that common law is the underpinning of the United States legal system, the reality is that administrative agencies in this country wield immense power. Consider the authority and power of the IRS in the lives of everyday people. Additionally, consider the breadth and depth of state and federal governmental agencies that you deal with personally. It should quickly become apparent to you that ours is, to a large extent, a government administered by agencies. Administrative agencies create law, which is often interpreted by administrative courts. This area of the law has become so important that law schools offer a course cleverly called Administrative Law that is dedicated to this subject.

KNOW WHAT TO EXPECT IN YOUR 1L CLASSES

Virtually every law school has the same first-year curriculum: contracts, torts, constitutional law, property, criminal law, civil procedure, and legal writing. Consequently, the more you can learn about what these subjects entail before you begin law school, the more likely it is that you will do well your first year. At minimum, you should know which courses you will be taking each semester. Although your professors will not post a syllabus until the very last minute, conduct some Internet research on your school's website to at least get a feel for the courses.

Your performance in these courses will likely determine whether you, in fact, get it and will set the tone of your entire law school performance. If you do well that first year, your second and third years will be immensely more rewarding. You will spend less time trying to understand the basics and more time learning and developing your craft, which will ultimately make the study of law (which will become a lifelong endeavor) more interesting and pleasurable.

Finally, these courses also constitute the core of most, if not all, bar exams. I realize that it is a bit early to be thinking about bar preparation! However, the point is that eventually your assimilation of this material will have a real-world impact on your effectiveness as a lawyer. If you do not grasp the fundamental principles contained in these courses, your bar preparation will be that much more difficult.

Your Law School Section

The incoming first-year class is divided into smaller sections, typically about 80 to 100 students. You will share the joy of all of your first-year classes with these people; however, your legal writing class will be subdivided into even smaller groups of about 20 students. At least in theory, you should receive fairly personalized instruction in effective legal writing.

Of course, upon being assigned to a section, everyone will worry whether they were assigned to the better section. I remember wondering whether Section A meant that you were on the A team (as in high school athletics) and if the students in Section B were less capable and placed there for remedial purposes. But your section assignment has nothing to do with much of anything, other than teaching economies. During your second and third years, you will not be part of a section. However, you will enjoy the benefit of substantially smaller classes and at most schools, the liberty of selecting courses you actually want to take.

Contracts

Contract courses deal with the enforceability of agreements between parties. The facts almost always involve a dispute between parties. The issues covered typically include:

- The requirements for an offer
- Acceptance
- The elements of an enforceable agreement
- Conditions to performance of one's obligations
- The Uniform Commercial Code (UCC)
- Breaches of an agreement
- Damages

This course examines when an agreement between parties is legally enforceable, as distinguished from an unenforceable promise. For example:

- A promise to make a gift (unenforceable due to a lack of consideration)
- Advertisements as offers (generally, an advertisement is merely an invitation by the merchant to a customer to make an offer)
- Voidable contracts (contracts with a minor or contracts made while incapacitated, such as by intoxication)

- Unconscionable contracts (these are the so-called contracts of adhesion; so one-sided, oppressive, and unfair as
  to be unenforceable)
- UCC "battle of the forms" (the Uniform Commercial
  Code, adopted by most states, dictates the rules of the
  game when merchants' form agreements disagree or
  contain additional or different terms)

When a party breaches an agreement, the other party is generally entitled to be placed in the same position as if that party had performed his or her obligations.

In class, most likely, you will never actually read a complete contract. You will probably never study typical sections included in most commercial contracts. You will not see a sampling of different types of contracts. Instead, your contracts course will teach you contractual principles of interpretation. The theory is that if you develop the critical thinking skills necessary to understand and interpret contract law, the ability to draft and interpret contracts themselves will follow.

Torts

Tort law cases often date back to Old English common law cases, complete with the accompanying arcane language and concepts. A typical tort case often contains amusing, entertaining, or even tragic disputes between parties. Typically, you will cover:

- Intentional torts
- The concepts of negligence and gross negligence
- Defenses

In a tort case, or civil case, a plaintiff (the person who initiates a lawsuit) can recover damages in a civil action from the defendant for wrongful conduct. In a criminal case, a third party—typically the local, state, or federal government (i.e., a district attorney)—brings the case to court and prosecutes a claim against a defendant for a violation of a statute.

Torts is arguably the simplest of law school classes. Generally, someone is injured and the question is whether someone else pays for it. However, some of the interaction of the concepts discussed previously, especially when interlaced into a single exam fact pattern, can become incredibly complicated and confusing. The ability to spot issues comes in especially handy on torts exams. This is because professors often throw in nonissue red herring facts in order to obfuscate the real issue(s).

The subject of torts is an excellent didactic starting point to teach new students about the law and legal analysis. There are abundant majority/minority positions regarding particular elements of causes of action. In addition, the facts in cases are frequently in dispute. Further, much of tort law involves the notion of public policy, which concerns the rightfulness or wrongfulness of holding someone accountable for his or her actions in a particular situation. As a result, there are always issues that can be argued both ways, either factually or legally. You will probably spend a great deal of time dissecting the various elements of particular torts.

For example, the tort of false imprisonment requires the tortfeasor (the person committing the act) to confine someone. However, the body of law around this area differs on whether that person must be aware of the confinement. This becomes a good basis for an exam question: a person is confined in a room. However, the room is unlocked and the person is, in reality, free to leave. The issue is whether that person was actually confined, at least in the legal sense. The common law intentional torts include:

- Battery (harmful or offensive contact)
- Assault (placing another in imminent fear of battery)
- Intentional infliction of emotional distress
- Trespass to property
- Trespass to chattels (*chattels* refers to personal property)
- False imprisonment

Key issues include:

- What intent is required to create liability
- Damages (note that unlike in the study of contracts,
  where damages are required in order to sustain a cause of

action, in torts no actual damages are required; a judge
or jury can award monetary damages merely to teach the
defendant a lesson, so-called punitive damages)
- Defenses (such as necessity, self-defense, and defense of
others)

Intentional Torts. You will spend a large amount of time understanding
the intent requirement for intentional torts (as opposed to the unintentional tort of negligence). The classic case, as described in the introduction to this book, is *Garratt v. Dailey*, 46 Wash.2d 197, 279 P.2d 1091
(1955), in which a five-year-old boy moves a chair that an arthritic old
woman was sitting in moments before, thereby causing her to ungrace-
fully pratfall as she attempted to resume her seat. This case is used to
illustrate the concept that the intent element for intentional torts does
not necessarily require the tortfeasor to intend to injure anyone. Instead,
the plaintiff only needs to show that the tortfeasor was substantially certain that his actions would cause injury. In *Garratt v. Dailey*, for example,
the boy was found liable for battery, because the court's view was that the
boy possessed the requisite intent (whether parents can be held liable
for the torts of their minor children is yet another discussion found in
the subject of torts). This is true whether the little angel intended to
actually harm the woman or not.

In torts, you will also discuss the concept of transferred intent, in
which the tortfeasor's intent to commit an act against a plaintiff can
be transferred to another plaintiff. For example, if a tortfeasor swings
a baseball bat at someone intending to hit them, but misses and hits
someone else, the tortfeasor's intent to hit anyone will suffice to form
the basis for a battery claim.

Negligence. Negligence refers to harmful actions that are contrary to
those of a so-called reasonable person. The legal standard for negligence
is whether the person knew or should have known that his actions would
result in harm. Recklessness refers to conduct which is so negligent that
it virtually rises to the level of intentional conduct. You may also cover
products liability, in which manufacturers of products (as well as resell-
ers) have a duty to provide safe products and to provide warnings on
products which are dangerous.

Property

This course deals with the ownership of real and personal property, although the vast majority of time will be spent on real property. The study of real property requires you to struggle with a series of arcane concepts, which you will learn stem from ancient England. As a result of the Battle of Hastings, the King of England allowed commoners, typically knights who had served him in battle, to own and utilize land (called a freehold estate). More importantly, this law allowed commoners to pass down land to their heirs. Prior to that time, the king owned all of the land and he merely allowed commoners to use it (called a leasehold estate).

As a result, a series of legal principles were developed in order to describe how property might be owned and transferred. The terminology is not intuitive, and you will simply have to read the cases carefully and memorize the concepts. However, the good news is that the study of real property more closely resembles what you became accustomed to in your undergraduate studies than any other first-year law school course. In other words, this course deals more with the memorization and regurgitation of information than in other first-year courses, as opposed to intricate legal analysis. Certainly, your final exam will consist of a fact pattern, however, you will be required less to argue the sides of the legal issue and more to identify the particular estates in land or to analyze a bequest of property against several rules (e.g., the rule against perpetuities, which essentially prohibits generational control over real property beyond a fixed period of time).

Much of real property involves arcane property classifications, which you will probably never use, other than on the bar exam. For example, *fee simple absolute* refers to the fact that the holder owns the property outright and can transfer all or part of it. A *life estate*, on the other hand, refers to the fact that the holder owns the property only for as long as he or she lives; and upon death, he or she will not transfer the holder's testamentary wishes, but will be in accordance with the bequest of the person who granted the life estate to begin with. Your property course will also deal with other interests in land such as leaseholds (you guessed it—this term refers to leases, which are possessory interests in real property), easements, licenses (the right to use the property of another), and bailments (entrusting your property to another, deed restrictions, and a variety of other concepts regarding real and personal property).

As with all of the first-year courses, property is also a multistate bar exam subject (the multistate bar exam generally represents about 40 to 50 percent of your overall bar exam grade, depending upon your state), and the material is virtually identical to that on which you are tested on the bar exam. So the time and effort you spend on learning some of the language of property, as with all of the first-year courses, will pay double dividends, both in law school and on your bar exam.

Civil Procedure

Civil procedure describes the prescribed rules of engagement by the parties to a lawsuit. All court systems, both state and federal, have procedural rules that attorneys must follow. In particular, you will spend a great deal of time on the rationale for determining the proper forum in which a plaintiff may file a lawsuit. The Federal Rules of Civil Procedure is the underlying text for this course, because these rules are used in all federal courts. In addition, the federal rules have become the model rules for many state courts. Of course, you will also have a casebook with a variety of cases dealing with procedural matters.

In order to bring a lawsuit against a party in a particular court, the court must have over the defendant the following two things:

1. Subject matter jurisdiction
2. Personal jurisdiction

It is interesting that the focus in this class is personal and subject matter jurisdiction. The reality in law practice is that these kinds of issues arise infrequently because a good plaintiff's attorney will always carefully analyze the factual issues that determine jurisdiction in his lawsuit. The last thing the attorney wants to do is to have to explain to his client that his lawsuit was thrown out because he filed it in the wrong court. However, the issue makes for a great intellectual exercise. And intellectual exercises are great fun for law professors.

Subject Matter Jurisdiction. Subject matter jurisdiction refers to the subject of the lawsuit. For example, generally speaking, a federal court decides questions under federal law (e.g., discrimination actions brought under Title VII of the Civil Rights Act of 1967). However, a federal court also has the power to hear claims brought under state law (e.g., intentional infliction of emotional distress, a state common law claim) if the claim is part of a bigger federal claim. This is referred to in the Federal Rules of Civil Procedure as supplemental jurisdiction.

Personal Jurisdiction. Personal jurisdiction refers to whether the defendant exercised sufficient contact in the jurisdiction in question to reasonably expect that he could be sued in that jurisdiction. For example, a company that is headquartered in New York but conducts business in Texas would likely anticipate that it could be sued in a Texas court (either a federal or state court located in Texas). *Venue* refers simply to the convenience to a defendant, as well as the court's locale and its effect on a defendant's ability to have a fair trial. Anyone who has followed a high-profile defendant trial in the past few years is probably aware of the change of venue motion.

Other Issues. Other issues that are usually covered in a first-year civil procedure course are pleadings and motion practice.

Pleading is as much an art as a science and in my opinion is one of the most gratifying areas of litigation practice. Understanding the various pretrial motions available, which can potentially result in the disposal of a case without trial, can save clients a huge amount of money and justify their attorney's fees. Examples of these motions include the motion to dismiss (for failure to state a claim upon which relief can be granted) and motion for summary judgment (filed at the end of the discovery phase of the litigation, which is when the parties conduct their investigations into the facts behind the lawsuit, e.g., depositions, document requests, and interrogatories). In these motions, the movant argues that, based upon discovery, there is no genuine issue before the court and no reasonable fact finder could, as a matter of law, find for the nonmovant.

As with contracts, in which you never work on an actual contract, in civil procedures you will most likely not draft a motion or supporting brief as part of this class. Instead, the idea is to teach you an analytical methodology. However, in your legal writing class, you will probably write at least one motion and perhaps more. Similarly, part of the moot court competition will likely be to draft a summary judgment motion on an issue. As an aside, I loved writing motions and supporting briefs in law practice. I found it exciting to know that words I used could convince a judge to take one particular action or another.

Most professors will also cover the first phase of a lawsuit after the initial pleadings are filed, including the conference between the parties to determine the likelihood of settlement of the case and in some cases, alternative dispute resolution such as arbitration and mediation.

Criminal Law

Criminal law is usually jurisdictionally specific and statute based; however, as with torts, there are certain principles that are universal to all penal code systems.

The Model Penal Code, or MPC, was drafted in 1962 by the American Law Institute and has been adopted in various versions by most states. The MPC codified many of the common law principles that had been in use prior to its adoption.

You will spend a great deal of time in criminal law discussing *mens rea* and the *actus reus*. In addition, you will learn the various levels of intent required and their effect on the levels of punishment for a crime, e.g., first-degree murder compared with manslaughter.

You will discuss specific crimes and their elements, including burglary, kidnapping, rape, embezzlement, larceny, and arson. You will probably also learn about the inchoate (or incomplete) crimes, such as attempt, solicitation, and conspiracy. As with property, most of the subject matter in criminal law can be traced to the common law of England.

In addition, criminal law will cover the traditional defenses to crimes, such as entrapment, insanity, and self-defense. Finally, criminal law deals with the subject of punishment arising from conviction of a crime.

Legal Writing

This course is probably of a greater initial benefit to you because of the class size more than anything else, as well as the fact that this class is devoid of Socratic dialogue. Generally, your section will be broken down into small groups of 20 to 30 students for your legal writing class. The small class size will afford you the opportunity to interact closely with your instructor, should you desire.

You will be given several writing assignments for each semester, typically a legal memorandum and a brief of some sort. As you will quickly learn, the difference between a legal memorandum and a brief is the degree of persuasiveness versus objectivity employed by the writer in each. A legal memorandum is designed to inform and help the reader assess risk, while a legal brief is designed to persuade the reader. Legal memoranda are documents designed for internal use and written in an objective format, whereas legal briefs are submitted to a court and written for the purpose of persuasion.

Many law students and new lawyers assume that because they are expected to think like lawyers, they are also expected to write the way so many lawyers before them have written—obtusely and voluminously and using large, lawyerly words. Further, law students read judicial opinions from 50 years ago and assume that the same writing style applies today. As a result, they are often unnecessarily verbose, using abundant multisyllabic words and hiding much of their substance behind legal jargon such as *hereto*, *herewith*, and *wherefore*. This writing is often indecipherable. The reality is that in today's world, lawyers are expected to write clearly and efficiently and communicate their points quickly and effectively to clients, judges, and other lawyers.

Another important aspect as you learn to write legal documents is the ability to properly refer to the authority upon which you rely to make a particular point. These references are called citations, which are the series of numbers and abbreviations following the case name that tell the reader precisely where a legal reference can be found, as well as other information regarding the lineage of the case. The standard citation format used by law students and lawyers is described in *The Bluebook: A Uniform System of Citation*, often referred to as *The Bluebook*. *The Bluebook* is a collective effort of the editors of the most prestigious law schools' law reviews: the *Columbia Law Review*, the *Harvard Law Review*, the *University of Pennsylvania Law Review*, and the *Yale Law Journal*. This book is the authoritative source for the proper citation of cases.

All of your legal writing will require citation, and almost everything you include in a document will have a source, either a factual or a legal source. Anything and everything you use that you did not create must be properly cited; otherwise, such use could constitute plagiarism. In law school, plagiarism is a very serious offense and one of the few things you can do to actually get thrown out of school. The only defense against it is to properly refer to the source of information contained in your writing. In order to introduce you to one of the basic currencies of communication in law practice, I have included a 1L legal memorandum in Appendix F of this book. Most legal memoranda follow the same general format. Citation is a skill you will use throughout your legal career, especially if you litigate and draft motions, briefs, and the like.

Taking Notes in Class

Throughout our undergraduate studies, we attend class. We read the assigned reading. We work the assigned problems. We write assigned papers. The professor explains the subject and answers students' questions. We simply write down everything the professor says—note taking is generally about quantity, rather than quality. The college student who does all this conscientiously will succeed. However, a different approach is required for success in law school.

Certainly, law school exams test your recall of information; but even more, exams test your ability to apply the law to a factual setting—identifying issues and application of law using legal reasoning. In fact, in law school the application is more important than the recall. If you possess sufficient legal reasoning skills but cannot remember the legal rule involved, you can usually iterate your way back into the rule, as long as you are able to identify the legal issue.

How to Focus Your Law School Note Taking. Your note taking should focus on the reasoning and insight gained in the class, instead of every detail that arises during class, especially unproductive details of the Socratic dialogue. Spend more of your time trying to understand where the professor is trying to take you, especially how it all fits into the big picture of the law.

In particular, you should understand where the assigned cases fit into the overall body of law. Like any good journalist, remember always to ask Who, What, When, Where, and Why? Asking Why is a particularly useful skill in law school and law practice. As you read each case, you should always ask questions such as:

- Why is this case important?
- Who are the parties and why are they before the court?
- What is the issue in dispute?
- Why did the court reach the conclusion it did?
- Is the case about the interpretation of a particular element of a rule?
- Is the case included to show how the common law has changed over time?
- Why did the professor assign this case? What was the point or points he was trying to illustrate?

As you will learn from the Pyramid Outline Method, much of the dialogue in class can be boiled down to one or two important legal principles. Use your notes to create memory triggers for key concepts that you have already established through your own study and outside reading, which are important to the subject. In other words, your goal is to capture what the professor, through the Socratic dialogue, conveys to be important topics and why they are important.

I encourage you to experiment with the degree of detail you capture in your notes, in order to determine what works best for you. By comparing your class notes with your other study activities (case reading, commercial materials, and so forth), you will be able to adjust your note taking in order to optimize it as part of your overall study plan.

In fact, you may even find that there are times in class where it is more productive to put your pen down and simply listen, in order to fully grasp what is happening and why. Note taking can be a type of security blanket for students. To let go and put your pen down (or close your laptop) and just listen to what is happening in the classroom can be scary if you have succeeded previously by noting every word the professor said. However, doing so will free you up to be able to truly listen, process the information, and decide for yourself the significance of the dialogue. In addition, doing so will help you to develop your recall, a critically important skill for lawyers.

Pros and Cons of Taking Notes with a Laptop Computer. Assuming that you can type faster than you can write longhand, taking notes with a laptop can be an effective tool in law school. In addition, with a laptop you can type your notes directly into your Base Outline, as discussed in this book as part of the Pyramid Outline Method. More importantly, having your laptop in class will give you easy access to your case briefs or summaries, your reading notes, your outlines, and other information which may help you better assimilate the information from class.

The risk presented by using a laptop is that you can get so caught up in all the content you have access to that you miss key information from the class discussion. In addition, technical issues while in class can be a real distraction. Sitting in class with nothing but a legal pad and a pen (and perhaps your casebook) may help you to focus on nothing but the classroom dialogue. That said, I find that a laptop is an excellent tool for integrating the entire learning process, your reading, your outlines, your notes, and outside materials into one easily accessible place. Having everything on your laptop gives you the ability to review any of your work at any time.

If you choose to use a laptop, it is critical that you back up your information frequently! Otherwise, you may find yourself in the catastrophic position of losing everything. I carried floppy disks with me to class and backed up my class notes and outlines after every class. Today, USB drives, external hard drives, or CDs are essential, practical, and affordable backup tools.

YOUR PRE-1L CHECKLIST

The following list includes suggestions to help you begin to develop your own preparation and planning process for law school. Again, you are investing a great deal of time and money in law school. You should take at least minimal steps to prepare before you walk in the door. I recommend that you accomplish these things the summer before school begins. By getting these basics out of the way early, in addition to the money issues discussed in chapter 2, you can focus on the real task at hand—learning the black letter law and developing an analytical framework with which to apply it to facts on your first-year exams. The basics:

1. Visit your law school. Tour the classrooms and any other facilities. Get a feel for the school. If at all possible, speak with second- or third-year students. Go to the library and meet one or more of the librarians. Look at some of the school's publications, such as journals and the law review. Visit your school bookstore. Check out the available commercial reading materials on the various first-year subjects. If available, purchase and review some of these materials in order to get a sense for your first-semester subjects.

2. Finalize your arrangements for personal issues, such as housing, transportation, parking, immunizations, and student health insurance.

3. Learn the basics of how the United States legal system works. It will save you a lot of time and stress in class and during your studying.

4. Become familiar with your first-semester and first-year curriculum. Obtain casebooks if your professor has posted his or her choice. If you get to the bookstore early, you may be able to purchase used books at a good discount. Review the tables of contents. Get a sense for how they are organized. Read a few cases to get a feel for how judicial opinions are written. Visit one of the many free law student websites. Numerous law students have posted course outlines on the Web. Read over some material, in order to gain familiarity with the first-year subjects before school starts.

    If possible, purchase your casebooks well before school starts. (Note: Many professors wait until the last minute to designate the casebook. If this is your situation, remember that the basic substance of each first-year course is pretty much the same. Contracts are contracts, regardless of the text, and so on.) Start your outlines as soon as possible, using the casebook's table of contents as an overall guide to the casebook and course. If you can't purchase your casebooks before school starts, you can still start outlines using commercial study materials or materials you find on the Internet.

5. If you don't have one, consider purchasing a laptop computer. It will be invaluable in taking class notes, building and distilling your outlines, and accessing databases, such as LexisNexis and Westlaw. Brush up on your typing skills, if necessary.

6. RELAX! Take the last two to three weeks prior to orientation off. Don't think about the law or law school. The next three years will be productive, stimulating, and extremely demanding. So commence law school relaxed and refreshed and ready to work.

Chapter 4

Your Law School Study Approach

BECAUSE FIRST-YEAR GRADES ARE so important in law school, it is critical that you proactively develop a study approach to utilize from your first day. This approach should incorporate active and aggressive learning techniques and a creative and effective exam writing method. By doing this, you can build your legal knowledge database with the principles, rationales, and black letter law you will accumulate from the very first day you begin to study. By forcing yourself to organize everything you read within your study framework, you will ensure that you understand how each piece fits together and will begin to develop the legal reasoning skills necessary to manipulate each piece.

Any legal education should, at minimum, have two outcomes: you learn the law and you learn how to analyze legal problems. Anything that does not yield to either of these two objectives is wasted time. Focusing on these two objectives will pay huge dividends in law school and in law practice.

Every first-year law student takes the same courses. You have to know the black letter law cold in order to do well on your exams. If you don't know the law, it is difficult, if not impossible, to spot legal issues. But a substantial portion of your first year is spent learning the legal reasoning process. This is why the first year can be so confusing to some students. Your professors are, in reality, teaching you a new way of thinking. In fact, your entire first year could be called Legal Reasoning 101. But no one talks about it in this way. In your second and third years, you will spend your time learning the black letter law in increasingly specific areas.

But first things first. This chapter will focus on the most important study tools and skills of your law school career, to give you a road map of this first-year process.

THE CASEBOOK EXPLAINED

The books you purchased for your undergraduate education were called textbooks. It is very likely that you will not hear the word *textbook* during the entire three years you are in law school. Unlike textbooks, casebooks are sparse in terms of actual declarative content. In particular, casebooks will not provide you with a summary of "black letter" law. A casebook is actually nothing more than a book comprised of a series of edited cases, each included by the editors to illustrate particular legal concepts. The casebook's purpose is to teach you how to think like a lawyer.

Whether you like it or not, you will be (or should be) spending a great deal of time over the next three years reading your casebooks. Casebooks are expensive and you will seriously question the value for this dollar; however, they form the core syllabus for almost every law school class. You will most likely highlight, underline, write in the margins, and generally use the casebooks extensively.

In your casebook material, you will not find summaries and other tools for use in exam preparation other than the table of contents. Instead, each case is included in the casebook to illustrate the law or an element of the law. Whether they realize it is happening or not, students read cases to learn the analytical thinking and reasoning that lawyers use in developing, analyzing, and arguing the law. Casebooks usually describe the judge's reasoning process in deciding a legal issue. And the judge forms his or her analysis from the lawyers'. So a case is really a double dose of legal reasoning. And this is the real difference between a textbook and a casebook. You read a textbook for information; you read a casebook to learn the reasoning method employed in the cases.

Cases Read in First-Year Classes

Most assigned reading in law school involves higher court appellate opinions that analyze lower court decisions (recall that *opinion, decision,* and *case* all mean the same thing—the document written by the judge which conveys the law). In fact, lower court decisions frequently do not result in written opinions because these judges are simply too busy to publish an opinion for each case. Appellate courts, on the other hand, make decisions by carefully scrutinizing the lower court decision, which in turn requires a careful articulation of the current state of the law. Usually, only one or two issues are raised in a judicial opinion. As a result, an appellate decision is an excellent teaching tool to describe particular elements of a given law. A written appellate decision may articulate and discuss in great detail a particular element of the law. Or it may simply articulate a change in the law, which is also useful for law study purposes.

In your first year of law school, professors frequently assign the classics, which are common law cases written long ago, but which illustrate fundamental legal principles, such as the discussion in *Garratt v. Dailey*. The basic rules of the cases covered in the first year of law school were decided long ago, and the doctrine of stare decisis has resulted in the holdings of these cases continuing to be good law. I should also add that there is a certain amount of snobbery on the part of the professors in assigning these types of cases; it's sort of like sampling a fine vintage wine instead of a recently bottled domestic product.

Further, these classics are simply a rite of passage for law students. Every lawyer has read them, everyone chuckles at them, and usually the professor uses students' obtuseness to clobber them in Socratic dialogue. There is absolutely no way you can anticipate which way the Socratic dialogue will go if your professor has assigned one of these arcane cases (and I promise you they will). These arcane bits of legal trivia can be used to illustrate any of a

Understanding the table of contents is essential to understanding the big picture of the course.

number of legal principles. My advice is to read these cases carefully, evaluate their placement in the casebook (that is, their location and context), understand the facts precisely, and follow the steps outlined below. More importantly, just relax and relish your role in history as yet another law student stumped by something written by someone who died decades ago or more.

The Important (and Often Overlooked) Table of Contents

An often overlooked aspect of a casebook is its table of contents. While students often skip right to the assigned case, the casebook table of contents is an excellent starting point for the outline you will need to construct in order to assimilate your class reading, case briefs, class notes, and other reading for the course, such as commercial outlines and hornbooks. Understanding the table of contents is essential to understanding the big picture of the course.

I suggest that one of the first tasks you accomplish before classes start is a careful review of your casebook table of contents. In addition, I recommend a periodic review of the casebook table of contents as you progress through the semester. This will enable you to see the trees as well as the forest in your courses. Keep in mind that your casebook table of contents may not follow the same order as a commercial outline or hornbook. This is not important; different authors and editors have particular areas of interest, and these interests are often reflected in the layout of the casebook. The only thing that is important is whether it helps you to organize and assimilate the information necessary to do well on the exam.

Further, you should frequently review the table of contents throughout the semester. This will help you understand where the assigned case fits into the overall body of law and why it is important. Think of the table of contents as a road map to your casebook, the cases, and the course. As discussed later in the book, the table of contents will also form the basis for your course outlines, using the Pyramid Outline Method.

The Format of a Judicial Opinion

Judges interpret and communicate the law through written judicial opinions, called cases by law students. These written opinions are recorded in volumes called reporters, which organize and record these opinions by geographic jurisdiction.

Before the electronic age, a lawyer had to look up cases through this elaborate indexing and recording system. Today, cases are available electronically through such databases as LexisNexis and Westlaw. With a well-constructed search query and a click of the mouse, the law student and lawyer can find a case relevant to any area of the law. Don't take this ability for granted. You might be surprised at the number of practicing lawyers who went to law school before the electronic age and cannot navigate these databases. The ability to do so will make you infinitely more efficient and effective in your legal research. Regardless, judicial opinions convey the current state of the law by the judge who has the jurisdictional responsibility to ascertain it.

In writing legal opinions, judges are, among other things, storytellers describing who the parties to the case are and what events led to the matter being brought before the court. They must marshal facts, organize their logic, and put the pieces of the litigation puzzle together in a way that makes sense and is also persuasive. The authority of these judicial opinions, the precedents they rely on, and the analyses they convey are of critical importance. If the law does not make sense, the law loses its credibility.

Most cases in your casebook will follow a predictable format, at least in terms of content. Cases may not follow this format in order, or the edited version may omit some of these components, in which case your challenge is to try and figure out what is going on in spite of the omissions. Here is the typical format:

1. Typically, the court first reviews the procedural history of the case. Next, the court will describe the facts of the case. Generally, most of the factual discussion in a judicial opinion involves relevant facts. However, a judge may also include other facts for other reasons, such as for use in signaling a potential change in the law.
2. The court deals with the legal issue before the court. Frequently, the court will simply designate this portion in the form of a question. For example, the judge may simply indicate: "Issue: whether plaintiff is liable to defendant for failure to perform under an agreement if plaintiff suffered no damages?" However, in law school casebooks, this key component is frequently edited out. Presumably,

casebook editors want you to figure out for yourself what
the issue is before the court.

Some judicial opinions are presented in great detail regarding the
state of the law. The writer will cite substantial precedent and other judicial opinions that support the judge's holding in this case. This can be a
very useful tool for the student (or lawyer for that matter) as a synopsis
of the current state of a particular rule. Other opinions simply get to the
point and state the law.

You will also hear the term *dicta* as you begin to read cases. Dicta
(the singular is *dictum*) are statements or facts included in the opinion
that are not legal authority or perhaps even relevant to the holding. In
other words, the writer included them for some reason, but they do not
deal with the holding or rule of law. However, dicta can often signal
a movement in the law or change in direction. For example, a judge
may indicate that if particular facts other than those in the instant case
had been present, the holding would have been different. Many students
mistakenly spend a lot of time trying to determine which parts of a case
are dicta and weeding them out. This is likely a waste of time. Instead, by
using the techniques described in this book, you should read and understand the case and the relevant legal principles. Dissecting out dicta just
for the sake of doing it won't teach you much of anything.

I'll discuss this in greater detail later, but a good thought to keep in
the back of your mind is to read the case as if you are trying to solve an
actual legal problem, rather than a theoretical one. This may help you to
focus on what is important.

Legal Analysis. Obviously, the legal analysis is an important component
of the judicial opinion. However, it may be difficult to actually isolate the
legal analysis in the opinion. The legal analysis may not be continuous
or in a discrete section of the opinion, but instead it may start and stop
at various points in the opinion. On the other hand, it may be a specifically identified segment of the case and even labeled as Analysis. If the
analysis is all over the place, don't worry. Simply try to understand the
point and the assumptions and logic used in reaching the conclusion.

However the analysis is presented, at this point in the opinion, the
judge has probably described the procedural history of the case and the

factual setting, and now turns to the law that is applicable to the case. Often, this is the biggest underlying dispute in the matter. One side believes that a particular law should apply; the other side does not. Or the proper interpretation of the relevant law may be in dispute between the parties. Generally, the relevant rule of law will be identified in the opinion, usually by citing the case precedent or statutory source.

Once the law is decided, the judge may then turn to the application of the relevant facts to this law. The application of the facts to the law is the essence of legal analysis. As you develop your case-reading skill, you will begin to identify and understand the analysis and reasoning process the writer uses in formulating the opinion. With older opinions, the analysis is frequently imbedded throughout the writing.

Frequently, in recently written opinions (say, over the past 20 years or so), a judge may simply label this portion as Analysis. The judge will then apply the relevant facts to the law and develop a holding and even label it as a holding. The holding is the judge's statement of the court's decision regarding the case. It is usually one sentence that reaches a conclusion regarding the facts of the case as applied to the law. This may be somewhat different than the rule of law, which is the synthesis of years of precedent.

For example, in a case in which the plaintiff has sued the defendant for battery where there was no physical injury, it is well settled that the rule of battery requires: (1) an act by the defendant, (2) harmful or offensive contact, and (3) the intention by the defendant to cause such contact. There is ample case law that indicates that casual everyday contact is not considered offensive. If the facts indicate that the plaintiff had a particular sensitivity to contact by others and the defendant merely brushed against her in passing, the court's analysis would likely conclude that these elements were not met. The court would find and indicate in the holding that the defendant was not liable under these facts.

Most judicial opinions have the above components in common. However, some of these components are frequently omitted from the casebook, either by design or poor editing, and you must be resourceful enough to fill in the blanks in order to fully understand the legal principle involved.

Summary Judgment Opinions

Generally, when an issue is before the court, both sides prepare briefs to argue the issue. Frequently, the issue is whether the case should be dismissed, without the need of a trial. There are a number of ways a party can get a case dismissed. One way to obtain dismissal of a case is to show the court that it does not have jurisdiction over the matter before it. For example, if the claim is based upon state law and the dispute is between citizens of that state, there is probably no good reason for a federal court to hear the case because, in the vernacular, there is no subject matter jurisdiction.

Another route to dismissal is through summary judgment. Summary judgment is a pretrial motion, which is designed to end the case before it really starts. Using a motion for summary judgment, a party moves the court to dismiss the case on the basis that there is no real factual issue before the court, and the movant is entitled to dismissal based upon the applicable law. Under most rules, the movant is required to submit a brief that explains the motion and provides factual detail and legal arguments in support of the motion. The opponent writes and submits an answer to the motion, and there may also be several exchanges in the form of court-filed documents by the parties before the court decides the motion.

Published summary judgment appellate opinions are useful as teaching tools. Typically in such opinions, a party has been either granted or denied summary judgment, and the loser has appealed the lower court opinion. The appellate court reviews the lower court's decision and affirms or reverses it. A summary judgment opinion is useful for illustration purposes because it often articulates a particular element or elements of the law in question in the lower court opinion. The appellate court reviewing an order granting summary judgment goes into great detail, carefully applies the facts to the law, and decides the issue before it. The detailed opinion can be an excellent educational tool and used to illustrate a variety of legal principles. As a result, many cases in casebooks address summary judgment opinions.

LexisNexis and Westlaw: Tools to Help You Read and Brief Cases

Ostensibly, cases are edited for the purpose of condensing and thus lightening your nightly reading load and to provide clarity as a teaching tool. However, key information is frequently omitted from cases, as edited by the casebook editor, resulting in a confusing jumble of facts and analysis. You may find that the unedited case is easier to understand. For example, most judicial opinions contain a procedural history of the case. Procedural history can help you understand why the court is even considering this case. Many edited cases may exclude the procedural history. Similarly, an edited opinion may omit an important argument, which could have assisted you in understanding the arguments before the court. Whether this is poor editing or intentional obfuscation is left to the reader's imagination.

As a law student, you will receive unlimited access to legal databases. Take full advantage of them!

Consequently, as a first step, I would suggest that you use your school-provided LexisNexis or Westlaw electronic access to obtain a complete and unedited version of the case you are assigned. As a law student, you will receive unlimited access to these legal databases. Take full advantage of them! They are particularly useful when you find a case that appears to make little or no sense. For that matter, Westlaw and LexisNexis also have voluminous legal encyclopedias, treatises, and other reference materials that can be used in lieu of commercial study aids (commercial study aids are described later in this book). Westlaw or LexisNexis unedited versions of the cases will contain headnotes, or synopses, of the cases and of the legal issues contained therein. These headnotes are a great guide to the key points of the case. More importantly, you may actually find that the unedited version of the case simply makes substantially more sense than the edited version found in your casebook. Keep in mind that very old cases, such as the English common law opinions typically included in your torts and property casebooks will not be available electronically. They are simply too old to have been included in the database. This is where a good commercial supplement will help you to understand the case and its purpose in the grand scheme of the subject matter.

And while you are at it, you might want to browse the treatises on these electronic databases. They are packed with incredible resources, not only for the practitioner, but for the law student. You may have to dig a bit, but you may be surprised at the useful materials available.

The Right Turns to Take When Reading and Briefing Cases

Generally, law students brief cases in order to distill out the most important portions of the cases and to be prepared for the Socratic onslaught in class. They typically use the IRAC (Issue(s), Rule, Analysis, Conclusion) format to summarize a case. This format has been used by law students for years. However, simply following this formula in a rote manner will likely lead to your missing the most important piece of the law school puzzle. You absolutely must first ask yourself, "Why am I even reading this case? What's the point of this case?" Any case is included in the casebook for a reason. Most likely its purpose is to illustrate a rule or element of the rule, a development in the law, or a counter-rule. You have to figure it out for yourself; the professor will not explain where the case fits in the body of law.

Step One: Determine Why the Case Is Important. The first thing you should do before you read a case is to try and understand why your professor assigned the case in the first place. Reading and briefing cases without giving any thought as to why they were assigned and why the case is important is like trying to build a house with no blueprints. Even without blueprints, you will eventually end up with a house. However, you will likely have to redo a lot of things, you will waste a huge amount of time, and the result will be a less than desirable house. Similarly, diving into your class reading without understanding why your professor assigned the case and where it fits into the grand scheme of things will result in your spending a huge amount of time reading cases without a lot to show for it. The following is a suggested process for reading and briefing cases.

A good first step is to determine where in your book the case is located. For example, one of the first cases assigned in my Civil Procedure class was *Pennoyer v. Neff*, 95 U.S. 714 (1877). *Pennoyer* is an ancient Supreme Court case, which is lengthy, wordy, and extremely difficult to read.

The professor usually assigns reading by posting a series of page numbers in the casebook. As a result, the temptation is to jump straight to the first page of *Pennoyer*, without looking around the book and especially without determining where the case fits in the casebook's table of contents (and the overall scheme of the course). If you jump straight to the case, you will waste a huge amount of time just trying to get your intellectual bearings. Instead, first determine where *Pennoyer* is located in the table of contents and look at the topics and subtopics around it. Try and get a sense of the big picture. In addition, take a few minutes and if included, read the introductory passages in the chapter, as well as any discussion questions or ancillary material in the chapter. (Professors rarely assign or discuss these passages and questions. However, reading them will produce dividends.) This step will take less than ten minutes.

Pennoyer is found in the section of your casebook that deals with personal jurisdiction. In fact, it is highly likely that *Pennoyer* is the first case in the chapter of your casebook entitled Personal Jurisdiction. It will probably be located near sections titled with such words as *power, constitution*, and *specific and general jurisdiction*. Simply by reading these contextual headings, it is likely that you could formulate a rough idea of the principle involved in *Pennoyer*, which is the constitutional principle that allows a particular court to hear a case. The overall concept of jurisdiction (both personal and subject matter jurisdiction) is a basic concept that is typically discussed early in the semester. A court must have some basis for requiring a party to submit to its jurisdiction. Generally, this jurisdiction may be found within the federal or state constitutions.

This example illustrates the value of a brief look at your casebook's table of contents before reading a case. Had you simply begun reading *Pennoyer* instead, without any investigation or evaluation as to its importance, you would have immediately been overwhelmed with a plethora of facts, procedural history, and other distracters that would have inhibited your ability to discern the real issue. Instead, by looking at the context of *Pennoyer*'s location within your casebook, you would be able to get a rough idea of why the case is important. Consequently, your actual reading of the case would be much more purpose-driven and meaningful. More importantly, you would be able to save substantial time reading the case, time which could be used in much more useful study activities.

Step Two: Develop a General Understanding of the Legal Principle(s) Involved. After you determine in which section of your casebook the assigned reading is located, try and get a sense of the legal principle or principles discussed in the case. A good starting point is to simply look up the term or terms in your *Black's Law Dictionary* (*Black's* is also ubiquitous among the 1Ls and a key tool in your law school process). Continuing with the above example, *Black's* defines *personal jurisdiction* as:

> The power of a court over the person of a defendant in contrast to the jurisdiction of a court over a defendant's property or his interest therein; *in personam* as opposed to *in rem* jurisdiction. See *in personam* jurisdiction. BLACK'S LAW DICTIONARY 6TH ED. (Reprinted with permission.)

The lack of *in personam* jurisdiction, according to *Black's Law Dictionary*, precludes a court from "issue[ing] a . . . judgment" over the defendant. In about six minutes, without ever reading the case, you now have a basic understanding of what personal jurisdiction and *Pennoyer* are about. If you understood the basic facts contained in *Pennoyer*, this definition, and nothing else, I'm betting you could fake your way through a Socratic exchange with your professor and maybe even an exam question on the subject.

Step Three: Review Outside Materials. A casebook is frequently as poorly organized as the cases within it. For example, most commercial outlines on contracts begin with a discussion of what constitutes an offer. My first-year contracts casebook started with numerous cases on damages—expectation, reliance, and restitution. The section that followed dealt with enforcement at equity. This organization, in my opinion, is counterintuitive and confusing. It makes much more sense to organize a casebook on contracts commencing with when a promise should be enforceable and what elements are required to create an enforceable promise. This is how events involving contracts typically unfold.

However, I should add that in the law of contracts, as you will learn, the bottom line is the damages incurred by the plaintiff. No one is going to sue for contract breach unless the breach cost them something.

Without damages, one cannot sustain a cause of action for breach of the contract. And perhaps this is why damages appeared first in my casebook.

At this point, you should use your commercial materials as a check and perhaps even a road map through the particular dead ends often presented by your casebook. Your first step is to locate either the term *personal jurisdiction* or the *Pennoyer* case in its table of contents or index and read the corresponding section. This will give you a deeper sense of the issues raised in *Pennoyer*. It will also give you a sense of where personal jurisdiction fits into the overall outline of civil procedure. Read through the material carefully. Also read the topics located nearby. You should be able to understand the significance of the topic fairly quickly.

Another alternative at this point is to use your unlimited student LexisNexis or Westlaw subscription and pull the unedited case. Read the headnotes. Compare the unedited case to the edited version found in your casebook. The unedited case may turn out to be a fairly simple read, especially with the headnotes to guide you (as they will in actual law practice).

Step Four: Read the Case. Now you have a good idea of the key issue or issues raised by the assigned case, where it fits in the overall subject, and why it is important. You now probably understand a great deal of what you need to know to apply the legal principle or principles to a fact pattern on a final exam. However, you should know that your professor might choose to focus on particular facts or details in the opinion, which are very specific. In fact, your professor likely has considerable firsthand experience in which of these facts or details students are likely to overlook. His or her Socratic dialogue will likely be tailored to capitalize on this phenomenon. As a result, you should always read the case thoroughly.

Recall that to most professors, class participation has absolutely no effect on your final grade. Therefore, the only reason you would prepare for class is to either avoid embarrassment in the event you are called on or if it will ultimately lead to a better comprehension of the subject matter, and hence a higher grade. However, being prepared for class does not necessarily result in a better understanding of the subject. It merely enables you to better follow the Socratic dialogue, either as a participant or observer. It's up to you to make the connection between what the professor focuses on in the Socratic dialogue and what you have already learned about the subject, as described in the preceding section. This connection will enable you to develop a deeper understanding of the subject and optimize your exam performance.

Reading and effectively analyzing cases are critically important skills for a lawyer. Case law is the currency of lawyers. Whenever an arguable point of law arises, the first thing you will do is to examine the state of the case law in the appropriate jurisdiction. You will find relevant cases and analyze them to determine precisely what the law is concerning the issue. As a result, you will clearly need to be able to read and make sense of judicial opinions as you practice law. However, you should also understand that to some extent the reading of cases while in law school is a game. The cases, especially in your first year, are often arcane opinions which are either poorly written or poorly edited and virtually impossible to decipher without supplemental reading, such as a commercial outline or treatise.

My suggestion is to approach the cases as you would approach them if you were a practicing lawyer (recognizing that the case may be so old that the legal principle has been modified by its legal progeny, which is subsequent decisions; determining whether your case is still governing law and analyzing its progeny is called shepardizing the case, and you will learn to do it with hard copy and electronic versions of published opinions).

Assume that you are reading the case in order to understand the current state of the law regarding the particular legal issue(s) addressed in the case. Admittedly, this is difficult in the theoretical orientation of law school. When you read a case in practice, you are typically looking for factual similarities in that case relative to your own facts at hand. The closer the case is to your real-life situation, the more confident you become regarding whether that case will control the outcome of the case at hand. This results in an intensely objective-guided reading of the case. In law school, you are reading the case merely to elicit a principle of law in a vacuum and in an abstract way, making your comprehension of the case that much more difficult.

Try and imagine the arguments made by both sides, in favor of and against the issue before the court. Get inside the court's thinking and attempt to understand its reasoning.

- Is this opinion largely about precedent or is the court establishing new precedent?
- What might the law have been prior to this decision?
- What were the circumstances surrounding this decision: who (if anyone) was suing whom and why?
- What arguments are the two sides making?
- Is there a public policy involved (you will learn that public policy often becomes the vehicle by which old law is interpreted to avoid an unjust result in modern circumstances)?
- Is this case still good law?

In law school, many students do not read the cases with a purpose, other than to avoid embarrassment in case the professor happens to call on them. But the truth is, you can't win that battle. The professor knows the questions and the answers. If the professors want to embarrass you, they will. Students respond differently to this apparent paradox. Some reread the cases, memorizing the minutest details. Other students mark, highlight and underline the cases, in the hopes of being able to recall the reading. Still others furiously brief the cases hoping that it will help everything make sense.

After I graduated and went to work for a law firm, I was often assigned legal research and memoranda writing in support of motions, such as a motion for summary judgment or a motion to dismiss. I read these cases with purpose—to find a law in support of my facts or facts in support of my law. A lawyer reads cases in order to find a precedent (*stare decisis*). And as with anything in life, when you do something with purpose, it becomes easy and almost automatic.

This is why when you read a case, try and imagine that you are a practicing lawyer. Ask yourself why the writer included a particular fact or a discussion of the law. Try and imagine how subsequent judges would interpret this particular opinion. Would it be upheld or overturned and why? In short, work the facts and work the law. The purposeful work will enable the material to stick with you much more than an attempt at brute memorization.

Step Five: Brief the Case—Summarize the Key Facts and Principles.
Briefing a case essentially means summarizing the case, which includes
the procedural history of the case, the key facts, issues before the court,
the court's legal reasoning and analysis, and the holding or decision
of the court. As previously discussed, the principle components of a judicial opinion are the following:

- The procedural history
- The relevant facts
- The issue(s)
- The court's analysis
- The holding of the case

These are precisely the sections that should be included in your brief
of a case. Whatever format you use, make sure that it works for you in
terms of comprehending the case. A case brief can be inserted into your
outline; however, as you distill the information down (using the Pyramid
Outline Method discussed later in this book), you will ultimately need to
articulate the essential holding of the case in a few sentences. This is the
real reason the case was included in the casebook by the editors.

Many students spend hours briefing cases because they hear other
students talking about their briefs and blindly follow accordingly. Law
students typically assume that they are supposed to brief cases—but as
with outlining, they have no idea why they're doing it. Many spend a
substantial portion of their time writing elaborate briefs with all sorts
of codes, abbreviations, and shorthand. However, like everything
else in the study of law, rote actions that do not actually lead to an
understanding of the material before you are a waste of time. Out of
frustration, or because they have begun to understand the legal reasoning process, many students abandon the practice after the first
year. Don't. Continue to brief cases. It enhances your ability to identify and understand legal arguments and reasoning. You will need to
experiment to determine the best way to brief, but more importantly,
to truly digest a case. I would suggest that you take your brief with
you to class and use it as a reference tool during the Socratic discussion.
Try to determine whether you captured in your brief the salient points of

the discussion and as always, where those points fit into the body of law. This will help you to develop your own effective briefing style.

The learning process involved in briefing a case is much more important than the output. No matter how great the brief is, no one other than you will ever read it. You won't get graded on your brief. Further, rote briefing of cases will likely not add much to your class preparation. Regardless, you need to develop your own process for digesting and understanding the assigned reading and extracting useful information from it. I always found it helpful after struggling with the case to ask myself what the exact proposition that the case stood for was and why it was included in the material (there's that Why question again).

Additionally, most casebooks include discussion questions at the end of each case or the chapter. Even if your professor does not assign these questions, you should read them and attempt to answer them. The casebook editors included them for a reason: to help you understand the case. I suggest that you write the questions and answers out and include them in your Base Outline as discussed later in this book. You can also include them in your brief, if you find that it helps you follow the Socratic dialogue.

Step Six: Reread the Case as Close to the Scheduled Class as Possible. The actual content of case law, as used in the law school context, is arguably short-term memory stuff. You will read so many cases that much of the information you glean will begin to run together as the semester progresses. After reading a case, you will quickly begin to forget the specifics. However, rereading the case and your brief and asking yourself the questions discussed in Step Four 10 or 15 minutes before class will pay off hugely in terms of aiding your memory.

More importantly, the reading process outlined in this chapter, when used in combination with the Pyramid Outline Method (discussed later), will enable you to analyze the cases effectively, see the legal big picture, develop a good understanding of the subject, and write a good exam. The few minutes spent reviewing before class will help alleviate your fear of being called upon in class.

A caveat: I do not advocate last-minute cramming as a substitute for a thorough reading and analysis of the case. You absolutely must spend enough time on the case (by reading the case and supplementary materials) to understand it. However, rereading the case just before class will improve your recollection, thus enabling you to enhance your engagement and comprehension while in class and ultimately minimizing the amount of time you spend in preparation for class. This will enable you to spend more time on the real grade-maximizing activities.

EARLY UNDERSTANDING OF LEGAL REASONING PRINCIPLES

"During Christmas break, I actually had to leave the room during family discussions because I was so frustrated," lamented one of my 1L classmates to another. "I can't believe how no one gets it," she said. "My thinking is so different now that I just cannot relate to them anymore."

The other classmate vigorously nodded her head in agreement. "I know exactly what you mean," she replied. "It's like they have all become suddenly so stupid."

Law students hear the almost ritualistic phrase "thinking like a lawyer" so much that they begin to believe that they will somehow be magically transformed by the casebooks, Socratic experience, and study group debates. I graduated from law school, have passed two bar exams, and have been in practice for a number of years now. I have yet to meet anyone that has articulated a workable definition of what "thinking like a lawyer" actually means. Instead, law students, law professors, and lawyers refer to "thinking like a lawyer" in an almost fraternal, secret society sort of way. Here again, this is like Justice Stewart's *Jacobellis v. Ohio* "I'll know it when I see it" reasoning.

Nonetheless, I'll take a stab at articulating a working definition: "Thinking like a lawyer" describes one's mastery of the legal reasoning process and legal practice: specifically understanding precedent, supporting a position with facts, using deductive and analogical reasoning, and anticipating both sides to an argument.

Further, thinking like a lawyer means being able to identify the discrete parts of every argument—the assumptions, the rationale, and the steps used to reach a conclusion. One of the biggest sins in law school is jumping to conclusions or "conclusory thinking." Going to step D before you have sequentially visited steps A through C can result in flawed logic based upon flawed assumptions.

Don't worry if you didn't take any formal logic classes in under-graduate school. You won't take any logic classes in law school, either. In fact, you will probably never hear the term *logic* even used in law school. Instead, you will constantly hear the term *argument.* Argument generally refers to the legal reasoning process that the writer (typically the judge writing a legal opinion) uses to justify his or her opinion.

However, it is important to have at least some familiarity with these principles of logical reasoning, specifically deduction and analogy. Understanding these logical reasoning principles will help you to identify key elements of an argument as you move forward in your studies.

Deductive Reasoning

Deductive reasoning relies on a chain of premises, also called *syllogisms,* to reach a conclusion. Deductive reasoning starts with a general (or major) premise, which is followed by a specific (or minor) premise. If both premises are valid, then a conclusion may be drawn properly.

For example, a classic deductive reasoning setup (also called an argument) goes like this:

> All cats are brown. (major premise)
> Whiskers is a cat. (minor premise)
> Therefore, Whiskers is brown. (conclusion)

As you may have learned during your LSAT preparation, there are numerous logical fallacies, which are arguments that appear to be legiti-mate, but are in reality illogical. The following is an invalid deductive line of reasoning:

> All cats are brown.
> Whiskers is brown.
> Therefore, Whiskers is a cat.

The logical fallacy in this argument is that other animals are also brown. Therefore, Whiskers could certainly be a cat but could just as easily be a dog or even a cow. In case law, deductive reasoning uses facts and law to lead the reader to a conclusion. For example:

> Intentionally stealing a car is a Class A felony.
> Mugsy McGee intentionally stole the car.
> Therefore, Mugsy is guilty of a Class A felony.

Much of the deductive reasoning you are exposed to will be based upon assumptions.

Assumptions Hidden Within Arguments. One of the biggest traps for the unwary law student is the imbedding of hidden assumptions in deductive reasoning. Assumptions used in arguments may be explicit or implicit. As a law student and as a lawyer, you must sensitize yourself to identifying and understanding implicit assumptions in everything you hear, see, and read. Failing to identify assumptions can lead to faulty assumptions, which can lead to erroneous conclusions.

Suppose that you are a practicing lawyer, and a client says that she wants to file for a divorce from her husband. The client indicates that she has three children, and she estimates that the joint property between her and her husband is approximately $2 million. She tells you that she wants the divorce to be amicable and as painless as possible. Under these facts, you assume that your client will seek to have the custody of the three children. As part of your litigation planning process, you begin to prepare documents seeking the custody of these children. However, the client later informs you that her three children are ages 27, 31, and 35. This additional fact strongly showed that your prior assumption was incorrect. Your assumption was that children meant minor children. You jumped to an incorrect conclusion. And this can lead to unbilled work, embarrassment, and (in extreme cases) malpractice liability. Part of learning to think like a lawyer is to constantly identify and test the validity of your own assumptions and those of others. In addition, it is important to identify any assumptions that you make in arguments and reasoning, in particular at exam time.

As you read a legal opinion, you should be able to comprehend and articulate the assumptions and reasoning process that lead to the author's conclusion. Similarly, in a law school exam, you must articulate any assumptions imbedded in the fact pattern or in your answer. This is the "showing your work" that professors expect from A exams.

For example, consider an exam question involving contracts that does not specify the applicable law. As you will learn, the law of contracts has evolved judicially through common law decisions. However, most states have now adopted the Uniform Commercial Code and in particular Article 2, which governs the sale of goods. As a result, if you are given an exam fact pattern that involves the sale of an automobile, the first issue that you need to identify and resolve is whether the common law or the Uniform Commercial Code applies. Assuming that most of your class time has dealt with the common law (as is typical in most first-year contracts courses), you would be tempted to analyze this question under the common law only. This would likely ensure a C grade. Instead, you must assume that either the UCC or common law could apply. You state as much in your exam answer and argue the potential outcome under both scenarios. This will show your professor that you have carefully sifted through the facts like a competent practicing attorney.

Analogical Reasoning

Analogical reasoning (or reasoning by analogy), as its name implies, refers to the prediction that the application of similar facts to similar law will produce similar results. Unlike deductive reasoning, which moves from the general to the specific, analogical reasoning moves from one general premise to another. If the two general premises are valid, a valid conclusion can be reached and the argument is logical. The form of analogical reasoning is as follows:

> Stealing a person's property is a crime.
> Betraying a person's trust is like stealing their property.
> Therefore, betraying a person's trust should be a crime.

If the two general premises hold water, then it is valid to say that betrayers of trust should be treated as criminals. You can see that reasoning by analogy leaves a greater amount of wiggle room than does deductive reasoning, in which the premises are more concrete and less subject to interpretation. Analogies are more subjective. Simply put, there are good analogies and bad analogies. Nonetheless, reasoning by analogy is a very useful jurisprudential tool, especially in the case of extending a law into new factual settings.

Reasoning by analogy is the basis for legal precedent. The logical principles of analogical reasoning tell us that similar facts result in similar outcomes. Analogical reasoning is important in the legal context because a party can gain judicial support for its legal position by showing the court that the facts in that party's case are either similar or dissimilar to prior decisions. The legal principle of stare decisis says that once a court has established the law, it will apply that law to all future cases, assuming similar facts. A proponent of a particular case's precedential value, for example, will argue that the facts before the court are analogous to those that were before the court deciding the precedent. The opponent will argue that the facts are sufficiently different such that different or new law should apply. The ability to think analogically and understand the critical similarities and differences between factual situations is crucial to your development as a lawyer.

EARLY MEMORIZATION OF BLACK LETTER LAW

Early on, many 1Ls don't understand the simple fact that cases are included in a casebook to illustrate a legal principle, or black letter law. The term *black letter* simply refers to the specific laws and legal principles that comprise the current state of an area of law. For example, in a tort case, there must be strong evidence of intent, which is an essential element to the black letter definition of assault. Or a contract case may contain an exemplary instance of the definiteness requirement for an offer, which is an element of a binding or enforceable agreement or contract. Other elements of contracts include acceptance of the offer and mutuality of obligations.

As a law student, you will extract these legal nuggets from various cases in order to determine what the actual black letter law is. Each case explains an element or elements of the law. Put together the legal principles found in several cases concerning what constitutes an offer, and voilà! You have captured the black letter law for this area of contracts law. Successful students teach themselves the black letter law in this way. They also use commercial study aids and outside reading, since these tools do this synthesis of cases for you. They are also a quick and efficient way to begin memorizing the black letter law. This is why some law professors hate commercial study aids. They believe that these materials do the students' thinking for them and short-circuit the learning process. And they may be right. This is why I recommend that law students wrestle with the cases themselves at least for a while, before turning to commercial materials.

However, commercial study aids are extremely efficient ways to (1) check your own thinking to make sure you are getting it and (2) learn a great deal of black letter law through a relatively small amount of reading. And as repeated throughout this book, you must absolutely know the black letter law cold to be able spot legal issues, which is the key to A's on law school exams. Early memorization and understanding of black letter law will enable you to spot legal issues raised by exam fact patterns. If you don't understand that something violates the law or a legal principle, it is difficult to determine that a set of facts presents a legal issue to be considered. Instead, a finely tuned understanding of the black letter law (see the above example of UCC versus the common law in a contracts exam) will also help you to spot the ambiguity raised by a fact pattern in an exam question. Frequently, an exam fact pattern will include an element not covered in class. For example, in a fact pattern involving burglary, the offense may occur in the middle of the day. If you understand the elements of burglary, you will be able to identify and discuss the fact that under the majority of jurisdictions, burglary can not occur during the day and that the requirement that the offense occur at night is the minority rule.

OPTIMIZE YOUR STUDY TIME

As mundane as it may seem, much of what goes on in law school is short-term memory activity. And if you think about it, this makes sense. Certainly, lawyers develop specialties and expertise. But sooner or later, any lawyer has to look things up. The law is simply too vast and dynamic for any human to master all of it or, for that matter, even a part of it.

In law school, professors assign cases shortly before class because the factual details, which are often key to the holdings of the cases, will be forgotten quickly. Professors need students to be able to recite these details, in order to optimize the Socratic dialogue as a teaching pedagogy. Similarly, for exam purposes, memorizing cases and facts early in the semester will probably be a waste of time. You will learn facts and rules and promptly forget them as the semester progresses and the demands of your classes increase. I wasted a good deal of time my first year learning case details well before class, only to have to relearn them a second and perhaps third time.

Fifteen-Minute Mini-Cram Sessions

You will learn that even a small increment of 15 minutes of concentrated study can have huge rewards. This is especially true as you prepare for class and the Socratic method. However, those small time increments can also be of great help as you begin to boil the information down into your Pyramid and Capstone Outlines and review and digest it, as discussed on page 133.

Certainly, there is no way around the time investment required of all law students. You simply must read and digest a large amount of new material. In addition, much of the vocabulary, terminology, and concepts are new and to some extent, foreign. However, I eventually learned to take advantage of those intense mini-cram sessions, such as the ten minutes before class, at lunch, while waiting for the bus, and so on. Memorizing material as it is needed will also make your studies less wasteful and more efficient. As you use the Pyramid Outline Method to begin to distill legal concepts into discrete components in an organized way, these small increments of time will become especially useful.

More importantly, using these small time increments will allow you to take a break periodically—an afternoon off to be with friends, go to a movie, take a walk in the park, or engage in some other emotionally and intellectually renewing activity. Additionally, frequent variation in your study methods and breaking things up will keep your studies interesting and effective. Like an athlete who engages in cross-training, you will hit your mental muscles in a variety of ways, thus making them stronger.

Exercise and Study

Most college students understand the value of exercise. The effect of increasing oxygen levels in the brain is well documented. By engaging in regular exercise, you will enhance your brain's ability to process and retain information. Many law students mistakenly believe that they simply do not have time to exercise. But exercise will improve your overall effectiveness during the time that you do study. As a result, exercise will actually save you time and pay for itself.

While in law school, I owned a treadmill that had an attached bookstand. During my first year in school, I did no exercise. However, during my second and third years, I ran on the treadmill for about an hour each day. During the run, I would review my outlines and class notes, notes from the assigned reading, or a commercial outline.

The results were pretty amazing. I found myself able to recall much more information. In addition, it seemed that my ability to grasp the big picture of a subject improved dramatically. I am convinced that exercise played an important part in the improvement from my first-year to second-year grades. I used this same technique while studying for both the Texas and Tennessee bar exams.

The kind of exercise you do is less important than the simple fact that you need to elevate your heart rate and respiration. The treadmill enabled me to combine exercise and study in an effective way. However, a simple run, time in the gym, aerobics, in-line skating, tennis, or any other exercise you enjoy can accomplish the same thing. Additionally, the more you enjoy a particular type of exercise, the more likely that you will continue with it.

Nutrition and Study

Similarly, research has shown that the foods you eat can have an impact on your studying effectiveness and brainpower. For example, there are well-documented studies that have shown that children who skip breakfast or eat a breakfast high in sugar perform more poorly in school.

Studies have shown that people who eat fruits and vegetables and avoid saturated fats do better in memorization and reasoning exercises. You might also want to consider vitamin supplements. Research has shown that certain vitamins help memory function. It might be beneficial to you to discuss good nutrition habits and their effect on learning with your doctor or a nutritionist.

Sleep and Study

Strive for as much sleep each night as you need in order to feel rested and alert each day. There are numerous studies that have shown the effect of rest on memory. Certainly, pulling all-nighters and cramming have their place in law study. However, if you follow the Pyramid Outline Method, there is plenty of time to do what you need to do academically and still get sufficient sleep.

STUDY GROUPS

At the core of virtually every law school curriculum is a grading curve. Simply, a curve means that there will be winners and losers. Grading curves, by definition, are comparative in nature, and comparisons lead to cliques. You will be absolutely amazed by how quickly these cliques begin to form. This is particularly true among insecure 1Ls. Because there is such a void of information during law school, many students eagerly grasp snippets available from any source. Beginning at orientation, other students will approach you, probably checking you out in order to test your potential as a study partner. Most people will act as if they are indifferent to the idea. But deep down inside, the study group plays to the law student's deepest fear: someone will somehow get a leg up on them.

And that is the secret behind the perpetual formation of study groups. Year after year, in an almost ritualistic way, new law students join study groups, afraid that if they do not, they may somehow miss something: the outline of all outlines, lore regarding the professor, or some other advantage to be secreted away until final exam time. I was amused to observe that some groups even had interlocking members, that is, they shared members between groups. I also saw repeated examples of law students shopping for notes among the better note takers. Eventually, these students are discovered by their peers, the sources dry up, and they are left to fend for themselves when they become ill or miss class for some other reason. For example, I knew of a fellow who was a member of three study groups. Unfortunately, he did not reveal his membership in each of these respective groups to his other groups. Apparently, his objective was to shop for the best notes, analyses, outlines, and other tools among his study groups. As first-semester exams approached, his duplicity was discovered and he was thrown out of all three groups.

Study groups are also a key source of the law school grapevine. The grapevine will tell you about the best commercial outlines out there. It will tell you how you should and shouldn't outline. It will tell you the best way to brief cases. It also often becomes the means through which law school legend and misinformation is communicated regarding classes, professors, grades, and anything else of concern to law students, who huddle together in a feeble attempt to stay warm. My advice to you is to avoid as much of the grapevine as possible. At best, the grapevine will likely demoralize you at times. At worst, it will cause you to waste time or distract you from your purpose-guided trek through the labyrinth.

In my opinion, study groups can waste a lot of your precious study time, especially if the time invested is to the exclusion of the real heavy lifting of your legal studies. Chances are, your classmates do not know more than you do (although they may not realize it), and you will spend a lot of time in endless debate, going nowhere. I have frequently heard study group stories in which one or two people dominated the discussion most of the time, attempting to win arguments and prove how smart they were.

On the other hand, studying with someone else may suit you, especially if long hours spent in solitude aren't your cup of tea. If you have a good friend who shares your work ethic and disposition, a dual studying arrangement may be effective. If you can find a few people who want to simply review class material a week or two before exams, it may be helpful in that they may have a slightly different slant on the material than you do. Further, participating in a study group just prior to exams can be a useful cramming technique, especially if the other members share the same objective. Additionally, I found that just having a variety of people to bounce ideas and interpretations off of is a good way to assimilate legal concepts (you will find that the ability to check your thinking and compare notes with others is critical to delivering superior legal advice).

Study groups can offer competing views on the facts and law (similar to what occurs when lawyers work together on a legal problem). Or they can result in a lot of pointless dialogue with fellow neophytes. My suggestion is that you use the study group as a check on your thinking after you have invested solo time thinking through the issues and learning the law.

I also suggest that your study group lay out ground rules for the process—what work is required individually before the group meets, the duration of debates, and other rules intended to reduce time-wasting. If you follow these ground rules, study groups can be an invaluable component of your study methodology.

If you decide to go the study group route, I recommend that you first spend sufficient time to learn the material, effectively outline and review, and develop your analytical skills. Then select your study group wisely and devote any remaining discretionary time to comparing notes and ideas with your study group. There is simply no substitute or shortcut for the assimilation process that must occur if you are to learn the requisite material.

In your study group, you should also be able to recognize free riders and note shoppers. The name of the game for these people is to mine information from their peers (also known as stealing), while giving up as little as possible to other members in the group. A friend of mine, let's call him Keith, told me about a student at his school, call him Joe, who illustrates this phenomenon at its worst. Keith types much faster than he writes longhand and, as a result, his laptop notes were generally more comprehensive than many students' handwritten notes. Apparently, Joe had decided that since Keith was conscientious and used a laptop, his notes would be hard to beat.

At the end of a contracts class, Joe approached Keith and said that he had missed some classes due to illness and he needed Keith's notes to fill in the blanks. Keith dutifully downloaded his notes onto a floppy disk and gave them to Joe; perhaps he was a little flattered that someone else would seek the wisdom that Keith just knew was contained therein.

The next semester, at the end of a constitutional law class, Joe approached Keith again. He said that he had missed quite a few classes because of job interviews for summer clerkships and could really use Keith's notes. Once again, Keith gave them to him. Keith ruefully concluded the story by telling me that Joe ended up with one of the highest grades in the class.

Of course, this was all obfuscation. Joe hadn't missed any classes. Keith later learned the secret to Joe's success. A fellow student told Keith that Joe would approach four or five students with laptop computers each semester and ask them for their notes. He would then compare and contrast their content and formulate his own super notes, which likely contained pretty much every detail and legal nuance presented in class.

The idea, at least on its face, was brilliant. By obtaining several students' notes from class, Joe was able to develop a much better understanding of the subject based upon the various perspectives of the note providers. The problem, however, was with Joe's execution of the concept, which was ethically challenged at best. Had the contributing students known what Joe was up to, they would have demanded a quid pro quo or an exchange of notes in which everyone would benefit. Instead, his sneaky technique was intended to give Joe a distinct advantage at exam time.

Needless to say, Joe's misdirection eventually caught up with him. One semester, word got around regarding what he was up to and students refused to give him their notes. As a result of his developing dependence on other student's notes, Joe had become lax in his studies, and his grades suffered dramatically that semester.

Whatever you choose to do, don't join a study group simply because "it's the thing to do" in law school.

COMMERCIAL STUDY AIDS

"Looks like you're having trouble."

I looked up from my crim pro (shorthand for criminal procedure) pre-class review to face Brian, a first-year classmate who was reading over my shoulder. I had been looking at my *Blond's Criminal Procedure* commercial outline in preparation just before class. Brian looked down at me in disgust; he appeared to be truly offended.

"Those books are kind of like *Cliff's Notes* for law school," Brian sniffed haughtily, "a sort of 'Crim Pro for Dummies.'" He turned and walked away quickly, obviously not wanting to be associated with the taint of someone who simply wasn't lawyer material.

The 1L Reluctance to Use Commercial Study Aids

From Brian's perspective, I obviously lacked the intellect to absorb criminal procedure without the assistance of what to him were analytical training wheels. This is not an uncommon attitude among first-year law

students. I had unwittingly violated several inviolable 1L rules by bring-
ing my copy of *Blond's Criminal Procedure* with me and reading it before
class. First, I had actually used a commercial outline. Second, I actually
admitted that I had, in fact, used a commercial aid. Third, I didn't even
attempt to hide it.

First-year students, yet to be humbled by first-semester grades, all
like to pretend that they are doing no reading other than their casebooks to learn a subject. This adds to the illusion that all one needs
to do to be completely prepared for exams is to carefully read the
assigned cases. Further, most first-year students believe that, as with
their undergraduate studies, if they attend class and do the assigned
reading, they will succeed. They think that if you need a commercial outline, you are probably lacking basic intellectual substance
and probably shouldn't have been accepted into your law school to
begin with.

Make no mistake about it, law school requires a large time commitment and a substantial amount of reading, note taking, and the digestion of large amounts of dense, difficult material. That said, there are
also tools you can and should use which will, despite law school lore,
enhance your overall learning and development. Traditional wisdom
has always been that the law student should struggle with the reading
and wrestle with the cases, to the exclusion of all else. This enables the
student to fully develop legal analytical and reasoning skills, or so the
rationale goes. This view holds that spending hours digesting a case will
ultimately make you a better lawyer. Commercial outlines and other
materials are viewed as a shortcut which has a detrimental effect on your
ability to learn to think like a lawyer. Many professors also perpetuate the
myth that commercial materials can actually hinder your development
as a lawyer.

But after grades came out that first semester, everything changed.
On the first day of school following the posting of first-semester grades, I
encountered a 1L, who I will call Rachel, who was sobbing at the copier
in the law library. I asked Rachel if she was okay.

Red faced and weeping, she replied between sobs, "I had a 4.1
undergrad GPA at Northwestern—a 4.1." She reached into her purse,
pulled out a tissue, blew her nose loudly, and continued sobbing. It
took me a second to realize what she was saying. Apparently, Rachel

was unpleasantly surprised by her grades that semester. This may very well have been the first time in her academic career that she had not achieved perfection. Rest assured that Rachel was not alone that day.

Unfortunately, many 1Ls are unpleasantly surprised by their first-semester grades. This is a natural consequence of the law school grading curve. As a result, the student arrogance toward commercial outlines quickly disappears and law students begin to scramble to the school bookstore to find the most effective study aids. It becomes every person for himself, and the shelves go empty. Like the pro athlete, striving for increasingly improved performance, students look for any and every advantage available. However, most students are still extremely reluctant to admit this weakness of using commercial materials. Further, once a student finds an outline that they think will give them an advantage, they will guard this precious secret with their life. (By the end of our second year, I happened upon Brian one day sitting in the library, furiously studying three different commercial outlines for his secured transactions class.)

Many students will continue to deny that they are using them. Regardless, the truth is that you will likely need commercial outlines or other study aids to assist you early in your legal studies as you weave your way through the labyrinth, blindfolded by the Socratic method.

The purpose of using a commercial outline is simple. It enables you to begin to quickly and efficiently memorize the black letter law.

Why You Should Include Commercial Aids in Your Study Approach

Commercial outlines and other study aids provide a synopsis of the law. They can be a sort of user's manual to your class on contracts or torts, or any other first-year course. Some are well organized with beautifully constructed tables of content. Others are poorly edited ramblings, a monument to some law school professor's zeal to publish, regardless of quality. Therefore, spend your money on good quality study aids, and use them—as their name suggests—as aids.

Do not overwhelm yourself with extra reading on top of the hundreds of pages you may be assigned each night, or you will overload an already overloaded hard drive. And do not use study aids as a substitute for wrestling with the material. You have to roll up your sleeves, learn the legal principles, and develop your legal reasoning skills through hard work.

Finally, most likely your law school student government will engage in an annual outline sale as a fund-raising activity, which involves offering outlines for various classes developed by prior students. Law students are smart. They would not spend money on commercial outlines if they weren't effective. This certainly seems to endorse the value of purchased outlines.

I believe that relying on the casebook as your sole means of study will waste precious time and ultimately leave you with sizable gaps in your legal knowledge. First of all, the cases in casebooks are frequently poorly edited, often leaving out key facts and judicial analyses. If you doubt this assertion, you can easily test it by simply comparing the edited case as presented in your casebook with the original version, as available on Westlaw or LexisNexis. As a result, you can struggle mightily with the court's reasoning and ultimately get nowhere because there are big informational gaps in the document, sort of like trying to finish a jigsaw puzzle with a number of pieces missing. And even if your casebook is a comprehensive guide to the subject, the degree to which your casebook covers everything you need to know at exam time is also a function of how your professor uses it. In other words, if your professor does not cover the entire casebook during the semester, you may find yourself with gaps in your knowledge of the subject. I wouldn't want to gamble my grades and career that the professor covers everything you need to know for exams during the semester. Recall the discussion earlier in the book on "hiding the ball." Whether it is deliberate or unintentional obfuscation by the professor doesn't matter; the fact is you need to have broad mastery of a subject in order to do well on the exam.

Overview of Commercial Outlines

The term *outline* is really a misnomer when it comes to commercial law school study aids. In reality, a commercial outline is a summary of the law written by a professor or practitioner, which provides the most important legal rules and elements and associated cases. Commercial outlines can be hundreds of pages long. There are also treatises, hornbooks, Nutshells (condensed treatises), and other books tailored for each law school subject. That said, you can waste a large amount of time and money trying to find the holy grail of law school outlines. Worse, you can become so consumed with reading all of these outlines that you overlook the cases themselves or waste precious time that could be used more productively. My suggestion is that you experiment with the various books to determine which are helpful to you.

Generally speaking, most commercial outlines follow the same overall structure and are substantively very similar. This is because the body of law, in particular for a first-year course, is largely well defined and well established. Simply, the law in these areas has not changed much in a number of years. And again, the topics covered by the Multistate Bar Exam (MBE) are typically the subjects of your first-year courses. In fact, the leading bar review preparation companies—BARBRI and Kaplan PMBR—have subject outlines for first-year course topics that are very similar in content and format to the outlines they provide for bar exam subjects. You can obtain a complete set of first-year outlines from BARBRI, and you can purchase the Kaplan PMBR first-year outlines (called the Kaplan PMBR FINALS series) in bookstores nationwide and through online booksellers.

I should also point out a very important resource frequently and ironically overlooked by law students. When I started law school, I was intimidated by our law library, primarily due to its sheer size. However, as you will learn, many of the volumes in your law library are actually reporters, which are the published records of cases organized according to geographic jurisdiction and citation number. Although you will be taught how to research case law using these volumes, in reality and in practice virtually all case law research you perform will be accomplished electronically. Regardless, most law schools, perhaps in tribute to a time-honored but outmoded tradition, feel compelled to teach you how to perform paper research. But the vast majority of space taken up in your law library is wasted with these reporters, which contain the same cases that can be retrieved at the push of a button. You will likely begin to think that the law library isn't of much use to you.

However, once you get past the intimidating volume of reporters in your law library, you will learn that it also contains many volumes of treatises, hornbooks, ABA materials, and other scholarly works which can help you learn a particular subject. If you look carefully, you will be amazed at the

If you look care-fully, you will be amazed at the number and quality of study aids that your law library offers. These materials are all free.

number and quality of study aids that your law library offers. These materials are all free.

Again, this is something that your professors will not tell you. Additionally, there is also a great deal of free information available at various websites on the Internet. Fire up a good search engine and you are on your way.

The point is this: you don't have to take out a student loan to obtain decent commercial materials. A treatise, outline, or hornbook can save you a tremendous amount of time when trying to get an initial grasp of a subject or topic of the law. Further, you should know that as a practicing attorney, it is likely that you will turn to a treatise first when faced with an unfamiliar legal topic. A treatise is a scholarly analysis, usually written by multiple authors, complete with annotations (that is, references to relevant case law). A hornbook generally refers to a scholarly work regarding a subject, designed for use by students. Hornbooks are usually shorter and less dense than treatises. However, the terms *treatise* and *hornbook* are frequently used interchangeably.

As you will also learn, your *Black's Law Dictionary* will become an invaluable tool, often your first line of defense when faced with a topic with which you are not familiar. Another great resource is *American Jurisprudence*, a legal encyclopedia, which is also available online through LexisNexis and Westlaw.

The following is a brief overview of the most popular commercial study materials used by law students:

West's Black Letter Law. The Black Letter Law series is published by West, a Thomson-Reuters business. It is a paperback series that covers all of your first-year subjects. Each book is generally keyed to the major casebook in the subject and provides a black letter outline, as well as a summary outline.

In addition, the series provides practice examination questions, both in multiple-choice format (to help you in recalling the material) and in some cases, practice essay questions. Finally, each book provides a disc with the outline of the course included.

This outline can also be used as the basis for, or in conjunction with, the Pyramid Outline Method. I found this series to be useful in understanding your first-year subjects, as well as for exam preparation.

Blond's Law Guides. The Blond's Law Guides series is published by Aspen Publishers. The series provides you with a summary of each case found in your casebook. The cases are organized and keyed according to the most popular casebooks. Blond's can serve a variety of useful purposes, including checking your own comprehension regarding a particular case against that of the summary's author. I frequently found the Blond's Law Guides established why and how the case was important in the overall subject, and in a way that made confusing subject matter click for me.

Nutshells. The Nutshell series is an excellent collection of mini-treatises of various subjects published by West. These pocket-sized paperbacks are particularly useful because they cover a wide range of subjects. Nutshells are fairly inexpensive and will give you a good overview of a subject, while also offering useful citations and explanations of particular topics within a subject. They are also generally an interesting read, which is fairly unusual in the realm of law school study aids. If I had never attended class or read a case for an entire semester and found myself faced with a final exam the next day, I would read the Nutshell before I read anything else.

This series is especially useful in your second and third years of law school as study aids for the more technical legal subjects such as tax practice and procedure, bankruptcy, and others where there was almost nothing else in the way of a subject overview available.

Glannon's Examples and Explanations. Glannon's Examples and Explanations series is published by Aspen Publishers. This series is very popular among students, presumably because they are very readable and take fairly dry subjects and make them interesting. Glannon's books get to the bottom line quickly and explain why a particular topic is important in the grand scheme of things. They also include discussion and practice questions, which are very useful in helping you to understand important topics. I found Glannon's very useful for my second-year courses.

West Hornbook. This hornbook series is also published by West. These are essentially treatises, written by the leading authors on the subjects. These books are especially helpful for understanding a particular area of the law in a fair degree of depth. In addition, they provide useful annotations that may help you to further understand the subject. These hardbound books are more expensive than the other study aids.

I would not consider these hornbooks as essential for first-year students, and the risk in using them is that you will get bogged down in the minutiae, without ever really understanding the big picture. However, they make a great addition to your legal library and can be used throughout your career.

Law in a Flash. The Law in a Flash series is published by Aspen Publishers. These are flash cards, arranged according to first-year subject. Although the idea of flash cards may be reminiscent of elementary education, in reality they can be a wonderful way to burn the black letter law into your memory, especially just before exams. In addition, they may provide the kind of study variety you crave after hours upon hours of reading, taking notes, and outlining. Law in a Flash has been around a long time and is used by thousands of law students each year.

Casenote Legal Briefs Education. Casenote was one of my favorites for the deeper second- and third-year subjects. The Casenote corporations outline is outstanding and provides a huge amount of useful information. It provides ample citations and explanation of the cases. More importantly, it provides detailed information regarding the most complicated aspects of your corporations course. In addition the securities regulation book was very useful. Casenotes are published by Aspen Publishers.

Gilbert's Legalines. Gilbert's outlines are published by Thomson-West and are popular among law students. They follow the order of the casebook, making the subject that much easier to follow and comprehend.

Matthew Bender Understanding. This series is sort of a mini-treatise series, which is not in an outline format. Matthew Bender goes into a fair amount of detail and explanation. However, these books are geared toward the law student and new lawyer and can be invaluable if you need in-depth explanations of a particular area of the law. I used the Matthew Bender book for securities law and found it extremely helpful.

Siegel's Essay and Multiple Choice Q & A. Siegel's Essay and Multiple Choice Q & A series, published by Aspen Publishers, is especially useful for helping you to practice your exam analytical skills. Working through hypothetical fact patterns and practice exams is critical to developing solid exam writing skills. I would suggest that you purchase these and begin using them as early in the semester as possible.

Always remember that although a commercial aid can jump-start your assimilation of the important legal concepts for a subject, it cannot replace the basic reading and wrestling with the material. Further, there are plenty of low-cost options available. As previously discussed, your law library contains a wealth of free study aids. I was amazed at the number of commercial materials on hand at my law library.

THE PYRAMID OUTLINE METHOD

Shortly after law school commences, you will begin to hear a lot from your peers about outlines and how important they are. You may hear of a holy grail outline for a particular course, authored by an apocryphal student who booked the course and has made the outline available to some of your classmates. As final exams loom in the not-too-distant future, anxious 1Ls begin to try to make sense of the entire process—the voluminous reading, massive notes, and intense discussion—and begin their outlines. The problem for most students is they have no idea what is important and what is unimportant, so they build huge outlines which contain everything, including the kitchen sink.

In one popular law school movie, the protagonist joins a study group that subdivides the content for a contracts course outline. The study group agrees that each member will outline a particular section of the course. At the end of the semester, they all get together and contribute their portion to the group's outline. The theory is that the group will have a super outline of sorts, but the resulting outline is hundreds and hundreds of pages long.

This is an extremely bad idea.

Aside from the fact that the movie study group members end up hating each other because of suspicion that other members are holding out information, a collective outline completely defeats the purpose of the exercise. Although you will hear a lot about how important *outlines* are, you will likely hear nothing about how important *outlining* is. The distinction I am making is about process versus output. Certainly, the output is important. An outline is the source of the black letter law for the course. However, your outline will not be graded. Most likely, no one else will even see your outline. You may never look at it again after exams.

The process of outlining is infinitely more important than the outline itself. This is because the process of outlining is an active learning process, which will force you to work with an amorphous body of information and make sense of it. The Pyramid Outline Method is a process that will give you the tools to succeed on your final exams. This process will enable you to take a large amount of information contained in your class notes, casebooks, commercial outlines, and other sources and distill it down to a manageable level.

By using the Pyramid Outline Method, you will increase your study effectiveness and assimilate information more efficiently, ultimately enhancing your class preparation and saving precious study time. You will spend less time preparing defensively for class. Instead, you will always have an eye toward the ultimate objectives—learning the law and performing effective legal analysis. Further, you will begin to see the trees in the forest. You will understand where the case reading fits into the overall subject matter. You will be able to determine whether the case is dealing with a rule, an element of the rule, an alternative rule, or an extension of the rule. You will learn to identify the ambiguities in the law, arguments, and potentially applicable factual situations, which will in turn greatly impact your ability to write a solid exam.

The Pyramid Outline Method is simply a holistic and systematic approach to your studies, which if followed will help bring the study of law together for you. Although it will also help you in your class preparation, you will focus on learning the law and understanding legal analysis. By exam time, you will use your knowledge of the law to identify legal issues and cogently discuss them. You will be able to articulate both sides of an argument and to discern logical extensions of the law.

Overview of the Pyramid Outline Method

The following is a schematic of the Pyramid Outline Method:

The first outline, your Base Outline, is your comprehensive outline. It stays intact throughout the semester—you add information to it but never edit it down. It will become your record of all of the information you gathered during the semester, whether from case reading, outside reading, or class discussion. It will contain all but the most irrelevant information. At the semester's end, it may easily total several hundred pages in length. The Pyramid Outline is derived from your Base Outline. Each week, you will boil down your Pyramid Outline.

The third outline, your Capstone Outline, is the shortest synopsis of the course and will be generally no longer than two or three pages. It will contain only memory-provoking points that will essentially summarize the entire course. You will begin to develop your Capstone Outline by distilling down your Pyramid Outline about two to three weeks prior to the exam.

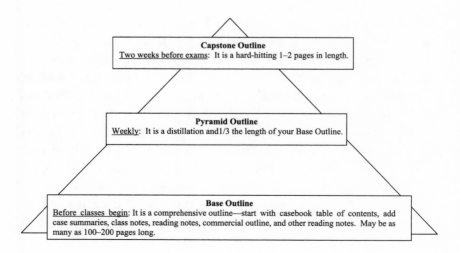

Capstone Outline
<u>Two weeks before exams</u>: It is a hard-hitting 1–2 pages in length.

Pyramid Outline
<u>Weekly</u>: It is a distillation and 1/3 the length of your Base Outline.

Base Outline
<u>Before classes begin</u>: It is a comprehensive outline—start with casebook table of contents, add case summaries, class notes, reading notes, commercial outline, and other reading notes. May be as many as 100–200 pages long.

You may already be groaning at the thought of developing not one, but three outlines. However, the process involved in constructing these outlines is more important than the output. This is because the process of digesting and reducing the broad information contained in your Base Outline is the method by which you will actively assimilate and learn the course material. The process of continually reducing the material will enable you to master the information you will need for your final exam. The Pyramid Outline Method requires regular, scheduled outlining work, which is reviewed and updated on a daily, weekly, and monthly basis. This method will give you a schedule and the discipline required to manage the vast amount of information you will receive during the course of the semester. And if used effectively, it will enable you to digest and recall the voluminous amount of information necessary to write your law school exams.

> **The process of digesting and reducing the broad information contained in your Base Outline is the method by which you will actively assimilate and learn the course material.**

The appendixes of this book provide examples of Pyramid and Capstone Outlines, as well as issues checklists. Here are the detailed steps involved in the Pyramid Outline Method.

Step One: Create Three Copies of Your Casebook Table of Contents. The first step in the Pyramid Outline Method is very simple. All you need to do is to create three copies of the table of contents contained in your casebook. The first copy will become your Base Outline, the second your Pyramid Outline, and the third your Capstone Outline.

As you prepare the foundations for your three outlines from your casebook table of contents, you should also think about the various headings and subheadings and why they might have been included in your casebook. Obviously, the casebook editors viewed these topics as important to the subject. Think about the cases referenced in the casebook's table of contents. Try and get an overall sense of the subject. As the semester progresses, you should also get a sense of your professor's view of the importance of these topics. Those the professor finds important will likely find their way into exam questions.

Step Two: Insert Case Briefs into Your Base Outline and Pyramid Outline. Brief the cases in your casebook and insert those case summaries into the appropriate sections of your Base Outline and Pyramid Outline.

If your casebook includes problems or discussion questions, work through them and write out your answers. This information should also be plugged into both your Base Outline and Pyramid Outline.

Step Three: Insert Class Notes into Your Base Outline and Pyramid Outline. While everything is still fresh in your mind (no later than eight hours following class), review your notes and insert them into your Base Outline and Pyramid Outline. This will enable you to determine with a fair degree of certainty exactly where in the overall course that day's classroom dialogue fits.

For the Base Outline, you should do very little editing other than to omit obviously irrelevant information and to ensure that you can understand the notes later. Keep in mind that different portions of your notes may need to be placed into different sections of your various outlines. Throughout the semester, your Base Outline will remain a comprehensive record and reference tool of all the information you learn, from all sources, throughout the semester. Using your word processing program, you should mark various headings and words and create and maintain current tables of contents and indexes for each outline. This will make your Base Outline that much more useful.

Step Four: Weekly Review of Base Outline and Condensing of Pyramid Outline. At the end of each week, take a step back and try to understand exactly what information the professor covered that week. Briefly review your class notes and your Base Outline. In addition, add information to your Base Outline and Pyramid Outline which you decide is relevant from your outside reading of commercial outlines, unedited cases, and hornbooks. Depending upon how informative a particular class is, you may lean much more heavily on your outside reading than class notes, and you should insert relevant information into your outlines.

Next, boil down the relevant sections of your Pyramid Outline for that week by two-thirds. This may seem a little scary, especially earlier in the semester when you are just beginning to grasp what may be important. However, you will always have any information you delete available in your Base Outline. This is why you need three outlines: one is for the recording of raw information, the second is for processing and digesting this information, and the third is your memory trigger at exam time. Additionally, your Pyramid Outline is your self-created textbook and reference source, which you can refer to at any point in your studies.

At some point, as you become more comfortable with the material, you may even want to rearrange the topical order, deviating from your casebook's table of contents order. If your professor clearly speeds through certain sections but spends a great deal of time on others, you may want to include the emphasized sections first in your Pyramid Outline. Or if the sections make better sense to you in a different order, you should rearrange accordingly. The point is to organize your Pyramid Outline in such a way as to optimize your integration and learning of the material.

Cutting out irrelevant topics in your Pyramid Outline will force you to identify the key concepts. More importantly, you will begin to see the "on the one hand" and "on the other hand" issues (either in competing common law or statutory law influences, or in factual distinctions), which are prime exam topics. As you review the material as part of this distillation process, ask yourself whether the law and facts could be argued both ways in an exam situation.

For example, as you organize your Pyramid Outline for contracts class, you will probably include sections on Offer and Acceptance, Consideration, Revocation, Performance, Defenses, Damages, and Breach.

As you contemplate performance, you will learn that under the Uniform Commercial Code (UCC), the perfect tender rule applies, which means that the parties have to do (or more likely supply) *precisely* what they promised. Anything less is considered a breach in performance of the party's obligations under the contract. However, under the common law, judges often held that as long as the party *substantially* did what he promised, then the other party was obligated to uphold his side of the bargain. Assuming that your contracts professor covers both the common law and UCC, you should have two subsections under your Performance section. The first subsection deals with performance under the common law and the second one addresses performance under the UCC.

In fact, it is likely that most of the sections in your contracts outline should have these two subsections, the common law view and the UCC rule. Divisions such as these in the law make for a perfect exam question. You may read a fact pattern that indicates that one party performed slightly less than promised and assume that the party was in breach. By understanding that there are really two sets of law governing (i.e., the UCC and common law), you would discuss both, thus scoring more points on your exam. Discussing only the UCC will rob you of substantial exam points. Most fact patterns on law school exams are ambiguous enough that either could apply. And this is where the Pyramid Outline Method will begin to help you earn big dividends on your exams.

Step Five: Monthly Review of Outlines. In addition to your daily review of class notes and your weekly review and editing of your Pyramid Outline, you should also schedule a monthly review of both your Base Outline and Pyramid Outline. These monthly reviews should enable you to better retain the course material. In addition, as you review the material, you should again think about the kinds of legal issues raised by the material.

Now is also the time to begin to think about testable legal issues. As you read the cases, get into the habit of thinking about other potential issues raised by the facts, as well as the arguments for and against the extension of the law relative to the case. Learn to anticipate potential arguments and break these arguments down into their basic assumptions, either explicit or implicit.

You can also look at your professor's old exams on file in the library, if you haven't already done so. This will begin to give you an idea of what kinds of legal issues your professor will test. If there are no exams on file for your professor, try to find exams from other professors who have previously taught the subject. If old exams are not available, it is still important to look at practice questions, and I would suggest that you use one or more of the commercially available materials, such as the Casenote Legal Education series or Siegel's.

Step Six: One Month before Exams, Develop Your Issues Checklist. At this point, you have probably covered approximately two-thirds of the material for exam purposes. You have also become familiar with the kinds of legal issues that are commonly tested. You should now begin to maintain a list of the kinds of issues likely to be tested on the exam. I would suggest that you phrase the issue in the form of a question. The purpose behind an issues checklist is to force you to begin to think of the law you have learned and its application to factual issues. This will facilitate your memorization of the law, but more importantly, it will begin to help you develop the critically important skill of identifying issues raised by the exam fact patterns. You must resist the temptation to simply memorize the law. Instead, you should always think of the law in terms of the issues it raises.

For example, under the topic of Consideration, an issues checklist might look something like this:

I. Is there evidence of consideration sufficient to make a
   promise enforceable?
   a. Was the promise actually a donative promise, i.e., a
      promise to make a gift?
      1. If so, can the party rely on promissory estoppel or
         was there detrimental reliance?
      2. Was the promise actually a conditional donative
         promise?
   b. Do the facts actually indicate past consideration?
      1. If so, was there a material benefit conferred?

By formulating your issues checklist as a series of questions, you will resist the temptation to assume facts and make unsupported conclusions. The more that you have thought through potential issues that may be raised, the more complete your issues checklist will become. I recommend that from the very beginning of the semester, you continually think about the issues that may be presented in an exam for the subject that you are studying. How the court resolves the issue of law (for example, by adopting the majority position regarding the law) or the issue of fact will often provide a clue as to the kinds of issues that your casebook editors and professors find important.

Developing an issues checklist will serve as a good memory prompter as you prepare for exams and as you eventually read through exam fact patterns. More importantly, by continuously thinking about your issues checklist, you will learn to anticipate potential issues and arguments, a key attribute of the successful law student and lawyer.

Step Seven: Three Weeks before Exams, Develop Your Capstone Outline. A few weeks before exams, you will make a copy of your Pyramid Outline and edit it down to a Capstone Outline, or summary outline, of no more than two or three pages, depending upon the subject. Some subjects, such as property, are rule-intensive and may require three pages. Other subjects, which are more principle-based, will require fewer pages.

The point of the Capstone Outline is an extremely brief synopsis, which will give you an overview of the subject with enough detail to prompt your memory more fully. Ideally, the Capstone Outline should be short enough that you can commit it to memory. Having the essence of the subject distilled and memorized will be of tremendous value as you read the exam fact pattern, spot issues, and analyze the issues.

As you reduce your Pyramid Outline down, refer to your Base Outline as well. You may discover that you have edited out information from your Pyramid Outline that should be retrieved, based upon subsequent learning during the semester. This will also give you an idea of how your understanding of the subject has evolved, thus providing better direction of how best to distill it down into your Capstone Outline.

Developing your Capstone Outline is the stage at which you will truly begin to own the material. You must simplify, rearrange, and distill it to the point that you are also committing it to memory. Remember that during exams, you will have almost no time to look anything up. Your Capstone Outline's purpose is to serve as a memory trigger for you as you study those last few days before the exam and when you are actually taking the exam.

Timing is important in this regard. Do not develop your Capstone Outline so far in advance of the exam that you promptly forget all of the material. Remember that the point of the Pyramid Outline Method is to help you assimilate the law. On the other hand, if you wait too long to begin the intense synopsis of the Capstone Outline, you may not have enough time to do a comprehensive digestion and summarization of the material.

EFFECTIVE LEGAL WRITING

In many ways, effective legal writing is like any other effective writing—you want to do it in a well-organized fashion, always keeping in mind the needs of your intended audience. And the sooner you begin to develop your legal writing skills, the better you will do on exams.

As previously discussed, you will be required to take a course on legal writing during your first year. Legal writing is usually a two-semester class, and you will meet in a small group of 20 to 30 students. In addition to your legal writing instructor, the class may also have second- and third-year students assigned as teaching assistants. You will be introduced to certain concepts associated with writing about legal issues, including citation of your sources and the proper organization of memoranda and briefs. Generally, you will work on one project per semester. My first semester, we worked on a legal memorandum, and the second semester, we worked on a persuasive brief. These are the two basic types of documents you will likely prepare throughout your career.

The legal memorandum is an objective as opposed to a persuasive endeavor. It is usually prepared for another lawyer or a client. It is designed to provide the recipient with the current state of the law regarding a particular legal issue. It describes both sides (or all sides, if you prefer) to a legal issue. A legal memorandum usually concludes with some sort of a recommendation to the recipient. Writing a law school exam in many ways simulates writing a legal memorandum. An example of a first-year legal memorandum is included in Appendix G of this book.

The other legal document you will learn to write is called a brief. The legal brief is typically a document filed with a court. Although it must accurately state the law, a legal brief is more persuasive in nature. For example, a common brief is one filed in support of a motion for summary judgment. The brief cites case law in support of the movant's position.

Regardless of the type of document you prepare, there are certain principles that apply to every legal document. The following is a brief discussion of these principles. These principles will also apply to your exams.

Write in a Clear, Concise, Well-Organized Fashion

In short, words are the currency of the lawyer. Arguably, writing in a clear, well-organized fashion is more important than any other aspect of legal writing. This is because the recipient of legal documents is typically required to read numerous documents on an ongoing basis. These recipients include other lawyers such as partners, opposing counsel, judges, and law clerks. A poorly drafted document simply will not achieve its intended results.

I recommend that you use fairly short sentences and short paragraphs. Avoid the typical legal jargon so common in much legal writing—the *thereins, hereinafters,* and *therefores.* Many law students make the mistake of following the poor examples found in many legal opinions written by judges. However, these examples are often old and arcane. Further, if they confused you, why would you want to emulate their writing style?

The single best way to organize your writing is to first develop an outline. You will likely find that creating an outline before you start writing will greatly enhance the organization of your memoranda and briefs. An additional benefit of approaching your writing in this way is that it will greatly improve your exam writing skills. If practiced enough, you will eventually be able to outline quickly and effectively. In fact, if you really master outlining, you will begin to approach your topic with an outline in mind, and during actual exams you will likely only need to make a few brief notes as memory triggers, rather than a complete outline. You will almost always use certain broad categories in your outline. For example, there will almost always be introduction and conclusion sections in anything you write. There will almost always be a facts section. There will always be some sort of analysis or argument section (a brief usually contains an argument section; a memorandum usually contains an analysis section). These sections are the heart of any legal writing and require the most thought and precision in drafting.

Use the Active Voice

In virtually any type of writing, using the active voice is always preferable to the passive voice. Active voice writing is easier to read, more interesting, and once you get used to it, it is actually easier to write. Essentially, passive voice places the subject of the sentence behind the predicate: "Harry rode the bike" becomes "The bike was ridden by Harry."

Law students tend to drift into a passive voice mode because it usually sounds more formal. On a subconscious level, I believe that students use the passive voice because it is less direct and presents, at least in their minds, less opportunity for contradiction. One of your first reviews of any draft should be for the purpose of eliminating passive voice in the document. It will make your writing much more effective.

Use Headings and Subheadings Liberally

Headings and subheadings can be fabulous tools to enhance an otherwise drab document. Headings and subheadings are excellent guideposts for your reader and may make your exam stand out in the crowd. These tools will make your paper more readable and may also serve the useful purpose of helping you to organize your ideas. One way to approach headings is to use your outline as the basis for determining your headings. You may decide to stop at a certain level in your outline; however, my advice is to liberally include headings and subheadings.

Chapter 5

How to Prepare for Final Exams

O**N A SUNNY, COOL** December day, I walked into the auditorium and took a seat for my first 1L exam—torts. Although I had sat in this room an entire semester, I was struck with what seemed to be its complete metamorphosis. Not that the actual room had changed, but it may as well have. The atmosphere was so completely different, I wondered for a minute whether I had inadvertently entered the wrong room. I looked around for a familiar face. Students were not sitting in their usual spots; instead, many had moved to the front of the room, presumably in order to concentrate. This was battle and everyone had suddenly become a "gunner."

No one spoke. The intensity in the room was palpable. The looks on some students' faces frightened me. They said: "I know this stuff cold and I can't wait to destroy the exam." Everyone appeared to have an exam strategy. I didn't really want to think about the look on my face. It was probably something resembling the look of a mouse just before being swallowed by a python.

The professor had indicated at the end of our last torts class that the exam was open book. When he said this, I thought that perhaps there was hope after all. Taking full advantage of the opportunity, I had lugged in to the auditorium my complete torts library. This included my casebook, my commercial outline, my hornbook, my class notebook, my *Black's Law Dictionary*, and everything else I could think of that I could use to look up the law during the exam. Another false lead in the labyrinth: anyone who has gone through first-year law school exams knows that there is no time to look anything up.

A proctor handed out the exams. I quickly read mine, hoping that I could at least initially make some sense of it. On its surface, it didn't look too bad. However, as I mentally tried to tally up the number of issues, I stopped counting at something like 30. I immediately realized that there was no way to discuss all of these issues in some sort of an IRAC format, as all of the books I had read advised. To do so would take much more than the allotted three hours for the exam. I assumed that some of these issues must be red herrings, included to distract me. Or alternatively, I reasoned that perhaps some of the issues might be dependent upon the resolution of other issues—in other words, some issues might go away, depending upon the outcome of other issues. This meant that I must also decide what the relationships *among* the issues were. Nonetheless, I realized one important point; there was nothing discussed in class that even remotely resembled this jumble of facts.

I looked around and people were already busily writing, brows furrowed in concentration. I started to panic. I thought I was the only person in the room without a clue.

How can people be writing already, when I haven't even decided how to begin writing some sort of an answer? I felt totally unprepared and as if I had been taken completely by surprise. Before the exam, I anticipated something more rote and undergraduate-like, a sort of regurgitation of the various laws and cases we had covered in class. I expected the fact pattern to present a legal issue in which an element of a particular cause of action was missing. I did not expect a confusing mass of facts, which appeared to be loosely related.

Now, merely identifying the legal issue or issues seemed to be impossible. The fact pattern was indecipherable. Somewhere, somehow, within this morass of verbiage was a legal problem or problems. I caught my breath and reminded myself that the exam had to bear some resemblance to what was discussed in class. Or at least I hoped it did.

THE ESSENCE OF A FINAL EXAM

Understanding the law is only the tip of the iceberg in preparation for law school exams. You must know the law (and the associated nuances) so well that the legal issues presented by fact patterns in exams virtually jump off of the page into your awareness. As discussed throughout this book, the way to accomplish this is by continuously working with the material. You do this by progressively distilling it down. Eventually, using the Pyramid Outline Method, you distill the information down to two or three pages into a Capstone Outline. If you take anything with you into the exam room (assuming the exam is open book) it is these pages and an issues checklist.

The essence of a final exam is this: you have a mere three hours to showcase your black letter law knowledge, analytical ability, issue-spotting, organization skills, and writing skills—in sum, your ability to write and think like a lawyer. The fact that you never missed a class, did all of the assigned reading, beat issues to death in your study group, and developed a cogent and comprehensive course outline is simply irrelevant at this point in the semester. Exams in virtually every law school are administered on an anonymous basis; who you are and what you have done during the semester are not factored into your grade. What matters at this point is whether you can convince your professor through your writing that you have mastered the subject in a lawyerly way.

Your law school professors grade exams on a curve. There are a predetermined number of A grades, B grades, and so on. To put it crassly, your classmates are the competition in the grading curve contest. This should tell you that at least part of your objective should be to differentiate yourself from the competition. As with virtually all exams, the secret is in telling the grader what they want to hear and in a way that they want to hear it. There is a tension between content and style that is critical. To illustrate, a student can properly identify every core issue, analyze the issue, apply the appropriate legal rule, and still get a

B, especially if the student's writing style is hard to read. On the other hand, a student who effectively organizes the same answer and writes an interesting essay that is easy to read will have a much higher probability of receiving an A.

A Typical Final Exam

Most first-year exams are three hours in length. You will most likely be given a series of fact patterns, each of which raises one or more legal issues. However, I have had final exams that were essentially one fact pattern—a convoluted winding mess of parties and causes of actions, but all contained in one big fact pattern. In many cases, you may not even be asked a question about the fact patterns. I have seen exams where convoluted fact patterns are given without any instruction whatsoever. It is simply assumed that you will discuss the legal issues presented.

As a result, do not expect to find questions at the end of the fact pattern such as: "Discuss the liability of Smith to Jones." You must assume that the facts themselves cry out to you the question. You are expected to showcase your ability to think like a lawyer and come up with the questions yourself. It's called spotting the issue. The facts, based upon your knowledge of the law, present a question (or problem) that needs to be solved. And the exam writer is not going to tell you the issue.

Arguably this is unfair, especially to the uninitiated 1L. After all, years of secondary education, undergraduate education, and perhaps even graduate education have laid down clear ground rules: You are given an exam. The exam has questions. You answer the questions. But then again, life isn't fair.

Most law school exams, at least during the first year, are organized in a similar fashion. A complicated fact pattern that entails multiple relationships between multiple parties is described. There may or may not be an actual question at the end of the fact pattern (if there isn't, then assume that you are to identify and analyze the issues contained therein). You will typically have three hours to complete the exam. You will either write in blue books (blank, lined booklets) or you may have the opportunity to take your exam by computer with software which blocks out all programs and files except a simple word processing program.

Exams are typically open book, meaning that you can bring books, notes, and pretty much anything in hard copy with you to the exam. However, the term *open book* is yet another false turn in the labyrinth. Unlike undergraduate or graduate exams that test your knowledge only and are almost always closed book, having the information at your fingertips for a law school exam will do you almost no good. The idea that you have time to look up the law, much less find anything useful, is ludicrous to anyone who has taken a law school exam. 2Ls, 3Ls, and law professors know that having books at your side during exams is virtually worthless. Most exams last three hours and will go by faster than anything else ever has in your life. You may remember that the LSAT was like this. The key to success on law school exams is in the application of the information and specifically the application of the rules of law to the issues raised in the exam fact pattern. In order to do well on an exam, the information must be beyond your fingertips, it must be etched into your memory, and your recollection of it must be triggered by particular facts in the exam. On these exams, you are much too busy reading the fact patterns, trying to make sense of them, and organizing an answer to consult your notes. The three-hour exam seems like 30 minutes.

Before you can analyze a legal issue raised by a fact pattern in an exam, you must first be able to identify the issue presented by the facts. The only way you can identify a legal issue is by first knowing the law. As a result, if you do not know the law (the rule and its elements and the various judicial interpretations discussed in class or found elsewhere), you will not be able to identify the legal issue. For example, on a criminal law exam, if you do not understand that the crime of burglary consists of the breaking and entering of the dwelling house of another at night with the intent to commit a felony, you will likely miss some important issues in the fact pattern. If you do not remember the intent element of the burglary rule, you will likely overlook any facts, or the lack thereof, which could apply to this element. If the fact pattern indicates that the would-be burglar broke in to a neighbor's garage for the purpose of retrieving a loaned tool, you may miss the point of the question entirely.

Law school exams can involve discrete subparts that contain one fact pattern for analysis. More likely, however, they consist of a complex fact pattern that involves multiple parties and multiple issues. These fact patterns usually omit key facts, which are so obvious that the risk is that the law student will assume them. If you assume these facts, you will overlook an opportunity to discuss potential issues and outcomes that may depend upon these missing facts, as well as the opportunity to score exam points.

Understanding the Grade-Point Bucket

During my first semester, while we were waiting for the professor to arrive for our class, a classmate leaned over toward me in a conspiratorial way and offered a rather startling theory about the professor's exam-grading methodology.

"I heard that last year, the professor's 16-year-old daughter graded his final exams," he whispered.

"What?" I hissed, "You must be kidding!" I was sure that this was some kind of setup to a punch line that would be shortly delivered.

"No, seriously," the classmate retorted. "He lets his kid grade all of his exams," he said.

I later heard this rumor reported, along with all sorts of silly variations, from students at other schools regarding their professors. Although obviously labyrinthian mythology, for the sake of the discussion that follows, I ask the reader to withhold judgment as to its accuracy. Let's just assume for a minute that it was true. If it were true (and even if it weren't), it would reveal a great deal about the construction of law school exams. Specifically, it would tell you that exams can be graded by someone who knows little, if anything, about the laws involved.

How can this be? The only reasonable explanation is that law school exams, in fact, bear a striking resemblance to undergraduate exams, at least in the way that they are graded. The only way someone who does not understand the law could grade a law school exam would be if he or she had a grading key, which could be used to count a predetermined number of criteria tested in that exam. This would mean that law school exams could be graded objectively, by assigning points to an answer's components, rather than a subjective system based upon the relative merits of each answer. As a result, a 16-year-old, or a trained monkey for that matter, could grade them.

Later, during my second semester, I spoke with a relative who was a law professor at a school in Texas. I asked him for the secret to good grades in law school. He thought about it for a good while before he answered. "You never know what is going to affect your grade," he said, almost wistfully. "Perhaps the professor had a fight with his or her spouse just before grading your paper. Maybe he or she just had a bad day," he said as he pondered the imponderable.

His response to my question was disconcerting. I couldn't believe that it was possible that something so meaningless and random could affect my grades.

Both of these conversations reveal a little-known secret about law school exams. Most exams are constructed in such a way as to allow the professor to categorize exam answers in order to assign points for correct issue identification and points for analysis in an answer. In this way, the tests can be graded objectively, rather than subjectively. Point-based grading makes grading on the curve infinitely easier. More importantly, it ensures that there is a rational basis for the grading curve. As a result, when you boil it all down, what appears to be a subjective exam situation is, in reality, objective. There is a template of legal issues and analysis (and to a lesser extent, conclusions) that goes with every test. The distracted grader is yet another minotaur in the labyrinth. This should tell you how important it is to so clearly write an A answer that even the most distracted of graders can recognize it.

Your goal, therefore, is to clearly match the template with the issues you identify and analyze, such that you accumulate the maximum number of points and the grader has no choice but to give you an A. Despite the fact that exams are generally in essay format, which seems subjective, almost all of them are actually graded in an objective format. With law school exams, it is primarily about earning points. Most professors, in constructing an exam, first decide which issues they want to test. They then develop facts around these issues. Each issue is assigned a certain number of points. Think of your exam analysis as a point bucket. When you identify the issue, you get to put points in the bucket.

That said, there is definitely also a subjective component to the exam. In addition to identifying and analyzing legal issues, *how* you discuss the relevant law and *how* you apply the relevant facts to this law are also assigned points. If you identify the relevant law, you get to put points in the bucket. If the law has some inherent ambiguity (such as the common law view versus the UCC view) and you discuss it, you get to put points in the bucket. You get points for how well you craft your arguments. If the facts and/or the state of the law (e.g., a split of authority or common law/UCC) are ambiguous and you discuss both sides, then you get to put more points in the bucket. The conclusion you develop is given points, and the professor may even assign points for the overall organization and quality of your work.

At the end of the exam, this bucket is dumped into your grade bucket, and your final grade is based upon the total number of points you scored. Therefore, to do well on an exam, you must score the greatest number of points. Clarity in your answer is your insurance policy against the professor that had a bad day (or for that matter, his 16-year-old daughter). Assuming that you can spot the issues, understand the law, and apply the facts (if you follow the Pyramid Outline Method and have written complete practice exams, you should be able to do so effectively), then the only thing that will potentially reduce your grade is your inability to clearly communicate.

You should also recall that your exams are submitted anonymously. You will be given a student number that identifies you to the school's registrar; however, the professor will not know the identity of the examinee. As a result, your dedication in attending classes, your diligent preparation, and your charming personality will have no impact on your grade. Instead, your grade is solely based upon the effectiveness of your writing during the exam period.

THE RIGHT TURNS FOR SUCCESS IN FINAL-EXAM PREPARATION

I suggest that as you approach exams, you first try to envision yourself as a lawyer, sitting in your office long after you have passed the bar exam. A partner or client comes to your office and explains a series of facts. He or she leaves your office in a huff. You must somehow make sense of it all. This is in essence the point of a law school exam: to test your ability to think on your feet as a lawyer. In addition to knowing the law, you must be able to identify issues and apply the law to the facts to resolve these issues.

Early Memorization and the Benefit of Cramming
This may seem oxymoronic, but in reality, early and methodical memorization and cramming actually go hand in hand in law school. One of the

benefits of knowing the rules early in the semester is that it will enable you to engage in legal analysis that much more quickly. Otherwise, it will be difficult to identify legal issues presented by an exam fact pattern. Using all of the techniques presented in this book, you must make sure that you know the law cold well before exam time.

When I began law school, I mistakenly believed that cramming was a sign of poor planning and preparation. Early in the semester, I had resolved that I would be so prepared at exam time that I could take the day off before exams and relax. Let the students who had procrastinated during the semester do their cramming. The fallacy of this thinking is that much of the detail and nuances of the law are retained primarily in the your short-term memory. You work with it for a little while and then promptly forget it.

This concept was driven home to me when I took my first bar exam in the state of Texas and a few years later when I took my second in Tennessee. As you will learn, the bar exam is a huge test covering your knowledge of numerous subjects and hundreds of laws. You may have no exposure whatsoever to some of the subjects tested while in law school. I took the BARBRI bar review course in preparation for both exams. I faithfully attended class. I worked old practice exam problems. I followed their prescribed study schedule carefully. The third day of the Texas exam included questions on secured transactions, a subject that I did not take in school. As a result, the only knowledge I had of the subject was what I learned during my bar preparation. Early that morning, around 3:00 A.M., I arose from a fitful sleep and decided to review the subject. Despite the fact that I had spent weeks on the subject, had written numerous practice exam questions, and had reviewed the material repeatedly, I could not remember one thing about secured transactions. I psyched myself out and became convinced that the reason I couldn't remember anything was because I had no foundation in the subject from law school.

A little well-placed cramming can help you hugely as you approach exams. It will reduce the short-term memory loss phenomenon and also increase your confidence.

After the initial panic wore off, I decided to simply review my Capstone Outline (I used the Pyramid Outline Method to prepare for the bar exam). Just looking at the outline calmed me. I spent the next two hours reviewing this one-page document. The concepts began to come back to me almost immediately. A bit later, the nuances began to drift back. By exam time, I was able to articulate credible answers and ultimately passed the exam. The point is this: a little well-placed cramming can help you hugely as you approach exams. It will reduce the short-term memory loss phenomenon and also increase your confidence. I am not recommending cramming as a replacement for the preparation you will do throughout the semester. Instead, I recommend it as a supplement to that preparation; sort of the icing on your studies cake.

Practice, Practice, Practice

Other than assimilating the black letter law, the single most important thing you can do in preparation for final exams is to practice identifying legal issues, analyzing them, and writing *effective* exam-style answers.

Old Exams. No other resource is more valuable to your final exam preparation than old exams. Period.

Your law school will very likely have old exams from various professors on file in the library. In addition, there may be model answers included with the exam. Some professors include the highest grade answer with the exam on file. I suggest you do as much as possible to find old exams with model answers. If there are none on file in the library, speak to your professor. If she is unwilling or unable to give you old exams, seek out other professors or search on the Internet at other law schools.

The most important thing is to develop a good idea of what a winning exam answer looks like. Chances are that the brevity of the answer will surprise you. A good exam answer simply identifies all of the issues presented, discusses them in a cogent, thoughtful analysis, and develops a conclusion. Looking at old exams will also give you an idea of the types of issues that the professor considers fair game on an exam. You will likely discover that professors love to raise issues not presented by the class materials. Their reasoning is that they are there to give you the tools to analyze new issues. This is why law professors enjoy believing that they teach you to think. Rather than recall and regurgitation, law school exams are designed to test your ability to apply learned principles to new situations.

By reviewing old exam model answers, you will also learn what effective legal writing style looks like. Winning exams do not waste the grader's time by discussing the history of the law and repeating the facts. Winning exams are neat and well organized, get right to the issues presented, and present clear and cogent legal analyses.

Complete the Practice Questions in Your Casebooks and Commercial Study Aids. If your casebook includes discussion questions, work through all of them and write out full answers. If you have commercial materials that provide practice questions, use them. Many study aids offer practice exam questions, including the Casenote Legal Briefs Education series outlines, Kaplan PMBR FINALS series, and Glannon's *Examples and Explanations*. The point is that you need to become familiar with how legal issues arise, what they look like, and how to resolve them.

Begin to Write Practice Exam Answers as Early in the Semester as Possible. As early in the semester as possible, when you feel like you have at least a grasp of the material, begin to write practice answers to questions. Of course, you will not be substantively equipped to analyze exam fact patterns until well into the semester because you will not have covered all of the black letter law. Regardless, I would advise you to at least familiarize yourself with the form and substance of exam questions and answers as soon as possible. This awareness will in turn drive your studying and make much of the reading that you are doing more relevant.

Repeated practice exam reading and writing, under timed conditions, will greatly speed up and improve your exam writing skills and enable you to focus on the more subtle issues presented in exam fact patterns. Grade your practice exam, or have someone else do it. Scrutinize the exam answer for organization, analysis, and readability. This is the territory where A and A+ answers are usually found.

WRITING AN EFFECTIVE FINAL-EXAM ANSWER

By exam time, most first-year law students understand that their exam will be in an issue-spotting format. Issue-spotting exams are constructed with dense, confusing fact patterns. These fact patterns raise legal issues, which the examinee must identify and analyze. Obviously, if you cannot identify an issue, then you will not be able to discuss it.

Issue spotting is a highly leveraging activity on exam day because once an issue is identified, the various sides of the issue can be discussed, and a rational conclusion can be made. If you completely miss any one of these steps, you will lose the opportunity to earn substantial points.

How do you know what your professor is looking for? One of the key ways is by analyzing the professor's emphasis during class. Did she spend a great deal of time on the UCC? Obviously, it would then be likely that a UCC-related question would be included on her exam. Try and get to know your professor and her interests. The professor may have a website with a curriculum vitae and a list of her published works, which may tell you something about her academic focus.

It is somewhat of a trap to think of an exam as a typical college question-and-answer exercise. Instead, you should think of the exam as if a client walked into your office one day with a story. Your job is to explore these facts and determine relevant law. You then perform an analysis that predicts the outcome of these facts in light of the relevant law. Finally, you advise your client as to his rights and obligations and recommend a particular course of action. This is essentially what you are being asked to do on a law school exam.

Always Look Over the Entire Exam Carefully before You Start Writing

During one of my second-year final exams, the professor thoughtfully included a blank page between two of the exam questions. At first glance, the entire exam appeared to be one relatively simple question, easily answerable in three hours. I blissfully wrote what I thought would be the best exam of my law school career. With about 30 minutes left in the exam, I realized to my horror that there were actually two more questions to answer following the blank page. I composed myself and wrote furiously, managing to answer the remaining two questions. However, these last two answers were nowhere near the quality of the first answer.

Needless to say, I learned a very valuable lesson: look over the entire exam before you do anything else. You must be sure that you plan to dedicate equal amounts of time to all parts of the exam. A brilliant answer to one of three parts of the exam and mediocre answers to the other two will likely result in a less than desirable grade.

Make the Phrase "On the One Hand/On the Other Hand" Your Exam Mantra

In law school, as in life, there are always two sides to an argument. Many students lose valuable points in their exam answers because they only make one side of the argument. It is likely that the reason this occurs is because these students assume the other side of the argument is incorrect. However, lawyers must always be ready to articulate and argue both sides to any argument. In fact, in most mock trial and moot court exercises, students are asked to argue the opposite side of an issue that they prepared for.

One of the most important skills of a good lawyer is the ability to see the other side of the story and anticipate what the other side will do in a given situation. Critically objective thinking is one of the most important skills a lawyer can have. This skill is arguably counterintuitive to the new law student, who has spent at least four years taking undergraduate exams in which there are almost always right and wrong answers. Good lawyers see the weaknesses in their own arguments and tactics, and they plan for those, as well as for the strengths and weaknesses of the other side.

Law school exams simulate and examine this skill in law students. You are given a series of facts. On the surface, the facts may appear to be indisputable. However, upon deeper examination, these facts almost always contain ambiguity. In the exam setting, remember to imagine yourself as one of the parties' attorneys in a lawsuit presented by the factual issues contained in the exam question. Find the potential weaknesses in the other side's case and exploit it. Perhaps the contact in a battery case was not offensive or harmful, but merely coincident to normal everyday contact on a busy commuter train. Next, take the opposite side. The contact was coincident to everyday contact; however, the defendant exceeded the bounds of normal contact. Or perhaps the plaintiff had special sensitivities that caused what would have been casual contact to become offensive. Even better, perhaps courts differ as to exactly what kinds of contact are harmful. The point is that as a soon-to-be lawyer, your professors expect you to begin to think and argue like a lawyer.

And this is what it means to think like a lawyer: You identify all of the facts of a disputed situation. You identify alternative explanations of the facts. You identify all relevant law. You identify alternative interpretations of the law. You then take a position, argue the facts, and argue the law. And you do all of the foregoing in a systematic, efficient way, using clear deductive reasoning and documenting it in a clear and understandable way.

During his Senate Judiciary Committee hearings, Supreme Court Chief Justice John Roberts made a great example of effective use of the "on the one hand/on the other hand" mind-set when the committee attempted to nail him down regarding his position on an issue. Roberts, arguably one of the least controversial Supreme Court nominees in recent history and one of the most capable jurists, was criticized by the opposing party for refusing to comment on particular issues. Instead, he stated that it would be improper for him to comment on cases or issues that might come before the Court. At times, his responses angered partisan members of the committee, who attempted to pin him down on procedural nits. Roberts, obviously a hugely successful attorney and judge, presumably reverted to his Harvard Law School days, just as any first-year law student would during a Socratic dialogue with an aggressive professor.

Customize Your Exam Answer Approach, Depending upon the Subject

Most books and courses prescribe a standard method for preparing for final examinations. I do not believe that a standard approach for all subjects will ensure the greatest likelihood of success. Instead, to obtain the highest possible grade, you need to look at each subject differently, just as lawyers practicing in different areas approach their work differently.

To illustrate, when confronted with a legal issue, a tax attorney will consider the Internal Revenue Code, revenue rulings, and opinion letters in his or her analysis. A personal injury plaintiff's attorney might consider the particular judge that he will be practicing before to be of critical importance. A corporate attorney, on the other hand, may spend a great deal of time reviewing the Delaware Corporations Code and supporting cases prior to opining regarding a particular issue with a client.

The point is this: lawyers do all kinds of work for clients and use all kinds of authority, experience, and resources. If the point of law school is to teach you to think like a lawyer, then I would advise you to approach any legal problem first with your common sense, and then get creative—judiciously. The reason clients pay exorbitant fees to some lawyers is that they are able to solve problems and offer creative solutions where less skilled lawyers cannot.

Write Your Exam Answer in a Clear, Organized, and Legible Fashion

Early in law school, I suffered from the misconception that professors agonize over grading as much as students do writing the exams. Nothing could be farther from the truth. Most professors grade quickly and efficiently and spend very little time on an individual exam. It would probably surprise law students that a professor would spend as little as one or two days grading 40 student essay exams. That works out to be about 20–30 minutes of grading for an exam that took three furious hours for the student to write. Because most exams are actually objective, as previously explained, it does not take a great deal of time to grade them.

One of the most important things you can do to boost your grade on an exam is simply to write legibly. Professors cannot grade what they cannot read. Further, a messy exam will give the professor a bad first impression of the paper, or worse, anger the professor because the paper slows down his or her grading process. I would advise sacrificing almost anything for the sake of legibility in your exam answer. If it means that you have to slow down, then you should slow down. If it means you have to write less, you should write less. If your handwriting is simply terrible, consider using the exam software that your school likely offers to type the exam. However, investigate the software well before the exam to ensure that you can use it and that it hasn't caused other examinees problems during previous exams.

The organization, style, and readability of your exam will either help or hurt your grade. For my second- and third-year exams, I disciplined myself to draft a cursory outline rather than writing furiously as soon as I finished reading the fact pattern. I imagined an effective heading for each key section of my answer. You are much better off with a shorter, well-thought out answer than blue book after blue book of rambling, inefficient prose which procrastinates until it eventually arrives at some sort of a conclusion.

At times, depending upon the question, I would even fashion my answer in the form of a legal memorandum. The professor became the senior partner of the imaginary firm, and I was the associate he or she had assigned to draft the legal memorandum. This approach was invariably received well by the professor. In fact, if you can use the professor's pet buzzwords or phrases in your answer, that's even better. Obviously, one way to determine what is important to the professor is the amount of time he or she spends in class on a subject. Be observant. Also, do some simple research on what topics your professor has published (most schools post professors' curriculum vitae and publications on the school's website).

A friend of mine booked our torts class, which was a very impressive feat, given the competitiveness among extremely capable students that first year. I asked him how many blue books he had written.

"Six," he replied.

A gasp escaped my lips as I tried to imagine how anyone could fill six blue books in three hours. He quickly added the word, "pages."

I had written nearly two blue books (or about 20 pages) and received a B+ in the class. Clearly, our torts professor prized brevity and presumably, clarity.

The Types of Issues You Will See on Exams

There are infinite variations and combinations of issues that your professor can use to construct an exam fact pattern. As a result, there is no formula that will ensure success on every exam. The most important thing you can do is to develop the mind-set of a lawyer: you are given a set of facts which raise an issue or issues, you then decide which is the applicable law or laws, apply the facts to the law in an analysis which determines the likely outcome of an issue, and advise your client as to recommended next steps. This is what lawyers are paid to do.

That said, there are certain types of issues which are classic exam fodder and which you will likely see on your exams. The following is a brief discussion of those types of issues.

Elements of a Rule Are Missing or Debatable. The most basic of exam issues consists of a fact pattern in which a particular rule of law is implicated, but an element of the rule is missing.

For example, on a torts exam, imagine you are given the following fact pattern:

John strikes Dave in the face, causing Dave to suffer a serious and painful contusion requiring medical attention. John suffers from epilepsy.

This obviously is a question that invites a discussion of the tort of battery. The elements of battery (at least based upon these facts) are: (1) intent on the part of the defendant to strike the plaintiff, (2) actual harmful or offensive contact, and (3) damages. With these facts, we know that John struck Dave in the face and that Dave suffered damages. We are given these facts, and the second and third elements of battery appear to be undisputed.

Never assume anything that is not at least arguably called for by the fact pattern.

Less obvious, however, is whether John possessed the requisite intent to strike Dave. Based on the facts given, we cannot know whether John actually intended to strike Dave in the face. Perhaps John was in the throes of an epileptic seizure. On the other hand, perhaps John was angry and struck Dave. You can see that the first element of the tort of battery is in dispute.

The relevant facts in an exam will almost always present an issue of fact or law that can be argued in at least two ways. These issues will raise more issues that can also be argued in multiple ways. The key to scoring points on an exam is to identify these issues and sub-issues and cogently discuss them in an interesting way. Don't argue for argument's sake. Don't assume facts or make silly, unrealistic arguments. Instead, explore all aspects of a factual setting as they relate to the interpretations of applicable law. In this case, you absolutely must analyze and discuss both possibilities, that is, the outcome if John's action was intentional or unintentional.

A huge mistake in writing this exam would be to assume based upon these facts that John intended to strike Dave. Never assume anything that is not at least arguably called for by the fact pattern. The facts do not indicate that this was this case, nor do they indicate that this was not the case. It would also be a mistake to assume other facts, such as that John had properly taken his medication (if he had not, he might be liable under a negligence theory) or that John was aiming at someone else and hit Dave (he might be liable under a theory of transferred intent, which you will learn means that as long as you intend to strike someone, you can be liable for battery to anyone you actually strike). It would also be a mistake to assume that John was acting in self-defense (which would eliminate John's liability to Dave). Each of these assumptions should be identified and discussed.

Split of Authority or Common Law versus Statute Issue. Now, suppose you are given the following fact pattern in a contracts exam:

> Buyer sends Seller a purchase order for 300 widgets, made
> with 50 percent molybdenum and 50 percent titanium,
> FOB[3] Buyer's warehouse, delivery no later than August 16,
> 2005. In turn, Seller ships Buyer 290 widgets, made with
> 45 percent molybdenum and 55 percent titanium.

You might be tempted to launch into a discussion about breach and damages, on the basis that Seller did not perform under the agreement. In this case, Seller clearly did not perform according to the purchase order. However, if you make only this argument on your exam, you have fallen for one of the oldest professorial tricks in the book. The professor creates a fact pattern that intuitively calls for only one conclusion, thereby tricking you into a particular variety of conclusory thinking— jargon for jumping to a conclusion based on erroneous assumptions, or at least not explaining your work.

Concluding that Seller breached the agreement requires a number of assumptions. The first assumption is that the applicable law in this matter is the UCC, rather than the common law. The UCC was adopted by most states to clearly establish the law of sales and eliminate variation from judge to judge and court to court in the interpretation of contracts. Under the UCC, the so-called perfect tender rule applies, which means

---

[3] FOB stands for "free on board," which means that the seller pays the freight and assumes the risk of loss of the goods until they reach the buyer's warehouse.

that the seller must deliver precisely what the buyer orders. Anything else is a breach. Under the common law, on the other hand, substantial performance is the rule. The only way to effectively answer this question is to argue both. Further, depending upon which law applies to this fact pattern, other issues emerge. If the UCC applies, then perhaps there is a battle of the forms issue, which determines whose terms prevail. We don't know whether Buyer actually accepted the goods. We don't even know who, if anyone, is the plaintiff in this matter. Any and all issues presented by these facts should be discussed. You must show the grader your reasoning process. Do not make the mistake many 1Ls make of assuming that the examiner inferred, for example, that you know that the UCC applies because virtually every state has adopted it. Show every single piece of your reasoning to make sure that the grader knows that you know that there are two bodies of potentially applicable law. You don't have to be verbose; a single sentence can accomplish this, thereby earning you valuable points without spending a lot of time writing. Show your work!

A split of authority occurs when different jurisdictions view claims differently. Although the majority common law rule is that substantial performance is sufficient, if another jurisdiction does not follow the majority rule, then the issue presents a split of authority discussion. Here again, you would use the "on the one hand/on the other hand" approach to this question.

Extending the Law Fact Patterns. Some professors enjoy testing your ability to analyze how far a law can be legitimately extended. For example, suppose you are given the following fact pattern on a criminal law exam:

> Joe is asleep in his Cadillac hearse while on vacation in Arizona. Moe peers through the windshield of the hearse and seeing no one in the car, breaks the windshield. He peers in and sees the six-pack of cola Joe has left on the front seat. However, the glass shards prevent Moe from reaching in and taking the six-pack. Instead, Moe grabs a passing armadillo, and holding the 'dillo by the tail, inserts it through the broken windshield. The 'dillo in

turn latches onto the six-pack. Moe withdraws the 'dillo,
pries the six-pack from it, and runs away.

At first glance, the facts appear so ambiguous that it is difficult to determine exactly what crime has been committed. You run through your Capstone Outline and checklist and find nothing in these facts that resembles any of the crimes you studied, other than perhaps some form of larceny. However, as you analyze these facts a little more deeply, it becomes apparent that the professor is looking for an analysis of burglary. The elements of burglary are: (1) the breaking and (2) entering of (3) the dwelling of another, (4) at night, (5) with the intent to commit larceny.

Here, the legal ambiguity stems from whether a Cadillac hearse would be considered a dwelling. On the one hand, Joe is sleeping in it, which appears to qualify it as a dwelling. One the other hand, we don't know if this was a quick nap or whether he slept in the hearse on a regular basis. There is ambiguity in the interpretation of what legally qualifies as a dwelling. In addition, we are not told whether the events in the fact pattern occurred at night. Regardless, many jurisdictions have done away with this element (resulting in a split of authority issue, as described in the previous section, which should also be argued both ways).

There is also the factual issue raised by the armadillo. Moe never actually entered the hearse. Does using the 'dillo as an instrumentality to enter qualify as entering? This too should be argued both ways. Another issue raised by these facts is the issue of Moe's intent. Did he form the requisite intent to steal the six-pack before he broke the windshield? This issue should be discussed and argued as well.

Six Steps to Writing an Effective Exam Answer

The following is a suggested procedure to follow in writing a final exam. However, keep in mind that you are solving a legal problem or series of legal problems. As a result, you should not blindly adhere to any particular format.

Instead, try and imagine that you are a licensed attorney presented with the same facts presented on your exam. The following steps will help you to isolate facts, identify issues, and make arguments and counter-arguments.

Step One: Take a Deep Breath and Relax. Resist the urge to begin writing, no matter what your fellow examinees are doing.

Step Two: Read through the Entire Exam. If there are multiple fact patterns or questions, read through all of them. If you prefer, make a few notes, but take no more than five minutes or so on this initial reading. Your purpose is to get an overview of and feel for the task at hand, namely the analysis you will write, for the next three hours.

Step Three: Make a Plan of Attack. Decide in what order you will answer each part of the exam, and then allocate the amount of time you will spend on each part. If there is a question that is discernibly easier, start there. It will warm up your writing process, build your confidence, and help ensure that you don't run out of time.

Step Four: Underline the Issues in the Fact Pattern. As you read through the fact pattern of a question for the second time, identify the issues and sketch them out briefly. Are there missing facts? Visualize who the players in the factual setting are. Why are they in court? What are the relationships among the parties?

If it helps you, make notes in the margin of the fact pattern. Some law school exam coaching programs advise you to cross out the irrelevant facts. I disagree with this advice, at least until you are relatively certain of your answer. Avoid marking the text itself until you are absolutely sure that you will not need to read it again, or you may end up with an exam fact pattern that is difficult to read.

Step Five: Identify the Broad Area of Law. After you have identified the first broad area of law, jot it down in the margin near the operant facts. You may even be able to identify an issue or issues raised by these facts. If you can identify issues, make a brief notation in the margin near the relevant facts. For example, assuming that the exam is your contracts exam, do the facts involve the formation of an enforceable agreement or is this an issue concerning damages for breach of a contract?

If the exam is open book, this is a good time to refer to your Capstone Outline or Issues Checklist, which may jog your memory as to possible issues.

Continuing to sift through the facts, identify the next broad area of law that the facts raise until you can no longer identify issues. Using the prior example, do the facts indicate that a breach has occurred, assuming an enforceable agreement was formed to begin with?

There is a very fine line between creatively identifying issues and creating or assuming facts that erroneously create issues. Don't add or assume facts. Instead, identify ambiguity in the facts given. Keep in mind that unless your professor intended that a particular issue be discussed, you will receive no credit for the issue, regardless of how creative or brilliant the analysis is.

Step Six: First Outline, Then Write Your Answer. At this point, you should have a list of issues to be discussed in your answer. Briefly sketch out your answer in outline format, based upon the issues presented.

I have known students who simply ran out of time during exams and turned in outlines of their answers and received decent grades. Certainly, that is not the purpose of this step; instead, the purpose is to organize your answer. However, if something catastrophic happens and you run out of time, this step will at least ensure that you have something workable to turn in. For example:

1. Did Moe commit burglary?
   a. Was Joe's hearse a dwelling?
      i. Majority/minority rule
      ii. Factual ambiguity—does Joe sleep in his hearse most of the time?
   b. Was there a breaking and entering?
      i. Did using a 'dillo to steal the cola constitute an entering?
   c. Did it occur at night?
      i. Majority/minority rule
   d. Did Moe have the requisite intent?
      i. If yes, was the intent formed before or after the breaking?

Include a heading in each discussion section of your answer. The headings should correspond to each heading in your brief outline. You may also want to include subheadings. Also, use your conclusion paragraph as an opportunity to enhance your exam answer and separate it from the pack. Write an interesting and cohesive conclusion.

What About IRAC, You Say? In theory, the student uses IRAC to remind herself to identify the issues, state the applicable black letter rule, apply the rule to the facts given, and conclude the likely outcome of the issue. You need to remember that IRAC has been around almost as long as the Socratic method. Most everyone in the exam room has heard of it and will probably be using it. If you solely rely on IRAC, then your exam will be indistinguishable from the competition.

Use it as an analytical tool only; craft your exam response in a lawyerly, insightful, and interesting way.

CHECKLIST FOR WRITING WINNING EXAMS

Here is a list of the suggestions I have provided in this chapter that will help you increase your chances of a good grade on your final exams:

- Know the black letter law cold. You simply won't have time to look things up and write an effective exam at the same time. Further, unless you have both a macro and micro perspective on the exam subject, you will not be able to effectively issue-spot, formulate an answer outline, and craft a cogent, winning essay in response to the fact setting. Know the common law, applicable codes, and majority/minority rules.
- Review old exams as early in the semester as possible, even before school starts! Your professor's old exams are best. Some professors frequently repeat questions. I knew a student who told me that he had scrutinized his constitutional law professor's old exams on file in the library. On his final exam, three out of the five questions were repeated from the year prior. (Disclaimer: simply reading your professor's old exams and answers will not adequately prepare you for final exams.) Remember that the key here is to become familiar with the format of law school exams so any exams will be immensely helpful.

If you are unable to obtain old exams from your school, then look online.

- Practice spotting issues as early in the semester as possible. Practice making arguments. This doesn't mean being persuasive. It means seeing and analyzing both sides of a legal issue. Conclusory analysis will cost you points.
- Don't forget your mantra! Always be ready to articulate and argue both sides to any argument ("on the one hand/on the other hand"). Good lawyers anticipate tactical moves by their opponents and plan for them. Simply put, a good lawyer can always see the other side of the story.
- Figure out a way to make your answer stand out from the herd. This could be as simple as using captions or headings. Don't forget to customize your exam answer based on the subject, or tell the professor what he or she wants to hear. Reiterating what he or she conveyed as important throughout the semester will likely win you some points. Good lawyers are creative, and good law students are creative as well. Whatever you do, keep it lawyerly; don't get cute.
- Outline your answer first, and then write it out clearly! There is no quicker way to anger an exam grader than to offer an illegible, disorganized, rambling exam answer.

Chapter 6

Summer Clerkships

CLERKSHIPS, DESPITE THE mundane-sounding nomenclature, are a very important step in the career of any lawyer. The term refers to law firm clerkships, in which the student lawyer engages in an apprenticeship of sorts. Most of the larger firms use the clerkship process as their sole assessment of candidates before making permanent job offers. In addition, many government employers hire through their clerkship programs. There are also judicial clerkships, which are extremely prestigious jobs for law school graduates. Law firm clerkships are generally the focus of your first and second summers while in law school, and they are a source of employment for new graduates.

THE LAW FIRM CLERKSHIP

Like most prospective law students, I had a somewhat glamorized view of law practice. I was an older-than-average student who had lost a lot of my naiveté through my years in the business world. Regardless, I still imagined that I would likely enter some sort of public interest practice and perhaps change the world. Many students like I was start law school with no real perspective on legal employment. However, eventually they decide to begin their legal careers in law firms, and then eventually move into an area of the law that they love.

Law firm jobs are desirable for a variety of reasons: law firms generally pay well and many new lawyers have substantial student debt, new lawyers have the opportunity to work with experienced lawyers in firms and receive excellent training, working in a prestigious law firm is a credential they carry for their entire careers, law firms can offer a variety of interesting work, and law firms provide a relatively collegial environment for the new lawyer. Additionally, it is relatively easy to move *from* a law firm into another area of the law. It becomes more difficult, however, to move *to* a law firm after having started your legal career in another area, for example public interest work. In other words, you will likely have more longer-term career options if you begin your practice in a law firm.

And because law firm clerkships are so desirable, the competition for them is fierce. Therefore, it is important to understand the process from the beginning of your legal studies, in order to maximize your chances of obtaining a law firm clerkship, assuming that a law firm is your career path of choice.

Depending upon the size of the firm, there may be a number of other law clerks working with you for the summer. You will likely be assigned a supervisor and/or a mentor who will provide you with your assignments, answer questions, and generally deal with issues that may arise during your clerkship.

Clerkships can be personally, professionally, and financially rewarding. Many firms compensate you at an equivalent rate to that which first-year lawyers in the firm are earning. In addition, you will likely have the opportunity to work on projects that have been especially selected for you because they are interesting and challenging work. Finally, clerkships have a courtship aspect to them, and you will likely be heavily entertained and treated to a variety of activities and events, in an effort to impress you (and as discussed later, evaluate you).

THE ON-CAMPUS CLERKSHIP INTERVIEW PROCESS

Sometime toward the end of your first year, your school's career services organization will likely contact you regarding its placement program. Many schools use a bidding type program, in which you are allowed to prioritize the firms with which you would like to interview. Firms rely heavily on this process to interview and select candidates for summer clerkship positions.

Most large law firms have a partner in charge of the hiring process. Additionally, these firms employ professional human resources personnel to develop and administer their recruiting programs. To these firms, recruiting top students from the top schools is an extremely competitive process, and they take it very seriously. If you are fortunate enough to be one of those sought after, you will most likely be heavily recruited by several of these firms.

If you are selected for an on-campus interview with the firm, you will probably be 1 of about 12 to 15 people interviewed for a clerkship position at your school. Most firms spend a day on campus interviewing, and the interviews typically last only 30 minutes. Depending upon firm size, you may be interviewed by more than one lawyer.

If you are successful in your first interview, you will likely be invited to the firm's home office for at least one more interview. Typically, this interview involves meeting with several lawyers within the firm and perhaps a social event, such as lunch or dinner. If you are recruited by an out-of-town firm, it will pay for the expenses associated with the trip and may even book your travel plans. After this interview, if the firm elects to extend a clerkship offer, you will usually receive a telephone offer, followed by written confirmation. This will be a very exciting time for you.

The Right Turns for Success in the Clerkship Interview

Interviewing with a law firm is not dramatically different than other job interviews you may have had, and many of the same rules apply. Studies have shown that the interviewer generally makes a determination regarding the candidate within the first four minutes of the interview. The balance of the interview is confirmation of the interviewer's initial determination. If you make a good first impression, you create a presumption that you are a desirable candidate. On the other hand, if you make a bad first impression, the presumption that you are undesirable will be difficult to overcome. As a result, how you greet the interviewer, what you wear, your grooming, your handshake, and eye contact are all very important during that first four minutes.

For more information about the particular nuances, intricacies, and niceties of clerkship interviews and other legal job interviews, pick up a copy of the aptly named book *The Legal Job Interview* by Clifford R. Ennico. It's a fantastic resource for law school students, newly minted JDs, and legal job career changers that covers all the topics you need to know before your interview. The book includes an inside look into what the lawyer/interviewers are looking for, what to do before scheduling and arriving at the interview, what to do (and not to do) to get that offer, strategies for dealing with common legal job interview questions, and ideas for using your interviewing skills after you've landed the job you want.

Here are some tips for success during your clerkship interviews.

Research the Firm. Firm websites are an obvious source of good information about the firm, as is the Martindale-Hubbell attorney and law firm directory, available for no charge at *www.martindale.com*. Look at major transactions or cases the firm has been involved in. Try and get a sense of what is important to the firm. Is the culture more conservative and traditional, or are they trying to convey an image of progressiveness and innovation? Every firm has a culture. You need to try and understand it.

If there are alumni from your school working at the firm, do not hesitate to make contact. However, you should keep in mind that anything you say will likely make its way back to the hiring decision-makers within the firm.

Research the Interviewer. Many students conduct research on the actual people that will interview them. This is a good idea. If nothing else, any discernable commonalities between you and the interviewer can help you, such as undergraduate alma mater and hometown.

Prepare Questions and Answers in Advance. Have answers prepared for the most common interview questions. You should also prepare your own questions to ask during the interview based on your research on the firm and the interviewer.

Probably the most commonly asked question during the interview process is about the connection that you have to the location of the firm. This inquiry is based upon two concerns. First, the firm wants you to have strong ties to the area because it is less likely that you will leave after you join. Second (and I believe this is the more important of the two to the firm), the firm views you as a long-term client development source. If you have a lot of family or other connections to the area, the firm can someday leverage these connections to develop new business for the firm. This is true whether or not you remain with the firm.

If the firm is located in your hometown, then your answer to this question is fairly straightforward. However, if the applicable city is not your hometown, your answer becomes a little more complicated. You need to be able to come up with something stronger than, "I always wanted to live in this town" or "I really like this city." Instead, your answer should focus on the connections you have to the city or your objective reasons for wanting to relocate there. Perhaps you have relatives or a significant other who live there. Or perhaps you view this particular geographic area as critical to your practice development. For example, if you have a strong desire to be an energy lawyer, a firm located in Houston would be a very good fit for you. If you are from Houston *and* want to be an energy lawyer, even better.

Dress for Success. Dress conservatively and groom carefully. If you have any questions regarding appropriate dress, consult your placement office or read any of the volumes of popular literature written on the subject. At the risk of stating the obvious, consider your personal hygiene and grooming. Facial hair, colognes, and perfumes are to be avoided. Take along breath mints for last-minute breath checks.

CHOOSING A CLERKSHIP

During the interview process, you may be offered multiple clerkships by different law firms. Be careful as you tread these waters. Some firms are very jealous of each other and insist that you clerk solely with them. Competition for top law school candidates in recent years has caused this attitude to largely dissipate; however, there are still old-school holdouts who may view your clerkship with a competitor as disloyal.

My suggestion is to broach the subject with the legal hiring coordinator after you have received a clerkship offer. Even if a firm does not require you to clerk your entire summer with them, some firms feel strongly that you should clerk with them during the first portion of your summer. The rationale is that if you choose them for the first portion, you are more likely to join them for permanent employment. Simply ask the firm representative for the firm's policy and/or preferences in this regard. But the important thing is to obtain the job offer; you can deal with the inter-firm logistical issues later.

TIPS FOR A SUCCESSFUL CLERKSHIP

The term *clerk* is something of a misnomer, suggesting that the law student will be performing menial, unimportant work. The reality is that the work is often important and may actually even be billed to the client. As a summer clerk at a law firm, you will be drafting legal memoranda that attorneys in the firm will rely upon as accurate and complete. You may even help to prepare legal briefs for use in court or corporate documents that will actually be filed with the proper authorities.

Make No Mistake, Clerks Conduct Real Legal Work for Real Clients

During a summer clerkship, I prepared a legal memorandum for a partner in the firm regarding the liability of partners for partnership debts. This was a big step for me. Up to that point, the only memoranda and briefs I had prepared had been in law school. They involved fictitious people in fictitious situations.

Consequently, I had approached the memorandum somewhat abstractly. I reviewed the facts as provided to me by the firm. I researched the relevant law. I prepared a memorandum, which I submitted to my supervising attorney, who in turn submitted it to the partner in charge of the matter.

Two days later, my phone rang. It was the partner, whom I will call Bill Towne.

Bill said, "Steve, I have reviewed your memorandum and it looks good."

"Thank you," I replied.

Bill then asked me, "What are you doing this afternoon?"

"My calendar looks open," I replied, omitting the fact that as a summer clerk, my calendar was almost always open.

"Great," Bill replied. "Let's go see Judge Jones at one o'clock."

Judge Jones was a state district court judge in Dallas County, Texas. Bill had invited me to a preliminary hearing in which the issue I had researched (and upon which he was now relying for legal authority) would be discussed.

I was in a state of shock. The research and conclusions I had developed and provided to Bill were to be a significant component in his armory, in battle against the plaintiff in the matter. I worried all afternoon. What if my legal conclusions were wrong? What if I had somehow overlooked an important case in my research? I'm sure that Bill had checked my work; if not, then a senior associate most certainly had. And as it turned out, we won the issue. That experience taught me a hugely valuable lesson—there is no grace period or learning curve in the legal education process. If you draft a memorandum for a law firm, it isn't necessarily an exercise. The work, even at the clerkship level, is important. The battle is real.

Don't Get Caught Up in the Clerkship Courtship

Large law firms spend substantial amounts of money entertaining their law clerks. I clerked for two large Texas firms and during the ten weeks that I was with these firms, there were only three evenings in total where I was not invited to a social event. The entire time is spent at dinners, sporting events, happy hours, and parties. The social events can be great fun and will provide you with an opportunity to experience new things and meet new people. More importantly, they provide insight to the firm as to who you are and whether you are a personality fit with the firm.

If you have been offered a summer clerkship, the odds are overwhelming that you will be offered a permanent job with the firm. Most firms extend offers to the vast majority of their clerks. Essentially, the offer is yours to lose. Some clerks make the mistake of assuming that a job offer is automatic. They misread the abundance of entertainment during the clerkship as a sign that the clerkship is not to be taken seriously and that the hiring decision has already been made. This is a big mistake.

I studied for the Texas bar exam with a student whom I will call Henry. Henry was articulate and bright beyond his years and very comfortable with people. He also talked too much. He was very open and unguarded and rarely appeared to self-censor much of anything he said; his honesty was his greatest asset but also his greatest liability.

In any environment other than the competitive realm of the law firm clerkship courtship, Henry would have been extremely refreshing in his candor. However, in the law firm clerkship environment, Henry's candor cost him dearly. Henry had indicated to several of the partners within the firm that he was excited about his second clerkship that summer. This infuriated that firm's attorneys, who wanted to believe that they were his preferred firm. As shallow and petty as it might seem, Henry did not receive an offer from the firm.

In an interview situation, things that the candidate does and says are often amplified by the interviewer beyond reason. A simple, innocent statement, a facial tic, or simply an impression may leave the interviewer cold about the job candidate. In the clerkship setting, this phenomenon is exacerbated; the clerkship process is essentially a 24-hour a day interview. You are constantly being observed. Most firms have hiring committees that meet regularly during the clerkship sessions and discuss the performance—project-wise, socially, and in other ways—of the clerk. So make no mistake about it—you are being scrutinized and reviewed on a weekly basis.

Law school lore abounds with stories of the clerk who flirts with the managing partner's wife at a firm cocktail party or the clerk who loses consciousness due to too much alcohol at a firm event. I heard about an East Coast firm event in which the bartender served margaritas specially designed by and named after various partners. There were something like 12 different margaritas for sampling. One clerk, apparently anxious to avoid offending any of these partners, consumed every one of their namesakes. He became violently ill in the parking lot of the establishment. Needless to say, he did not receive a job offer. Although the firm certainly provided the means to complete and utter intoxication for its clerks, it clearly did not intend such a result nor appreciate such intoxication. The point is this: do not mistake the firm frivolity as a license to reprise Bluto in *Animal House.* You aren't in college anymore. A firm event isn't a kegger. Instead, the entertainment aspect of clerkships acts as a subtle test on the maturity and character of the clerk. If given the opportunity, and even if firm lawyers are partying hard, will a particular clerk go insane, or will they act responsibly? Be sociable, but always keep your wits (and sobriety) about you.

The quality of the work you perform during your clerkship is also obviously important. While some assignments are primarily for the purpose of evaluating the quality of your work, you will be responsible for doing serious real-world tasks. If you do sloppy work, misstate the law, or fail to perform assigned tasks, you won't get a permanent offer. But never forget that as long as you work hard and carry yourself in a professional manner, the odds are very strongly in your favor. The fact that you are clerking for the firm is a good indication that they believe you have the skills and personality they want.

RESOURCES OTHER THAN YOUR SCHOOL'S PLACEMENT OFFICE FOR CLERKSHIP JOBS

It is more difficult to find summer employment for most students after their first year than after their second year. The reason for this is that many firms do not hire summer clerks that first year. The belief is that clerkship programs for 1Ls are not worth the expense because there is too much time left until graduation and the actual employment decision is made. As a result, competition for those first-year summer jobs is fierce.

Regardless, there are numerous ways to find summer employment in addition to through your school's placement office. Assuming that you want to clerk that first summer, I would encourage you to take active control over your search. I found my first-year summer clerkship on my own and without the assistance of my school's career services department. Following the clerkship, I received an offer to return the next year. First and foremost in your research should be the Internet. The Martindale-Hubbell online directory of attorneys and law firms can be sorted geographically and by practice area and firm size, and it is a good source of leads. This directory is invaluable because it provides a synopsis of the firm's practice areas, the size of the firm, and email links to individual attorneys. There are also numerous other Internet job boards which may be useful.

Another good source may be through your state bar association. Many state bars now also maintain their own websites with attorney information and search capabilities. In addition, there are several good websites that focus on law student and lawyer placement. Still another source may be your own contacts or those of your family and friends. My experience has been that most attorneys are willing to help law students in their employment searches. The legal profession is essentially still a family and lawyers take care of their own. I would not hesitate to make contact with lawyers who may be able to either employ you or help you find employment.

Chapter 7

Your Second and Third Years

AS YOU COMMENCE YOUR second and third years, much of your near-term future has been settled, and you may even have a clerkship under your belt. You will no longer be part of a section. Your class size will be much smaller, and you will have the opportunity to actually get to know your professors. Adjunct faculty, who are typically practicing lawyers working in the areas that they teach, may teach some of your classes; they will likely view you as a colleague more than a student. I actually enjoyed my second and third years of law school because I found that there were abundant classes and activities which provided me with ample opportunity to delve into practice areas that interested me.

Some students focus much of their energy on a publication, such as in the law review or a journal, moot court (also called mock trial), or other scholarly activities. I found that my second and third years enabled me to study subjects in which I had a genuine interest, perhaps even a passion. In my second and third years, I could see the specific benefit of the knowledge that I gained. I focused much of my time on business transaction and securities-related law courses, such as securities law (studying both the Securities Act of 1933 and the Securities Exchange Act of 1934), because I thought they would be of the most use to me in practice.

SELECTING YOUR COURSES

All law schools have required courses for the first year and at least a few required courses for the second year. Depending upon your school's curriculum, you may have much flexibility in picking your second- and third-year courses.

Many law schools have fairly stringent curricula, with only a few courses left to the selection of the student. This is one way that they are able to maintain high bar passage rates. Requiring a student to take secured transactions and commercial paper courses virtually guarantees a better bar exam performance.

Assuming that you will attend a law school that allows you flexibility in selecting courses, how you select your courses involves balancing several variables. First of all, you should assess how important the grade you will receive is to you, in comparison with what you would like to actually learn from the course. Second, as previously discussed, you should assess whether a particular course will help you prepare for the bar. Third, you should consider how important the course would be to your future practice. Fourth, you should consider the particular professor who teaches the course.

CHOOSING PROFESSORS

It is axiomatic among law students that "you don't take the course, you take the professor." I'm not exactly sure if this is a reference to the desirability of the professor's grading policy, or if it means that the messenger is more important than the message. Regardless, a lousy professor will make for a very long and arduous semester. Worse, bad professors are more prone to write unfair exams. These exams are characterized by questions that have nothing to do with material covered in class. Or they present questions that exhaustively cover legal areas on which you did not spend much class time.

The reality is that in law school, you largely teach yourself the subject matter. A professor's job is to provide you with the canvas upon which you will create your own intellectual masterpiece. If you decide that the particular course is important to your development as a lawyer, you may decide to take your chances with a marginal professor. But due diligence helps you make an informed decision.

I recommend an investigative consumer approach when it comes to drawing a bead on your prospective professors. Check out the professor's curriculum vitae on the school's website. Where did he go to law school? Which judges, if any, did he clerk for? What do the professor's published works say about her perspective? Does the professor have nonacademic experience? Is the subject the professor's true passion, or is he merely fulfilling his teaching obligation to the school?

Talk with second- and third-year students. However, be careful in relying too much on the opinion of previous students. Obviously, how well the student did in the class will affect his or her perspective.

Look at the professor's old exams. This will give you an idea of the subjects she may cover in class, and it will also give you a perspective as to how she approaches exams. The professor's grading history should be available through school resources, either in the library or your registrar's office. Try to sit in on a class to get a sense of how the professor interacts with students. If you decide to do this, you may want to seek the permission of the professor. Talk to other professors. If you feel particularly courageous, talk to the professor in question. He or she will admire your chutzpah.

Finally, if you find yourself in a class with a surprisingly bad professor, do not be afraid to drop the class. Most law schools are small enough to accommodate fairly liberal add/drop policies. Generally, you will have ample time to settle upon a class schedule with professors to your liking.

ESSENTIAL SECOND- AND THIRD-YEAR CLASSES

Although it may seem a bit premature at this point to begin thinking about classes beyond your first year, many law schools do not offer every course each semester. As a result, it is important to have some idea of the courses that you plan to take. This will help you to effectively plan your schedule.

This list of courses is not intended to be comprehensive, but instead a sampling of the kinds of courses which may be available to you your second and third years of law school. I would encourage you to talk with your registrar or check the website regarding the course offerings of your particular school.

This is also one of the few areas where students who have gone before you can offer you insight. They can tell you about the value of the courses. I would also suggest you talk with practicing lawyers, especially those practicing in your area of interest, regarding courses they took while in law school that they felt were useful in practice.

Finally, remember that you are investing a great deal of money in your legal education. One of the objectives of any legal curriculum should be to expose the student to various practice areas with which they may not be familiar. Don't be afraid to take courses simply for the purpose of finding out more about the area. It may actually have an impact on your choice of career direction.

Evidence

Most people are familiar with the subject matter of evidence through the common refrains of TV lawyers in the heat of a courtroom battle: "Objection! Counsel is leading the witness!" "Objection! Argumentative!"[4] Evidence deals with the various issues arising from the introduction of evidence into a judicial proceeding. Concepts such as the hearsay rule, the best evidence rule, and other important legal principles of evidence are covered. This course is usually taken during a student's second year in law school. It is also a multistate bar subject, and that alone is a good reason to take it. Evidence tends to be more akin to your first-year courses. Professors tend to still use the Socratic method in an effort to drill the concepts into the student.

If you plan a career in litigation, this course is obviously an important part of your curriculum. Most schools require an evidence course as a prerequisite to mock trial. And even if you don't plan to litigate, it will give you useful insight into the rules of evidence. My own view was that

---

[4] After you have taken your evidence course, you will view these objections from an entirely different perspective. I personally enjoy the creativity with which some television writers and screenwriters create new and entirely invalid bases for objections to a witness's testimony. Although legally flawed, these make for great courtroom drama.

to go through the entire law school experience without some meaningful exposure to litigation would be cheating myself of the opportunity to learn firsthand an area of the law practiced by a majority of attorneys. And as an in-house lawyer, I find that I frequently use much of what I learned in litigation-related courses, such as evidence, civil procedure, and the like.

Business Organizations and Entities

This course deals with the various forms that businesses may take, including corporations, partnerships, and limited liability companies. (It may also be referred to simply as corporations or business organizations.) Issues such as agency law and officer and director fiduciary obligations are usually covered. There are various issues raised by the form an entity takes, including tax issues, management of the enterprise versus ownership, and liability risk.

The purpose of this course is to teach you the fundamental advantages and disadvantages of the various entity forms, such as sole proprietorships, partnerships, corporations, and limited liability companies, as well other common issues faced by those entities. Additionally, this course may deal with fundamental business law concepts such as the fiduciary duty of directors, director liability, and the business judgment rule. Generally, this course is a prerequisite to securities law and other corporate law courses.

If you plan a career in transactions, this course is essential. If you plan to work as in-house counsel at some point in the future, you should definitely take this course. If you plan to ultimately practice on your own, it is important to learn these fundamental business entity concepts. And even if you plan to litigate, this course can help you understand the technicalities regarding how a corporation is formed, which will in turn help you ensure that proper parties are involved in a particular lawsuit. In short, I would suggest that you seriously consider taking a business entities course.

Securities Law

Securities law is often broken down into two courses but may be offered as one course. Essentially, securities law deals with the issues surrounding the purchase and sale of securities (usually stocks), such as investor disclosures required, illegal activities like insider trading, and the various capital-raising vehicles.

This course may also be referred to as the Securities Act of 1933 and the Securities Exchange Act of 1934. The Securities Act of 1933 was the congressional response to several catastrophic stock market crashes at the turn of the 20th century, which resulted in serious economic depression for the United States. The Securities Exchange Act of 1934 established the Securities Exchange Commission. If you are planning on becoming a corporate attorney, this course is an absolute must.

There are a number of issues raised by securities law, including what constitutes a security, the rules regarding selling securities, and informational requirements in securities offerings. In addition, the crucial topics of insider trading, tipper/tippee liability, and gun jumping are explored. Ever since the collapse of Enron and the passage of the Sarbanes-Oxley Act of 2002, there has been a resurgence of interest in the area of securities law, and it will likely only grow following the cataclysmic fallout that Wall Street is experiencing.

I found this course extremely interesting, both because I had a great deal of respect for the professor and because of my prior IPO career experience. IPO is an abbreviation for initial public offering, which refers to the first time a stock or other security is offered to the public for purchase. IPOs are always of interest to business people because, if successful, they can be an excellent way of raising capital and an opportunity for the investor to reap a substantial return on his or her investment. In addition, the number of IPOs can also be an indicator as to the general health of the economy. In short, IPOs are generally thought of as the glamour children of Wall Street. I particularly enjoyed learning about the requirements of public offering against the backdrop of my knowledge of the inner workings of the IPO in which I had participated. This course taught me the whys of the rules as they relate to these types of offerings.

Federal Tax

Federal tax is the introductory course on the tax laws and the Internal Revenue Code, Revenue Rulings, and important case law and legal principles of taxation.

Many law students view this course as one of the most difficult and therefore avoid it; however, I suggest you take it. It represents an opportunity to delve into one of the most complicated and lengthy codes within our system of government. Taxation issues affect almost every aspect of transactional work. Additionally, tax issues frequently arise in litigation. Exposure to this subject will probably serve you well in any future area of practice. It is also a prerequisite to the other business tax courses, such as corporate and partnership tax. I found that this course unraveled a great deal of the mystery surrounding the Internal Revenue Service and the rules it promulgates. And who knows? You might actually enjoy the subject, thus setting the stage for an extremely lucrative career in tax law.

Partnership and Corporate Tax

Usually, partnership and corporate tax are divided into two courses. Corporations are, in essence, taxed two times. The first time is when the corporation makes a profit. The second time is when the corporation pays a dividend to its shareholders. The dividend is considered taxable income to the shareholder. Partnerships, on the other hand, are taxed only once. However, the corporate form also insulates its owners (shareholders) from much liability. Partners, on the other hand, are liable for the actions of the partnership. As a result, a business must consider numerous issues when choosing its entity form. These courses are a must for anyone considering corporate practice.

Employment Law

Employment law deals with a variety of topics faced by many corporations and business entities. Major topics include employment discrimination, collective bargaining, employment agreements, and other issues.

This area of the law is a fairly popular career path; you should at least consider exploring it. Additionally, many lawyers who practice employment law eventually end up in corporations in a variety of lucrative careers, including as human resources professionals.

I practiced employment law for several years and found it to be a very interesting area of the law. Federal law is the linchpin of this practice area, and you will work with the Fair Labor Standards Act, Title VII of the Civil Rights Act of 1964, the Americans with Disabilities Act, the Age Discrimination in Employment Act, and other federal and state laws designed to protect employees' rights. Keep in mind that there are lawyers practicing on both sides of these laws—the employer/defendant side and the employee/plaintiff side.

Wills, Trusts, and Estates

The wills, trusts, and estates course deals with the creation of an enforceable will, estate planning, and trusts. It also covers key will provisions, as well as challenges to a will's validity. For the sole reason that this is the subject that every family member and friend will ask you about, I suggest that you take it. Additionally, this is a bar exam subject with specialized concepts and terms, and you can reduce your bar exam stress by having familiarity with the subject.

Antitrust Regulation

Antitrust regulation deals with federal and state regulation of competition. Core legal issues including price fixing, restraint of trade (both horizontal and vertical), and other anticompetitive activities by businesses are discussed.

Because certain anticompetitive activities carry criminal penalties, it is critical for anyone who plans to provide legal advice to businesses to take this course. It is also a must for anyone planning on practicing corporate law. Recent developments in antitrust law make this a very interesting course because the law is definitely changing in this area. I have found this information to be extremely useful in my current in-house practice area of commercial law. I frequently advise salespeople and other business managers regarding the dos and don'ts of antitrust law.

Copyright and Intellectual Property Law

This subject may be divided into two courses and deals with legal issues arising from intellectual property, the United States Patent and Trademark Office (USPTO), and the United States Copyright Office. In addition, it may also deal with other federal and state regulation of intellectual property, including the law of trademarks. Some schools offer a comprehensive intellectual property course in conjunction with copyright law. Trademarks and copyrights have a variety of applications, including entertainment law as well as intellectual property licensing and are overseen by the USPTO.

This is a fairly specialized area of law; however, by all means consider taking it if you have any interest in practicing intellectual property law. As an aside, admission to practice before the USPTO requires a separate requirement, distinct from your license to practice law.

I have also practiced in this legal area and found it to be extremely interesting. Intellectual property is often among the most valuable assets of businesses. To many companies, their trademarked brands are the single most important means of communication with their customers. As a result, these companies zealously manage and protect their intellectual property.

Family Law

Family law is a popular course that deals with legal issues associated with marriage, paternity, divorces, child custody, community property, and other issues. This subject is usually a state-specific bar exam subject; however, the course may often be too general to be of much use for bar exam preparation purposes. Regardless, many students find it interesting and useful.

Negotiation

Many law schools now offer negotiation, usually in an abbreviated seminar format, lasting a few weeks for an academic credit of one hour. If you have little prelaw exposure to negotiation, this course is useful. Negotiating is as fundamental to the practice of law as is anything else you will study while in law school. I found it to be an extremely worthwhile course, even though I had been negotiating for many years in various business activities prior to school.

Effective negotiating skills are an important weapon in any lawyer's arsenal, regardless of where they practice in the legal spectrum, from corporate law to criminal law. If your law school does not offer a course on negotiations, you should consider taking a commercially available course. It will serve you well throughout your professional career.

Professional Responsibility

Professional responsibility (may also be called Ethics) is typically a required course in law school and covers the various governing rules and regulations concerning lawyer ethics. In addition, the subject matter is the same as that covered on the Multistate Professional Responsibility Exam, a requirement for law practice. I heard a professor explain once that your law license is your most precious possession and that you should take all steps necessary to protect it. This course will provide you with a basic ethical framework, an analytical process from which you can make the critical ethical decisions you will be faced with throughout your career.

SUMMER STUDY PROGRAMS

Many law schools also offer summer study programs. You might want to consider one of these programs your first summer, when clerkship opportunities are scarce and you have the time to participate.

These for-credit programs, usually offered in cooperation with an international law school, combine international legal study with international travel. They are a wonderful opportunity to travel with fellow law students and professors while earning law school credit.

LAW SCHOOL PUBLICATIONS

In addition to law review, most law schools typically have at least one or two publications called journals, which, although lesser in prestige than law review, may also be important credentials to future lawyers. These journals are designated according to their primary subject, such as transnational law, law and economics, and other equally esoteric subjects. Journals also provide the opportunity for you to serve as an editor your third year, and this requires a note from all members. Depending upon your school, there will also be several other publications for which you may be eligible. However, these publications deserve some due diligence before you make the leap. Any publication will essentially require two to four classes worth of work, and yet only compensate you for one class. As a result, the choice to participate should not be automatic.

On the positive side, a publication may enhance your writing skills, which are critical to your overall skill set as a lawyer. You will also learn to deal with the drudgery of cite-checking and other menial editorial work required for all publications. This too may enhance your skill set as a lawyer, especially in your early years of practice. However, participating in a publication could also mean foregoing a class that you wanted to take, or it could even cause your grades to suffer. Grades are everything to recruiting law firms, and publication or not, a 2.9 GPA will seriously hurt your chances of employment after graduation. Therefore, the question of whether to participate in a law school publication should be carefully considered.

If you are wondering whether you should participate in law review, the short answer is yes. Law review is a credential that will virtually guarantee interviews with top firms. Although one of the most impressive credentials, law review certainly requires a substantial amount of work, especially during your second year of law school. You will spend inordinate amounts of time cite-checking. Basically, as a new law review member, you will be assigned someone else's work to review for citation errors. Citations are the shorthand identification of the case and the various reporters (the reference books with judicial decisions) where they can be found.

The Bluebook: A Uniform System of Citation, discussed earlier in this book, is the authoritative source for the proper citation of cases. Proper citation is precise and nit-picky, which is why new law review members are assigned to do it. Although it won't add much to your substantive skills, cite-checking will greatly increase you ability to read carefully and you will become much more nit-picky, both skills that are important to lawyers.

In addition, during your third year, you will have the opportunity to serve as an editor. Having served as an editor on law review is an impressive credential. All law review members are also required to write a note, a scholarly article about a particular subject.

MOOT COURT

Moot court (sometimes referred to as mock trial) is a competition that usually occurs during the first semester of your second year. You and a partner will brief and argue an appellate case, usually before an ersatz U.S. Supreme Court. The Court is usually composed of professors and local lawyers and some moot court board members. You must survive several elimination rounds in order to be selected for moot court. Some schools, especially those that view their mission as the preparation of law students as litigators, take moot court very seriously and engage in a variety of inter–law school competitions.

Although not as impressive a credential as law review, spots on moot court are very much sought after. It's one of those credentials that many lawyers refer to in their biographies long after they have graduated from law school. Further, the amount of work required for moot court is substantially less than that required for law review. If you are planning a career as a trial lawyer, you should seriously consider participating in moot court.

During the moot court competition, the competitors are divided into teams of two. Each team prepares a brief, and then engages in a series of rounds in which they argue their brief. In addition, the teams may also be required to argue the opposite side. The arguments occur before a panel of judges and simulate Supreme Court arguments. Teams progress through the series of rounds, and ultimately the last people standing are selected for moot court.

A law school friend of mine, whom I will call Sam, participated in the moot court competition successfully and immensely enjoyed the experience. His partner, Carol, was a 26-year-old student from Nevada. Carol was very intelligent, but did not have a competitive bone in her body. She was wrestling with whether she even wanted to practice law. She had seen enough of the cliques, competitiveness, and ruthlessness of the law school environment to decide that she likely didn't want to spend the rest of her life with these kinds of people. Law school had been rough on Carol, who had entered like many students with an idea that she wanted to change the world. The moot court competition was her last-ditch effort to find her niche in law school.

Sam and Carol's appellate case dealt with the constitutional issues surrounding the separation of church and state. This issue was perfect for the moot court competition. It was controversial; there had been a long line of cases that gradually defined the law on the issue. And it dealt with esoteric case law on which the Supreme Court had articulated a variety of tests and appeared to be far from unified. In particular, the issue before the court was the extent to which local churches could administer after-school programs. The plaintiff in the case had sued the school board because she wanted it to offer non-religious after-school care. The school board, on the other hand, had implemented the program because it had no budgetary dollars to fund the program itself. The real question was to what extent a state actor, the school board, could affiliate itself with a religious organization.

Sam was an incredibly intelligent and articulate student and had spent several years working for a well-known senator as a staffer. And yet, as he approached the podium to make his argument before three law students in the initial round, he was terrified. The fear emanated from the fact that, generally speaking, there is no way to fake your way through the argument. You must understand the facts, you must understand the law (including arcane opinions), and you must be able to effectively connect the two.

Sam began his opening statement:

"May it please the Court," using the time-honored phrase as a term of respect. "My name is Sam Wills, and my co-counsel Carol Thompson and I represent the appellant in this matter, the county school board."

He looked up at the stone-faced panel of judges.

He looked over at Carol. She averted her eyes and appeared to be perspiring heavily.

After Sam made his argument, it was Carol's turn.

When she stood up, her armpits were drenched with sweat. She smiled a silly smile and promptly froze for what seemed to be ten minutes. Sam coughed loudly as a not-so-subtle prompt and Carol began her argument. But she never quite got past those impassive judicial countenances.

Carol made it to the semifinal rounds, which is certainly a worthwhile résumé credential, and Sam was elected to the moot court board. Most importantly, they would both be better lawyers for having gone through the process.

If you plan to litigate, you should definitely go for it. Additionally, the brief-writing exercise is extremely useful in developing your writing skills; unlike most of the somewhat contrived and basic writing exercises in legal writing, the brief you write here will be a real-world brief, using real case law and legal situations. And best of all, Carol and Sam remain friends to this day; they share the common bond of having survived the moot court crucible.

RESEARCH ASSISTANTSHIPS

Research assistantships for professors are abundant at most law schools. They are a great way to broaden your horizons a bit and gain exposure to the law from a different perspective. Most research assistants can receive either hourly compensation or class credit for the work they do. It may be an excellent opportunity to work closely with a professor on a new scholarly work.

Some cynics view research assistants as nothing more than slave labor for professors in a hurry to publish. However, my perspective is somewhat different. I found the experience to be very rewarding in terms of developing skills such as research and writing, and I thoroughly enjoyed working with the professor, an extremely talented securities lawyer.

During my second year, I served as research assistant for my corporate law professor, who had invited me to work with him on a project. Based upon my prior corporate experience, the professor thought I might have some insight into the themes involved in the project. The project was a scholarly work regarding the theories behind executive compensation, and in particular that of chief executive officers of U.S. companies as compared with CEOs in the rest of the world. I was flattered because this professor, in my opinion, was one of the very best in the school.

I found the experience extremely worthwhile and interesting. It afforded me the opportunity to work with one of the leading influencers in this particular area of the law. I learned a great deal about legal research and writing on this project, and the professor provided abundant feedback. My experience was that this type of activity is definitely more collegial than the typical law student/law professor interaction. In some ways, as the professor's assistant on a project, you are treated more like a peer and less like a student. Additionally, I got to know the professor on a personal level, and he remains a friend to this day. We stay in touch and have lunch periodically, and he has been a wonderful coach and mentor. The professor gave me surprising leeway regarding the direction of the research involved. In addition, he allowed me to take a stab at writing and editing sections of the article. My research assistantship was truly one of the bright spots of my legal education. I learned an immense amount about the practice of law, legal reasoning and analysis, legal research, and writing style.

The reason why I am discussing research assistantships in this chapter is because it will be difficult to take on a project like this during your first year. You will simply be too busy keeping up and learning an entirely new reading and analytical protocol. In fact, many schools discourage 1Ls from doing much more than the mandatory first-year classes.

However, after your first year, you will have some time to pursue different activities. If you are interested in a research assistantship, there are several ways to go about seeking one. Many professors advertise these positions. In addition, most professors welcome inquiries from students. As a result, I would suggest that you draw a bead on professors that you share academic interests with or believe that you could enjoy working for. Make an appointment to speak with the professor about whether he or she has any pending projects that require a research assistant.

I would avoid making these inquiries of your current professors. Requesting to serve as a research assistant for a professor who is also responsible for grading your final exam could be viewed as self-aggrandizement at best and a conflict of interest at worst. You are better off approaching a professor after you have completed the class, or professors with whom you are taking no courses.

LEGAL CLINIC

Law schools typically offer a free legal clinic, or legal services, to the community. Students are assigned cases under supervision of a faculty member who is a licensed practicing attorney for clients who cannot afford legal representation. In legal clinic, you learn basic lawyering skills, such as interviewing clients, negotiation, case preparation, and trial and appellate practice. It's an excellent orientation to the operation of the United States legal system. Plus, it will provide you with real-world experience into the practice of law, with the safety net of a supervising lawyer. Not only will you develop crucial lawyering skills, but you will also have an opportunity to help others in a way that will be difficult to duplicate in actual practice. Additionally, if you have any doubts about whether you will enjoy the practice of law, a legal clinic is an excellent way to test the waters.

Some clinics focus on specific issues, such as the protection of children and the indigent. Other clinics are more akin to a general practice. Many law schools offer more than one clinic. Typically, there are more students desiring a clinical position than there are slots. As a result, you may have to wait until your third year to participate.

Regardless, the experience you gain will most likely be worth the wait. If you have the time, I strongly encourage you to participate in your school's clinical program. Speak with your school registrar and the professor who supervises the legal clinic to find out more information regarding the program and any requirements you may need to fulfill prior to enrolling.

JOINT DEGREES

Many universities now offer joint degree programs. Typically, these schools offer a JD/MBA, but many also offer law degrees with other curricula. Generally, these programs require an additional year of studies, plus the usual three-year law curriculum and the corresponding pro rata increased tuition for the additional year.

In my opinion, one should make the decision to pursue a joint degree carefully. If you ultimately want to practice law, a joint degree may impede your ability to clerk and ultimately work in a law firm. Because most of the job-yielding clerkships happen the summer after the second year, a joint degree candidate may find herself at a disadvantage. Law firms may question your commitment to the law. A joint degree may, erroneously or otherwise, signal to the firm that you have longer-term career aspirations than to be a partner in that firm. In addition, your schedule will be one year out of sync with those of your classmates.

On the other hand, if you have researched your chosen career path and have decided that a joint degree is a requisite, it may make sense. If your goal is to work, for example, as an investment banker immediately upon graduation, a joint degree may make great sense. Be prepared, however, for a fairly different educational track from your more traditional law firm–bound classmates. Although generally your first-year schedule will be the same as that of your law school classmates, after the first year it will change dramatically. However, some joint-degree students choose this path because they know precisely what they want to do upon graduation. A joint degree is a logical path for these students.

There are numerous joint degree programs. I had a friend who pursued a joint degree in divinity and law. Another good reason to obtain a joint degree while in law school is that it will actually save money and time if your plan down the road is to pursue an additional degree.

However, my experience was that law school alone was an extremely challenging curriculum. I'm not sure I could have handled the additional requirements presented by a joint degree. That said, many students pursue joint degrees every year. My advice is to do your due diligence early in the process, in order to understand the cost and benefits of a joint degree well before you begin law school.

CONSIDERATIONS FOR
NONTRADITIONAL STUDENTS

The median student age for most law schools is 24 to 27 years old. The vast majority of law students are fairly recent undergraduates, with perhaps a few years of postgraduation work experience. I graduated from law school at the ripe old age of 47, after a 20-year career in industry. My last job in that world was as chief operating officer of a billion-dollar business. I had money, prestige, and power and gave it all up to pursue a longtime dream of law practice. I had been a mediocre undergraduate student; however, 20 years in the workplace had instilled a fair amount of discipline and dedication to the task at hand.

As a 44-year-old 1L, I was by far the oldest student in my class and at the school, for that matter. There were a few people in their 30s; however, 20-year-olds were the vast majority of the law school population. While many people earn their MBAs in their 30s, 40s, 50s, and beyond, very few enter law school at this point in their lives. The reason is simple. Whereas an MBA actually builds upon the student's business experience up to that point, a JD is actually a start-from-scratch proposition. In the practice of law, you simply must begin at the beginning. There are usually no career shortcuts. You must graduate, pass the bar, obtain your license, and commence practice, usually in a law firm. Once in the law firm, you will become a first-year associate. In your second year, you will be a second-year associate, and so on. In the practice of law, there are simply predetermined hurdles you must overcome each step of the way in order to realize your potential as a lawyer. In this way, the practice of law resembles an apprenticeship of yore. As you advance in your career, you require less supervision and eventually begin supervising others.

To the older student, evidence of the youthfulness of law study is all around you: there is the weekly ritual, typically called bar review, where law students congregate at a local pub for the purpose of drinking into oblivion. There are Blackacres or some similar designation, which are weekly happy hours, in which law students can "party 'til they puke." There is the Barrister's Ball, which bears an eerie resemblance to your high school prom.

I befriended a young law student during a clerkship in Texas; I'll call him Edward. After the summer clerkship was over, Edward and

I went our separate ways, both back to our respective law schools for our third and final years. One afternoon, I got a call from Edward. I could immediately tell that he was upset. As he spoke, his voice cracked and he sounded as if he was out of breath.

I asked him what was wrong and he explained, "I was at the Blackacre last week and got totally wasted."

I replied, "That wouldn't exactly make you unique among law students, Edward."

Edward said, "True, but afterward I left and got arrested."

"What?" I replied, pretty shocked at what I had just heard and thinking that this was Edward's idea of a joke.

"I left Blackacre and was walking down the main drag near the law school campus when I somehow passed out in some bushes. The police found me and I apparently got pretty unruly. Anyway, they arrested me."

Edward was one of the nicest, gentlest, and smartest people I have ever known. But as sort of a legal Doogie Houser, he just hadn't completely grown up yet. He understood the law, legal process, and the philosophy of law. But as with most students of any discipline, the devil was in the application. In addition to the various opportunities to abuse alcohol, there were numerous other reminders of exactly how young my peers were (and how old I was). Many students' first real-life exposure to contracts is the lease they sign for their law school apartment. Most students are unmarried. Most students have excellent academic credentials but little actual work experience.

Many law schools offer what are essentially clubs for nontraditional students. There are student organizations focusing on the needs of minority students, gay and lesbian students, and other traditionally underrepresented groups. I would suggest that you get involved in one of these organizations, in order to develop or supplement your support system.

To the older students contemplating law school, I suggest that you consider schools with part-time programs, even if you plan to attend full-time. These schools tend to be populated with older and second-career students. There are some fabulous law schools out there with part-time programs.

Because of the competitiveness, law school can be a very lonely place. It can be even more so for nontraditional students. You should carefully choose your law school, based upon its demographic history. If the median age of your school is 26, and you are an older student, you may have a difficult time finding your place. However, law school is also what you make of it. If you are willing to involve yourself in activities and take advantage of the programs your school offers, you will likely carve out a place for yourself.

Chapter 8

The Bar Exam and Beyond

AS ONEROUS AS LAW school can be, it is actually only the first step in the labyrinth. A law degree is just that, a degree. In order to practice law, you will need to obtain a license from the licensing authority in the state in which you intend to practice. Although each state has its own licensing authority and requirements, there are some commonalities among them. Most states require a degree from an accredited law school, either approved by the American Bar Association (ABA) or state authorities.

If you are like most law students, you will not give much thought to the bar exam until approximately three months before it is administered. You will be required to register to take it in the middle part of your third year of law school.

One of the first hurdles in obtaining your license is the lengthy application process. The application requires extensive and precise (and frequently personal) information about you from much of your life. You will be required to establish that you have the requisite character and fitness to practice law by virtue of providing the authorities with references and comprehensive information about yourself, for purposes of a criminal background check.

A very large part of the application is devoted to information regarding your character and fitness to practice law. You are required to provide virtually every address you have lived at. The bar examiners want to know every place you have ever worked. They want to know if you have ever been arrested or convicted, suffered from alcoholism or drug addiction, filed for bankruptcy, or were a party to a civil lawsuit. The reason behind this exhaustive background check is ultimately for the protection of the public. Examiners are rightfully concerned about the potential for a lawyer's abuse of clients.

You should take the process very seriously. Any misrepresentation of information will virtually assure that you will not be admitted. The examiners are interested in your *present* fitness to practice law. A lie on the application, even a small one, is indicative of a character issue, which would likely preclude your being admitted, at least for a while. It is much better to clearly and positively communicate past indiscretions and explain them if necessary.

You will also need to pass a series of written examinations and in some states, oral interviews. When you are in the middle of the exam preparation process, it is difficult not to become overwhelmed with the stress of it all. You may think, "If I don't pass, I've just wasted three years of my life and many thousands of dollars." However, the greatest likelihood is that you will pass. Most states have approximately 70–80 percent passage rates for first-time examinees. If you take the exam seriously and invest an appropriate amount of time preparing for it, you will pass.

THE MULTISTATE PROFESSIONAL RESPONSIBILITY EXAM (MPRE)

The first step in obtaining your license occurs either at the end of your second year or sometime during your third year, when you will take the Multistate Professional Responsibility Exam, or MPRE. The MPRE is a requirement for bar admission by just about every state and is administered by the National Conference of Bar Examiners, or NCBE.

The MPRE is a two-hour exam consisting of 60 multiple-choice questions. The test is typically administered three times per year (usually March, August, and November) and will likely be administered at or near your law school. Essentially, the MPRE is an ethics exam, which is based upon the Model Rules of Professional Conduct. Most, if not all, ABA-accredited law schools require you to take a professional responsibility course, often referred to as your ethics course.

I suggest that you plan to take the MPRE at the same time you take your ethics course, which is usually in your second year. Preparation for the MPRE will help your ethics grade and vice versa. It will also be one less thing to worry about that third year, which at least on a calendar basis is the same year you will be preparing to take the bar exam. The MPRE is not nearly as taxing as the bar exam itself, and the threshold passing score is achievable with a reasonable amount of preparation.

BARBRI offers a one-day review course and preparation materials as part of your law-student package, which many students sign up for their first year of school. Kaplan PMBR has a separate MPRE package that includes a one-day course, two online workshops, a practice exam, and a customizable question bank.

The NCBE also administers the Multistate Bar Exam (MBE). By taking the MPRE early, you will also get a good feel for the level of difficulty of Multistate Bar Exam questions. Multistate Bar Exam questions are somewhat akin to LSAT questions. Generally, you can narrow down the answer string to two viable possible correct answers. However, it is almost impossible to distinguish between the two possibilities. By developing a feel for these types of multiple-choice questions early, you will be in a better position to prepare for the Multistate Bar Exam later. And again, given that you will likely take the bar exam shortly after you graduate, getting the MPRE over in your second year means one less thing to worry about.

That said, most students don't stress over the MPRE very much. It's offered three times a year, so you have at least six chances to pass it during your second and third years of law school. In addition, most states only require that you pass the MPRE within a certain period of time following your passage of the bar exam. However, I wouldn't take it too lightly because you cannot obtain your license to practice law until you present proof that you have passed the MPRE. Further, taking it early and getting it out of the way will help uncomplicate your third year and build your confidence as you approach the bar exam.

COMPONENTS OF THE BAR EXAM

Bar exams and bar exam stories are almost apocryphal among recent graduates preparing to take the test. The security procedures at most bar exams are extremely intense. Many states require multiple forms of identification and very strict rules regarding what you can and cannot bring into the exam room with you. Seating is frequently assigned and proctors patrol the exam room vigilantly. The stories regarding the actual exam grow in scope and magnitude until they assume almost mythological proportions.

For example, in Texas, examinees are prohibited from wearing baseball caps in the exam room. According to legend, this is because one examinee wrote crib notes inside the bill of the cap. (I find this legend hard to believe. It seems to me that, given the breadth and depth of exam subjects tested, the bill of a baseball cap—even a Texas-sized cap—would be a pretty futile repository of exam notes. When compared with the potential ramifications of being caught, it's hard to imagine that anyone would actually take this risk. Nonetheless, it certainly makes for interesting bar exam preparation bull sessions.) Bar exam stories and lore abound near exam time; their number and content are good indicators of how all-consuming the bar exam will become for you and your peers.

Each state sets up its own requirements for admission to the bar, which means that the components and content of the bar exam vary from state to state. That's why you can't just pass the bar in Kansas and practice law in Wisconsin. You must pass the bar for each state you wish to practice in. Some states (like New York and New Jersey) have reciprocity agreements that allow lawyers who passed the bar in one state to practice law in another state without have to take a full bar exam again.

However your state structures its bar exam, you can be assured that you will be required to understand and apply a substantial amount of material. Most states administer bar exams toward the end of the months of February and July. Generally, recent graduates take the exam in July. Your exam will likely be either a two- or three-day affair.

The Multistate Bar Exam

The Multistate Bar Exam is developed by the National Conference of Bar Examiners and administered by the participating jurisdictions—only Louisiana, Washington, and Puerto Rico do not use the MBE. Because the MBE is a standardized test, it *must* be administered on the same day across the country. That day occurs twice a year on the last Wednesday in July and the last Wednesday in February. The MBE is a 200 question multiple-choice exam that is divided into two three-hour sessions. The subject matter tested consists of exactly the same subjects that you take during your first year of law school: contracts, torts, property, criminal law and procedure, constitutional law, and contracts.

Most people find it challenging at best and impossible at worst. On the first day of the Tennessee exam, I was startled when time was called. A disheveled-looking fellow seated at the table in front of me abruptly stood up and, shaking his head, said, "That's it. I'm out of here." Apparently, he had run out of time and left something like 20 questions blank. Believing that he would be unable to recover from that morning's performance, he simply walked out.

However, what most people do not realize is that the median national performance on the MBE is only something slightly better than 50 percent correct answers. The questions are extremely nit-picky, and often your answer choices boil down the better of two poor choices. As with the LSAT, using process of elimination of answer choices is by far one of the most important test strategies you can utilize. And as bad as it may feel at the time, if you have prepared dilligently you will do fine on the MBE.

The Multistate Performance Test

The Multistate Performance Test (MPT) is a kind of applications testing protocol in which you are given an ersatz case file and are expected to review materials and write a cogent brief or memo. There are two 90-minute questions that test how adept you are at lawyering tasks—from legal analysis and problem solving to organization and communication. The MPT is developed by the National Conference of Bar Examiners and is administered in all United States jurisdictions except Maryland, Washington, Wisconsin, and Puerto Rico.

The Multistate Essay Examination

The Multistate Essay Examination (MEE) consists of 30-minute essay questions covering business associations, conflict of laws, constitutional law, contracts, criminal law and procedure, evidence, family law, civil procedure, property, torts, and trusts and estates. The NCBE provides nine questions per examination, with most jurisdictions selecting six questions from the nine. The MEE is also developed by the NCBE and administered by the participating jurisdictions—Alabama, Arkansas, D.C., Hawaii, Idaho, Illinois, Kentucky, Mississippi, Missouri, Montana, Nebraska, New Hampshire, New Mexico, North Dakota, Rhode Island, South Dakota, Utah, West Virginia, and Wisconsin, as well as Guam and the Northern Mariana Islands.

BAR EXAM PREPARATION

As I explained earlier, most law students don't even think about exam preparation. After they complete the application, they forget about it until their review course begins.

BARBRI is the largest full bar preparation company out there. A full bar preparation includes preparation for both the multistate and state-specific portions of the bar exam. Many of the larger firms will pay your review course fee. BARBRI will provide you with substantive outlines of the black letter law for all subjects tested in your state, as well as lectures and hundreds of old exam questions and model answers for practice. More importantly, BARBRI will provide you with a good study schedule and a plan to assimilate a huge amount of information. BARBRI begins promoting its services during your first year of law school. For a modest amount of money, you can register and lock in your bar course tuition rate. The rates have increased steadily over the years and locking in is a good idea. After you sign up, BARBRI will give you a series of first-year outlines, which are essentially the same outlines you will receive for the MBE.

In addition to BARBRI, another popular preparation course is Kaplan PMBR. For more than 30 years, PMBR was the leader in Multistate Bar Exam preparation. In 2006, it joined with test prep titan Kaplan to become Kaplan PMBR. Two years later, Kaplan PMBR announced the launch of full bar preparation options for New York,

New Jersey, and Florida. Featuring traditional outlines, printed materials, and a student-focused approach, Kaplan PMBR is a great resource to turn to as you prepare for both law school exams or the bar. It also features the latest in cutting-edge technology through the online Qbanks. For the MBE, PMBR offers lectures for three days and five days, which smartly do not conflict with the BARBRI lecture series. Additionally, I found the Kaplan PMBR review materials, such as their flash cards, to be extremely useful.

As I indicated earlier in this book, doing well in your first-year subjects has an added benefit: it will put you that much farther ahead in your bar exam preparation. As an aside, I would also suggest that during your second and third years, you take a modest amount of time to review your first-year courses.

SELECTING AN AREA OF PRACTICE

After more than three years of hard work, you have now been rewarded with a law degree and license to practice law. The issue you are now faced with is what do you want to do with your life and career? A law degree affords you a wide variety of employment opportunities, from large law firm to solo practitioner and everything in between. If while in law school, you participated in the clerkship ritual, perhaps you have an offer from a firm. Or perhaps you are now trying to decide where you want to go from here. The following section deals with the kinds of opportunities out there for newly minted lawyers and what you can expect as you seek employment.

ASPIRE TO FIND A PRACTICE AREA YOU WILL BE PASSIONATE ABOUT

Choosing a practice area is something that deserves serious consideration, especially if you are bound for a large law firm. The problem is that most large law firms do not allow new attorneys to switch among the various firm practice areas. It's simply too costly; the firm has invested heavily in the new associate and requires an immediate return on its investment. Learning curves are frowned upon.

After graduation, I joined a large Texas international firm in corporate practice. I have to confess that as a prospective law student, I
had hoped to change the world. Needless to say, the actual law school
experience and summer clerkships dramatically changed my perspective. As a former corporate executive, I decided that I was best suited
to do corporate work. However, I had always been interested in at least
exploring litigation. I felt that a lawyer should, at minimum, know his
way around the courtroom.

At the same time, I commenced my legal career shortly after the
wave of corporate scandals that had begun in the mid 1990s. Congress
had recently begun a massive initiative of corporate accountability and
responsibility legislation, referred to as the Sarbanes-Oxley Act of 2002.
The net result was that many corporations, for a time, halted all but the
most essential major transactional activity, in particular IPOs, mergers,
and acquisitions. Consequently, I found myself practicing transactional
law at a time when there were few transactions. Additionally, as an older-
than-average law graduate, I felt the constant pressure to accelerate my
learning curve as quickly as possible. The dearth of transactional work
available to me at that time made this impossible.

As a result, I joined a smaller boutique firm that specialized in corporate defense litigation. I was among a fairly rare group of lawyers who
had the benefit of both transactional and litigation experience. While at
the boutique firm, I immensely enjoyed litigation; however, I felt that to
some extent, I was wasting much of my education and experience, having spent a considerable amount of time learning corporate law. On the
other hand, the collegiality at a smaller firm is hard to beat.

Ultimately, I found my way back into the corporate environment.
Today, I am corporate counsel for a large publicly traded corporation.
I thoroughly enjoy my job, and I have ended up in an area that I love.
However, reaching this point has required a lot of work. I probably could
have avoided much stress had I known more about my potential choices.
More importantly, if I had established a career goal before I graduated,
I likely would have also had a plan to help me get there. Regardless, I
have been fortunate to be able to practice law in both the litigation and
transactional contexts.

Certainly, it may be unrealistic to expect that law students will know
their practice area when they enter law school. In many cases, unless

you actually do the work, it is impossible to know whether you will enjoy it. However, as soon as you understand the basic demands of a practice area, you will be able to begin to assess its attractiveness.

Much of what lawyers do is common to all practice areas. For example, almost all lawyers engage in some form of negotiation. Most lawyers spend a lot of time reading and writing, problem solving, and planning. However, different practice areas require different skills and personality characteristics.

For example, if you really enjoyed your legal writing class that first year, then you might find motion practice very rewarding. On the other hand, if you found yourself immersed in the tax code, perhaps you would be more gratified by corporate or tax practice. It is almost axiomatic that trial lawyers require a sort of stage presence, a flair, and persuasiveness. Much of their success depends upon their ability to sway a judge and/or jury of the correctness of their position. Transactional lawyers—lawyers who form business entities, negotiate and prepare complex agreements, and perform due diligence in anticipation of mergers and acquisitions— are typical of a more patient variety. Their work often requires plowing through mountains of disjointed documents, and they may be called upon to persuade management of the correctness/incorrectness of a particular position. Litigators are also frequently required to review numerous documents.

The point is to try and understand how your skills, experience, and interest would be best served by a particular practice area. However, my experience is that many lawyers change practice areas repeatedly throughout their careers. They find themselves in a particular area because it happens to be a high-demand area—for example, as estate planning became high demand in the 1990s as a result of the maturing baby boom generation. The practice of law is a career in which there is immense flexibility and it is never too late to develop new expertise.

From the Horse's Mouth: Speaking with Other Attorneys
Many attorneys would be happy to hear from you and entertain your questions and can provide a lot of excellent advice regarding career direction. You can find attorneys through the Martindale-Hubbell directory, available at no charge at *www.martindale.com.* The Martindale-Hubbell website and lawyer directory is an extremely useful tool in this regard.

In addition, the directory provides email links, which you can use to initially make contact with the attorneys.

Ask attorneys a variety of questions about their practice areas. Ask them to tell you about a typical workday. Do they enjoy this practice area and why? In which other areas, if any, have they practiced? How did they come to practice in this area? What do they believe are important skills and personality characteristics for this practice area? Just as with any important decision in your life, you need to research and understand the profession and practice of law, in order to make an informed and meaningful career decision.

If you are not sure where your practice interests lie, you should at minimum talk with lawyers involved in litigation and lawyers involved in transactional work. These are the two broadest practice areas and where much of the employment market rests. In addition, talk with lawyers in large firms and lawyers in small firms.

The best advice I can offer regarding selecting a practice area is that you absolutely must manage your own career. Do not rely on your firm or other employer to take care of it for you. You should establish short- and long-term goals for yourself and ensure that the experience you receive while on the job will help you to move toward those goals. For example, if your longer-range plan is to eventually move in-house with a corporation, you should try to determine the kinds of experience required of in-house counsel. And then set about gaining it.

WHAT DO LAWYERS REALLY DO ALL DAY?

You may wonder what the practice of law is really like. Perhaps you know someone who is a practicing attorney. Or like many law students, you may have no real idea of what being a lawyer is like, other than what you have seen on popular television shows or read about in novels.

Grouping everything that lawyers do into one designation is misleading. In reality, lawyers specialize in hundreds of practice areas. A lawyer who enjoys litigation may absolutely detest transactional work. Similarly, a corporate lawyer may have absolutely no interest in seeing the inside of a courtroom.

There are plenty of practice areas that can lead to career satisfaction. Some students enter law school with an eye toward pubic interest work. After graduation, they frequently land employment with state or federal government agencies. Other students have business leanings. They graduate and go to work for corporations or large law firms with corporate practices. Some new lawyers enjoy broad practice areas and join smaller firms or go into practice for themselves.

The possibilities are virtually limitless. Unlike many careers, a lawyer can change direction (and arguably should) numerous times throughout his or her career. This might mean a career path of ever-increasing specialization or an entirely new direction. Some lawyers start their careers in the private sector and later enter the public sector.

The following information is intended to give you an overview of some of the more common practice areas. This information is not by any means complete. However, it will give you at least an idea of the major areas where most lawyers work. If an area of interest is not included below, you might consider contacting a practicing attorney in that area. An excellent reference source is the Martindale-Hubbell lawyer directory, which is free and has a search engine that can sort by practice area, geographic location, and other options.

Solo (or Sole) Practitioner

According to published statistics, the vast majority of lawyers practicing today are doing so either as solo practitioners or working with one or two other lawyers. Most of these lawyers are generalists and engage in a variety of practice areas. However, much of their work involves litigation.

Real Estate Law

Real estate lawyers typically advise clients in the purchase and sale of real estate. Much of this work involves the drafting of contracts and other documents. In addition, real estate lawyers may review information contained in public records regarding the chain of title to property. In addition to residential real estate, these lawyers also work on commercial transactions, such as commercial leases.

Corporate Law

This is a broad area; however, much of what corporate lawyers do focuses on the buying and selling of businesses. Lawyers advise clients in these negotiations and prepare agreements to support these transactions.

Transactions can involve small, privately owned companies or huge corporations. If the businesses involved are publicly traded companies (e.g., shares traded on public stock exchanges), a series of documents must be prepared and filed with governmental authorities. Lawyers also advise these companies on compliance with federal securities laws, including the recently enacted Sarbanes-Oxley Act of 2002.

Labor and Employment Law

Congress has enacted a variety of laws governing the workplace. These include Title VII of the Civil Rights Act of 1964, the Fair Labor Standards Act, the Family and Medical Leave Act, and others. Attorneys practicing in labor and employment law advise clients on compliance with these laws and may also engage in litigation in these areas. In addition, lawyers may help clients train their supervisory employees and develop policies. A sub-practice area is workers' compensation law, which involves litigation regarding payments to injured workers under state law.

Litigation

This is a broad area, which as the heading implies, involves lawsuits. Virtually all of the other areas have some litigation aspects; however, litigation requires special skills that can be gained only through practice. As a result, many law firms assign a variety of cases to their litigators. Litigators spend a great deal of time negotiating, arguing, preparing persuasive documents, and managing lawsuits.

Criminal Law

The pursuit of justice has been glamorized through numerous novels, television series, and movies. Needless to say, the reality of criminal law is frequently much more mundane and deals with petty crimes and indigent defendants. Nonetheless, this is a fascinating practice area which often involves the core legal principles upon which the United States was founded.

Family Law

Family lawyers deal with disputes arising from familial relationships, including marriage, divorce, and child custody. Typically, these lawyers engage in substantial negotiation between parties; however, most family lawyers are also very familiar with the courtroom. Much time is spent on divorce and child custody matters, which can be emotionally draining for all parties and their lawyers.

Education Law

Education lawyers typically spend much of their time advising schools and school districts, in particular with regard to elementary and secondary education. Issues generally include curriculum determination, religion and public education, and equal educational opportunity.

Tax Law

Tax lawyers are essentially transactional lawyers who spend much of their time advising clients as to the tax implications of a particular transaction. Many tax lawyers today have LLMs, which are advanced legal degrees with a focus on taxation.

Intellectual Property Law

This is a fairly specialized practice area. Typically, intellectual property lawyers must pass the patent bar exam in order to practice before the United States Patent Trademark Office. In order to sit for this exam, you do not need to have graduated from law school; however, you must have a technical undergraduate degree or substantial technical education credentials. IP attorneys help clients protect their intellectual property through registration and help to enforce their rights in this property.

Estate Planning

Lawyers involved in this practice area help clients prepare wills and trusts and advise clients on the means to transfer and protect property, both in testamentary transfers and *inter vivos* transfers (while the client is still alive).

Appellate Practice

This is a fairly specialized practice area in which the losing party appeals the decision or verdict to a higher court. It involves substantial brief writing and much time spent researching legal issues and preparing documents for submission to the court.

LIFE IN A BIG FIRM

After graduation, I joined a large firm in Texas of approximately 500 lawyers. I felt honored to have been selected by the firm, whose partners included heavy-hitting Texas and federal government politicos. I had clerked there for about half the summer before and got to know a number of associates and partners. I also had offers from two other firms and felt that the firm I joined would help me to develop the most quickly and effectively as a lawyer in transactional work, my chosen specialty.

One the One Hand . . .

Frequently, students join large firms after graduation. The economics of law school are such that students need to earn six figures immediately in order to handle their student debt load. Large firm salaries for new lawyers have increased dramatically in recent years and at a much faster rate than many other employment areas. These jobs are highly sought after by new graduates. The credentials you earn by working for a large, prestigious firm will stay with you your entire career. However, large firm life certainly comes with a cost. You will be expected to work and bill a very large number of hours. The environment is largely sink or swim and as with law school, you will be left to your own devices to figure things out.

But as difficult and demanding as practice in a big law firm can be, it is by far the best environment for new lawyers to learn the practice of law. You will be exposed to a broad area of practice but may also have the opportunity to specialize. You will be surrounded by more experienced lawyers and have the legal resources to enable you to develop expertise. Large law firms also have substantial resources at their disposal that you might not find in a smaller firm. Typically, large firms have excellent law libraries, complete with professional librarians who can advise you and help you to obtain reference materials. The firm I joined in Texas sponsored weekly CLE luncheons (you will learn that a requirement to maintain you law license is continuing legal education, usually 15 hours of accredited training per year).

Large firms also typically have the largest clients. You will be exposed to high-end legal work and most likely some interesting clients. Unlike the business world, where leaner is meaner, law firms can often become more competitive by merging with their competitors. Frequently, the combination of a firm's clients will result in synergy from a client base perspective, and it will enable the firm to counter the business cyclicality found within many businesses, which in turn affects the law firm's revenue. Firms that are able to attract top law students are as a result able to attract top clients. Top clients make a firm more attractive to top students. The net result is that firms are willing to pay top dollar for top students.

In addition, if you ever plan to move in-house, a large firm may be the best pathway to do this. The relationships you develop and the work you perform will insert you into the pool of people that firm clients most like to draw from. Further, your firm, ever mindful of you as a future client, may even help you to go in-house.

On the Other Hand . . .

Certainly, working for a big law firm has a downside. You will be required to bill a minimum number of hours, typically between 2,000 to 2,200 hours per year. A new associate simply cannot bill every single hour that he or she works. Some of their hours will be written off because the billing partner realizes that the intrinsic value of the work performed is less than the amount billed. Some clients receive billing discounts. For whatever reason, it is likely that you will spend 10 to 14 hours per day in the office and work frequently on the weekends.

You should also be aware that turnover of employees within large law firms is extremely high. Statistically, within three years of joining a large firm, a substantial portion of new lawyers will leave, voluntarily or otherwise. Coming from a business model where high employee turnover is thought of as costly and inefficient, I was amazed when I first heard this statistic. However, in the corporate world, companies spend a lot of money training and developing employees who eventually provide a return on the investment. In the legal realm, a firm expects the new associate to provide a return on investment immediately. The billable hours equation ensures that the return happens. As a result, the high turnover of associates does not affect the firm's bottom line as dramatically as it does in the corporate world.

Another issue facing associates in new firms is making the partnership track. In many firms, the track has extended and associates may wait for eight years or more to become partners in the firms. Further, many junior partners are surprised at their compensation, having imagined that the leap to partner would bring a substantial increase. The reality is that equity arrangements vary, and from at least a compensation perspective, all partners are not created equal.

The Verdict

Despite some big obstacles, the experience you will gain in a large law firm will exponentially accelerate your learning curve. You will work on a wide variety of projects with a wide variety of people, which will in turn enhance your development as a lawyer. In many ways, working in a large firm is almost a rite of passage. Many lawyers do it, and it will enable you to begin to develop your network of colleagues and relationships that will last for the remainder of your career.

In addition, your compensation with a large law firm will likely be higher than almost any other avenue. Law firm salaries have risen dramatically in the past ten years or so, primarily because the top students are increasingly sought after. This is in turn due to the fact that firms have merged and grown increasingly larger in order to become more competitive.

Therefore, I would strongly encourage you to consider working for a large firm initially following graduation. The training you receive from other practicing lawyers guiding you, reviewing your work, and helping you to develop your skills will be invaluable throughout your career.

LIFE IN A MIDSIZED OR SMALL FIRM

After I left the large Texas firm, I worked for a small firm of about 25 attorneys in Memphis, Tennessee. I had decided to explore litigation, which had always interested me. The firm I joined was a boutique labor and employment law firm in Memphis that specialized in corporate defense work for national corporations. We handled Title VII discrimination lawsuits, as well as a number of other client problems. I found the small firm environment refreshing.

On the One Hand . . .

In midsized or small firms, associates are given much more responsibility at the outset. In addition to taking on a greater role, you will likely also have the opportunity to work on a broader range of cases. Access to partners is easy, and most small firm partners will view you as a resource and a colleague, as opposed to a mere subordinate.

On the Other Hand . . .

If you are interested in transactional work, small firms generally do not maintain the caliber of clients that large firms can. Most large, multinational companies prefer and have long histories with the big-name firms. As a result, if your goal is to work on a $10 billion IPO or mergers between Fortune 500 companies, you should consider a large firm.

Small firms also simply cannot afford to pay associates at the levels offered by large firms. As a result, if you are laden with heavy student loan debt, you may decide that a large firm is desirable. In addition, opportunities for advancement within small firms are generally less than in big firms. And while the billable hours are generally less in smaller firms, my experience was that they were not *proportionately* less relative to the compensation involved. For example, my billable hour requirement at the large firm was 2,100 hours and at the small firm was 1,900 hours, a differential of about 10 percent. However, the compensation differential between the large and small firm was almost 30 percent.

The Verdict

Midsized to small firms are excellent choices for many law school graduates, but clearly the decision to go with a midsized or small firm will likely be based upon something other than the work requirements. It may be based on access to partners or collegiality.

LIFE AS AN IN-HOUSE COUNSEL

After several years of law firm life, I decided to move in-house with a large corporation. As counsel for a company, a lawyer's responsibilities are varied and at times unpredictable. The work is interesting and rewarding. And there are no billable hour requirements.

There are days when I spend a large portion of my time revising contracts and advising businesspeople regarding potential transactions. There are other days when I analyze and advise regarding intellectual property issues. There are still other days when I spend a lot of time on litigation awareness and prevention, as well as the management of pending lawsuits. I also advise my client (the company) on compliance issues, including securities laws and commercial laws such as the FTC Act, Title VII, and other federal and state statutes. In addition, I also become deeply involved whenever the company is considering merger and acquisition activity.

With the wave of corporate scandals in the late 1990s, corporations became concerned that they comply with not only the letter, but the intent of the law. And Congress, by enacting the Sarbanes-Oxley Act, clearly signaled to corporations that a new day regarding shareholder protection was at hand. As a result, after a hiring lull in the 1980s and 1990s, corporations began once again to recruit attorneys.

The job is interesting, diverse, and also fulfills my need to help people. Certainly, it is not helping people who are indigent or unjustly accused of criminal activity, but it is helping people nonetheless. Nothing can sidetrack a career faster than committing the company to a bad deal or getting the company sued. I take a lot of satisfaction each day in helping company employees avoid both. I also enjoy the variety of work and the fact that I am allowed to be a generalist. In the law firm environment, you are almost certain to become a specialist in one area of law.

On the One Hand . . .

As an in-house lawyer, you are essentially a captive solo practitioner, whose responsibility is to provide legal advice and perform legal work for the various departments within the corporation. You will work for a variety of professionals, including executive, sales and marketing, engineering, human resources, manufacturing, accounting, and corporate compliance people. Many in-house lawyers are hired by their clients, who, after working abundantly with the lawyer, are impressed with their skill and desire to have them join the client's company.

There are many other benefits of working in-house. From a benefits perspective, most corporations have substantially better benefits than law firms. While this may not mean much to you when you are 30, when you are 60 it will mean a lot to you. In addition, corporations frequently offer stock options and other performance incentives.

Regardless of what anyone tells you, you should largely forget about vacation time if you work for a law firm. The billable hour requirements pretty much make vacations impossible your first few years. In the corporate environment, most companies understand the value of recreation and encourage their employees to take vacations. That said, law firms may offer you tremendous upside potential in the form of equity, should you become a partner.

Another benefit to going in-house is that chances are good that after a few years, you may also have the opportunity to work in other areas of the company, such as management. Many senior corporate managers are lawyers. Companies recognize that the rigors of obtaining a law degree and practicing law are effective screening tools and that those few who are successful can contribute to the bottom line in a variety of ways.

On the Other Hand . . .

The downside is that as a corporate attorney, you will most likely be among a few lawyers in a company populated by nonlawyers. In the firm environment, lawyers surround you. As a result, in a firm there is an intellectual and, to a lesser extent, an emotional support system that will help you to accelerate your growth as a lawyer. This is why many people work in a firm for several or more years before going in-house.

The Verdict

The decision to go in-house is, like all other career decisions, purely personal. However, having done it, I can tell you that it can be very rewarding, both personally and financially. Working in-house can offer an attorney a wonderful lifestyle and career path. It can also be a way to use your law degree as a rung to commence your climb up the corporate ladder.

OTHER CAREER OPTIONS

As I have explained throughout this book, the way one learns how to practice law is to practice it. As a result, I would encourage you to seek employment in which you will actually practice law, at least early in your career.

Government Agencies

If law firm life is not for you, there are scores of government agencies, at the local, state, and federal levels, which offer numerous positions for lawyers.

The Federal Government. Some of the better known federal organizations include the Internal Revenue Service, the Securities Exchange Commission, the Office of Management and Budget, the Environmental Protection Agency, the Occupational Safety and Health Administration, the Equal Employment Opportunity Commission, the Federal Trade Commission, the Central Intelligence Agency, the Federal Bureau of Investigation, and the United States Attorney's Office. All of these government agencies hire newly minted lawyers.

State Governments. State governments also have numerous agencies which require lawyers. City governments all have city attorneys who represent the city in a variety of actions, from employment disputes to defending the city in civil lawsuits. State and local governments also have law enforcement organizations which employ numerous lawyers, including district attorneys and prosecutors.

Judicial Clerkships. In addition to government agency positions, there are numerous judicial clerkships, primarily in state and federal courts. Clerkships, especially at the federal level, are often prestigious and interesting work. Frequently, these positions are highly sought after and the competition is fierce to secure them. However, I would not be deterred from exploring these opportunities if your grades are not stellar. There are numerous and varied positions out there in this sector which are available and should be explored.

Nonlegal Jobs

If you ultimately decide that the practice of law is not for you, there are numerous nonlegal jobs for lawyers. The great thing about having a law degree is that there are an almost infinite number of things you can do with this degree. Lawyers learn how to solve problems, and as one partner in a firm told me, "We are paid to worry for our clients." Legal skills are transferable to many professions, and over time you will be amazed at the people you meet in a variety of occupations who are lawyers.

Lawyers are writers, journalists, and news anchorpeople. Lawyers are chief executives, politicians, and administrators. Lawyers are teachers and businesspeople. The possibilities are only as limited as your imagination. Whichever career direction you choose, your law degree will enhance your ability to systematically think and reason your way through challenges in a way that would have otherwise been impossible.

If you are seriously considering a nonlegal career, I would suggest you read *Nonlegal Careers for Lawyers*, by Gary Munneke and William Henslee (American Bar Association, 2006) or *The Lawyer's Career Change Handbook: More Than 300 Things You Can Do With a Law Degree* (Avon Books, 1998), by Hindi Greenberg. These books describe alternative career paths for the legally trained individual who does not want to practice law.

The difference between a legal career and other careers can be evaluated by the flexibility that lies within them. You can do so much with a law degree. More importantly, you can accomplish much with the skills and knowledge gained in pursuit of that degree.

WHY DO PEOPLE HATE LAWYERS (OR AT LEAST THINK THAT THEY DO)?

At the outset, I should say that I don't think most people really hate lawyers. Instead, a lot of people merely think they hate lawyers. No chapter on life after law school would be complete without a discussion on this subject. As a soon-to-be member of the profession, you should understand how many of your clients may perceive you. And the fact is, people love to hate lawyers. Lawyers are stereotyped and "lawyer joke" has a permanent place in the American lexicon.

And yet, books, movies, and television shows about lawyers are consistently among the most popular of their genres. John Grisham has sold over 250 million books worldwide. Before Grisham, there were a number of hugely successful lawyer-authors including Scott Turow and Earle Stanley Gardner, whose novel was adapted into a long-running television series that many lawyers have cited as the inspiration for their choice of profession.

Other television series about the law have ranked consistently among the most popular and beloved shows of all time. Movies about lawyers have earned millions of dollars in the box office. It would appear that

America (and arguably much of the world) has a love-hate relationship with the legal profession. Why?

1. **Lawyers are the only people who can do what they do.**
   Recently, there has been a proliferation of software for certain legal tasks (such as creating your own will), but for the most part, if you have a legal problem, you need a lawyer to solve it. There is simply no way around it. The law is vast, complex, and extremely technical. In fact, most lawyers today are actually specialists, similar to medical doctors.

   It takes a determined and intelligent person to traverse the law school labyrinth and become a lawyer. Simply put, lawyers are focused and smart. I am not going to go into why anyone would hate someone simply for being intelligent and dedicated. Suffice it to say, good old-fashioned jealousy could very well play a role.

2. **Lawyers are trained to argue both sides of any issue.**
   As lawyers, we are trained to identify issues, anticipate issues, and break the issues down into seemingly infinitesimal sub-issues. Laypeople are generally not trained to spot these issues. And there is nothing that can make you feel stupider than having someone point out something you missed—even worse if they point it out during a fight. It reminds us of our own shortcomings. But we don't do it to show off, and we don't mean anything personal by it. This is just how lawyers are trained.

3. **Most people's exposure to lawyers is limited to an adversarial setting.**
   Generally, litigation is a zero-sum game and there are winners and losers. Divorces, personal injury, property disputes, contract claims, product liability and warranty matters, and other matters of this nature are, by definition, adversarial.

   And unlike the cost of medical care, which can be managed through health insurance, there is generally no insurance to protect against having to pay tens of thousands (or even hundreds of thousands) of dollars in legal fees. Even the winners usually end up with substantial expenses. (There are other countries that employ the "loser pays" rule, in which the losing party pays the legal fees for both sides. As you would expect, this is a strong deterrent to would-be plaintiffs bent on filing a frivolous lawsuit.)

Lawyers are, by necessity, in the middle of these disputes and typically become the face of the lawsuits. Over the years, I have worked with hundreds of lawyers, all zealously dedicated to representing the interests of their clients (which, by the way, is their duty). In their zeal, some of these lawyers did things I didn't like. In fact, they angered me. But no one ever did anything that was unethical, immoral, dishonest, or even unfair.

When you're in the middle of a fight, you want the best person you can find in your corner. And a lawyer is almost always going to be that person. Sometimes the result of the fight is not pretty, but some people hate the lawyer because of it.

So we Americans hate our lawyers, and yet loved to be entertained with stories about them. But the bottom line is that when most people are faced with a legal problem, especially when the stakes are high, they look to find the very best lawyer they can. And secretly, we appreciate and respect the work that most lawyers do for us.

Conclusion

ASSUMING THAT YOU HAVE made the decision to become a lawyer, I must congratulate you. You have chosen what is in my opinion one of the most worthwhile and challenging professions. There are a few certainties that accompany this career choice. You will always learn and you will always be challenged. Law school is the first step in this lifelong educational process. I hope this book has given you a methodology to follow as you traverse the labyrinth. I hope it will provide you with some comfort and insight from at least one student who has gone through the labyrinth before you.

If you are reading this book, you have most likely accomplished much in your life. Take satisfaction in these accomplishments. Take the time to enjoy your successes as you traverse the labyrinth. Endeavor to use your education and skills for good purposes. The tradition and history of lawyering is, despite popular wisdom, noble and a legacy rich in service to others. As you enter practice, strive to positively affect your clients and colleagues. Know that to your clients and to some extent the public, you represent this time-honored profession. Cherish this opportunity to use your specialized education and skill for good purposes.

And finally, thank you for allowing me to accompany you during this portion of your journey through the labyrinth. I wish you much success in your legal studies and career. If you have any questions regarding the material contained in this book, or if I can help you in any way in your law school endeavors, feel free to contact me via email at *stevensedberry@msn.com.*

Appendix A

First-Year Issues Checklist: Constitutional Law II (Individual Rights)

THE FOLLOWING ISSUES CHECKLIST is somewhat of a variation on the style of the criminal law issues checklist presented in Appendix E. Because constitutional law contains a substantial amount of evolving law, I chose to include quite a bit of case law in this checklist, for the purpose of tracking the evolution of the law and its current state. The case law included in this checklist should trigger the "on the one hand/on the other hand" line of thinking that professors love. This, in turn, enables you to spot issues, while also keeping track of the law in the same analytical step. Additionally, because constitutional law is so steeped in legal precedent, this is probably the one area where you should actually cite case names in your exam answers, in order to show your understanding of the subject.

The point is that you should customize your outlines and issues checklists, depending upon the subject matter and more importantly, your own thinking process. Your issues checklist is the final step in your exam preparation. Think of it as the thing to bring if you were allowed to bring only one document into the exam room. Then design your issues checklist to optimize memory triggers on the law and its application to typical issues, in order to tackle the exam aggressively and effectively.

Fourteenth Amendment §2: "Nor shall any State deprive any person of life, liberty, or property, without due process of law. Nor shall any State deny to any person within its jurisdiction the equal protection of the laws."

1. Start with explaining that the protections under the Bill of Rights have been selectively and largely incorporated by the 14th Amendment's Due Process Clause, as described by "fundamental liberty" in *Palko* and explained in *Duncan v. Louisiana*.

2. Explain that the "rights" spoken of are not positive rights but actually negative rights; that is, the right to be free from unwanted governmental interference.

3. *Has the right been incorporated by virtue of the 14th Amendment?* The Court has found these rights to be incorporated:
   - First Amendment in its entirety: freedom of speech
   - Fourth Amendment in its entirety: search and seizure
   - Fifth Amendment, except for requirement of grand jury indictment in criminal prosecutions
   - Sixth Amendment in its entirety: speedy trial
   - Eight Amendment: cruel and unusual punishment

4. *If not, is the liberty interest fundamental?* Due process, per *Duncan v. Louisiana*, means "fundamental to the concept of ordered liberty." Most of the cases following are trying to define what this means.

> **Broad view of fundamental liberty interest**

Further, under *Meyer v. Nebraska* (1923), "liberty" includes: "not merely the freedom from bodily restraint but also the right of the individual to contract, to engage in any of the common occupations of life, to acquire useful knowledge, to marry, establish a home, bring up children, worship God according to the dictates of his own conscience, and generally to enjoy those privileges long recognized at common law as essential to the orderly pursuit of happiness by free men." (This ties into the history and traditions approach used in *Bowers v. Hardwick*.)

So the Court's substantive due process analysis would focus on determining whether the right is fundamental or not, or in the case of equal protection, whether the right is fundamental or if the classification of individuals is fundamentally unfair, a "suspect classification." (See #7 and #8.)

5. *Is the action government regulation of private conduct?*
    a. Congruence and Proportionality (Does the government have the authority to broach private conduct? The Court has held that the government does not have the authority to regulate private actor conduct, unless it violates the 13th Amendment.) (*Morrison*, Civil Rights Cases)
6. *Is the action a state action or a private action?* (Note: Whether or not something is a state action is a fact-intensive analysis. While the Court has used all of these analyses, whether or not a state action exists is a function of the specific facts.)
    a. *Public function?*
        i. *Is it a function traditionally reserved for the state?* (liberal standard)
            - *Marsh* (1946): Company town. (This was the first and earliest case to bring in private actors. The more public the town becomes, the greater the obligation.) "The town and its shopping district are accessible to and freely used by the public in general." (By monopolizing all governmental functions within the town, the company had taken on the character of a governmental actor.)
            - *Evans* (1966): Park is a public function, even if operated by private parties. (Really broadened public function.)
            - *Logan Valley* (1968): Shopping mall is a public function because it was a "functional equivalent of a business district." (REALLY broadened *Marsh*.)
            - *Lloyd Corp.* (1972): Overruled *Logan Valley*.
            - *Rendall-Baker* (1982): School for maladjusted students that received 90 percent of its funding from the state in order to educate children who had been removed from a public school is not a public function.

ii. *Is it an exclusive function of the state?* (conservative standard; limits public function)
  - *Jackson v. Metroplitan Edison* (1974): Cut off service w/o process. Held: Must be traditionally exclusively reserved to the state public function.
  - *Flagg* (1978): Warehouseman's lien enforcement not exclusive public function (most recent case).

b. *Nexus—is the state so heavily involved in the action that it becomes a state action?*

  i. *State enforces the action?*
    - *Shelley v. Kraemer* (1948): Court enforces discriminatory covenants. Held: Enforcement makes it state action. (Note: This case has been limited only to situations where a court deprives a property owner of exercising his 14th Amendment rights.)
    - *Evans* (1970): Limits Shelley. State enforcement of a testamentary action not state action re: due process. (Thus, all state enforcement isn't state action.)

  ii. *Symbiosis? Mutually beneficial activity?*
    - *Burton v. Wilmington* (1961): State must be involved to a "significant extent." What does this mean?
      a. Licensing not state action: *Moose Lodge.*
      b. Use of public property? Maybe, under *Gilmore.*

  iii. *Entanglement: Is the state a joint participant?*
    - *Blum v. Yaretsky* (1982): Nursing home. State actor when government coerces or encourages.

Most recent decisions

    - *Leesville* (1991): Uses a multifactored analysis (governmental assistance, governmental function, governmental authority).
    - *Lugar v. Edmonson Oil* (1982): "Our cases have accordingly insisted that the conduct allegedly causing the deprivation of a federal right be fairly attributable to the State. These cases reflect a two-part approach to this question of 'fair attribution.' First, the deprivations must be caused by the exercise of some right or privilege created by the State or by a rule of conduct imposed by the State or by a person for whom the

State is responsible. Second, the party charged with the deprivation must be a person who may fairly be said to be a state actor. This may be a state official, because he has acted together with or has obtained significant aid from state officials, or because his conduct is otherwise chargeable to the State." (Note: This is not a new test. Instead it highlights those factors that are significant in a fact-bound inquiry.)

- *NCAA v. Taranian* (1988): The NCAA imposed sanctions on a state university for recruiting violations, resulting in Tarkanian's firing, who claims due process rights violated because of the state school and the NCAA's actions.

7. *Is the action a 14th Amendment "substantive" due process violation?* (Note: A law can be constitutional from a "procedural" due process perspective but unconstitutional from a "substantive" due process perspective.)

  a. Substantive Due Process: Has the state actor violated the individual's substantive interest in life or liberty?

Is the liberty interest a "fundamental" interest, i.e., an interest in life or liberty?

| Substantive due process |

  i. Strict Scrutiny Analysis (Burden of proof on government to show compelling governmental interest and "tight fit.") (Note: If Court uses "strict scrutiny," the law is almost always struck down.)

  ii. Steps in a strict scrutiny analysis:

| If answers to 1–3 are no, then go to "rational basis" analysis. |

  1. Is the interest in question one that qualifies as a *protected liberty* under the Due Process Clause?
  2. Is the protected liberty one deemed *fundamental?*
  3. Does the challenged law interfere with the fundamental liberty in a serious enough way to *impinge on* or *unduly burden* that liberty, thereby triggering strict scrutiny?
  4. If a fundamental liberty has been impinged on or unduly burdened does the law substantially further a *compelling government interest? What is the governmental interest?*

5. Has the government chosen the *least burdensome means* of achieving its compelling interest?

Note: The Court may avoid some of these tests to avoid having to decide whether or not something is a fundamental liberty interest (*Cruzan*).

iii. Cases of fundamental rights using strict scrutiny analysis:

A. Broad extra-constitutional view of fundamental rights (*Duncan*).

- *Meyer v. Nebraska* (1923): See above; the broad view of rights under the concept of ordered liberty.

- *Pierce v. Society of Sisters* (1925): The Court relies on *Meyer* to overturn an Oregon law that compelled parents to send children to public rather than private school. The statute violated due process because it "unreasonably interfered with the liberty of parents and guardians to direct the upbringing and education of children under their control."

Note: Both of these cases involved minorities (German immigrants and Catholics). Under Footnote Four, these would have received only a rational basis analysis. However, you could easily argue strict scrutiny, justified on an equal protection analysis.

B. Right to privacy in marriage (After *Lochner*, the Court exercised restraint for many years in substantive due process cases, at least in part to Footnote Four from *Carolene Products*. *Griswold* marks the return of an activist court in these cases. That activism continues today.)

- *Griswold v. Connecticut* (1965): Court strikes down statute banning advice on contraceptives. Court uses penumbras of various amendments, creating a new right to privacy in marriage from the resulting zone of privacy. Court uses strict scrutiny and rejects the statute without any consideration of the state's possible justifications for it.

> **Current state of the law seems to be that fundamental liberty interests are the Footnote Four interests and the right of privacy. All others seem to be non-fundamental.**

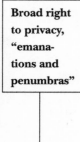

> **Broad right to privacy, "emanations and penumbras"**

Justice Douglas says that the right of privacy in marriage lies within these penumbras, hidden in the shadows of the First Amendment's right of association, the Third and Fourth Amendment's protection of the home, and the Fifth Amendment's guaranty against self-incrimination. On the one hand, this is consistent with Footnote Four and is a different rationale than the dreaded *Lochner*. On the other hand, how the heck do you determine what a fundamental right is from this? Note: Three members of the majority agreed to a right to privacy in marriage, but supported it with the Ninth Amendment argument: "The enumeration in the Constitution of certain rights shall not be construed to deny or disparage others retained by the people." (presumably including the right to marriage privacy)

Right to privacy continues to evolve.

However, the Court expressly declined to revive *Lochner* and made it clear that the rebirth of substantive due process was limited to the sphere of personal liberties. The Court said that it would not "sit as a super-legislature to determine the wisdom, need, and propriety of laws that touch economic problems, business affairs, or social conditions."

C. Right to an abortion (Also called right to personal autonomy. Perhaps also viewed as a liberty interest in one's health and the right to choose medical procedures; this lineage leads to the "right to refuse unwanted medical procedures" analysis.)

- *Roe v. Wade* (1973): Texas law outlawing abortions. The Court holds that the right of privacy in matters concerning procreation and family "is broad enough to encompass a woman's decision whether or not to terminate her pregnancy." By impinging upon the woman's liberty to choose an abortion, the law triggered strict scrutiny. As a result, Texas had to show a compelling government interest.

While the Court agreed that Texas had two compelling interests in maternal health and protecting potential life, the Court held that neither of these was compelling at the outset of pregnancy. Instead, interest in maternal health becomes compelling at the end of the first trimester (because it is safer for a mother to have an abortion then). The state's interest in protecting potential life becomes compelling at the end of the second trimester. The result is that the state can increasingly impose restrictions, the farther along in the pregnancy. And while the state can't prohibit abortions, it can regulate procedures. This led to enactment of various procedures such as "informed consent" requirements which would be disputed in future cases.

- *Planned Parenthood v. Casey* (1992): Upholds mother's right to autonomy (and the core holding of *Roe*) but created "undue burden" test as a balance for state's equally compelling interest throughout pregnancy. Under strict scrutiny, if a law impinges upon, or unduly burdens a fundamental right, it will be upheld if it is the least restrictive means. This new test appeared to increase the level of protection given to the abortion decision. However, a law can only be found to impose an undue burden if its purpose or effect is to place a substantial obstacle in the path of a woman seeking an abortion before viability. But if the state's purpose is to "persuade the woman to choose childbirth over abortion," this purpose is not satisfied. Thus, almost any law could be argued to be intended to "persuade" not "place a substantial obstacle," and the state has a right to favor nonabortion. The Court is also concerned about the reliance issue, as well as its legitimacy. This was a divided decision.

> **Right to an abortion, as long as you can afford it**

- *Maher*. While you have a right to an abortion, you do not have an entitlement, i.e., state funding. Thus, you have a right to an abortion, as long as you can afford it.

Right to Marriage

- *Loving v. Virginia* (1967): "The right to marry is a part of the fundamental 'right of privacy' implicit in the Due Process Clause." Typically trigger strict scrutiny, i.e., laws prohibiting noncompliance with child support orders from marrying. However, traditional state requirements that delay the right, i.e., minimum age laws, are upheld. (Note: "Right to marry" cases may also be Equal Protection cases.)

Is the liberty interest a nonfundamental interest, i.e., merely a property right or economic legislation?

i. The shift of economic legislation from strict scrutiny to rational basis analysis. The Court, at the turn of the century, engaged in activist scrutiny of Populist legislation and routinely struck it down. It held effectively that *the freedom of contract was a fundamental right*.

> **Economic legislation**

A. *Lochner* (1905): Court examined the right to contract as a fundamental right and overturned this economic legislation. Criticized for engaging in "extra-consitutional" analysis. Court uses strict scrutiny, says that the "means/ends" fit not tight enough. (Court uses strategy of finding "special circumstances" to justify judicial interference.)

- While Court suggested a deferential approach, it closely scrutinized the means/ends relationship and said that there was no "direct relation" and "substantial effect upon the health of the employee to justify calling this a health law."

- Thus, there were other ways (less restrictive means) to accomplish the governmental interest.
- Further, the trade of baker was not considered unhealthy, therefore the state's interest in the health of the baker could not be considered a compelling governmental interest.
- Another view is that the Court was looking at this as a labor law, which redistributed wealth from the employer to the employee and was as such unconstitutional.
- The Court did acknowledge that "governmental interest was permissible if it was on behalf of those who, as a group, were especially vulnerable and unable to protect themselves in the struggle for existence." (Arguably, this became the seeds of *Lochner*'s own destruction later in *Muller* and *West Coast*.)
- Holmes famous dissent said that "a constitution is not intended to embody a particular economic theory, whether of paternalism and the organic relation of the citizen to the State or of laissez faire," and that "the word 'liberty' in the 14th Amendment is perverted when it is held to prevent the natural outcome of a dominant opinion."

B. *Lochner* rationale begins to lose support in the Court:

- *Muller v. Oregon* (1908): Only a few years later, the Court upholds a maximum work hours law for women. This would support the notion that the Court was substituting its judgment for the legislature's in *Lochner*. The counter is that women have special needs (however, given our views today, this probably more supports the argument that the Court was legislating).

- *West Coast Hotel v. Parish* (1937): The Court upholds a state law setting minimum wages for women and children. In doing so, it overruled *Adkins v. Children's Hospital* (1923), a *Lochner*-era decision. The Court rejects the elevation of the freedom to contract to what amounts to fundamental liberty status. C. Justice Hughes: "The Constitution does not speak of freedom of contract. It speaks of liberty and prohibits the deprivation of liberty without due process or law . . .[A] regulation which is reasonable in relation to its subject and is adopted in the interests of the community is due process. This essential limitation of liberty in general governs freedom of contract in particular."

- *Nebbia* (1934): While not expressly overturning *Lochner*, it uses a "reasonable relation to proper legislative purpose" and says that as long as the "law is neither arbitrary nor discriminatory it satisfies Due Process" and upholds the statute. (Note: All economic legislation today is analyzed per "rational basis.") The Court said that in determining whether or not a law violates the Due Process Clause, "every possible presumption is in favor of its validity." (The Court analyzes only the means, not the ends.)

- *United States v. Carolene Products* (1938): The Court first articulates the "rational basis" test. Court rejects a substantive due process challenge to a federal law excluding nondairy milk producers from interstate commerce. Held: "A law affecting ordinary commercial transactions" is valid as a matter of substantive Due Process, as it "rests upon some rational basis within the knowledge and experience of the legislators." Justice Stone's famous Footnote Four: "More rigorous judicial scrutiny is called for only

---

United States v. Carolene Products Footnote Four: (1) limits S.D.P. strict scrutiny to B. of Rs. (2) and (3) suggest strict scrutiny for E.P. claims.

in three exceptional situations: (1) If legislation appears on its face to be within a specific prohibition of the Constitution, such as those of the first ten amendments; (2) if legislation restricts those political processes which can ordinarily be expected to bring about repeal of undesirable legislation, such as impairments of the right to vote; and (3) if legislation is aimed at 'discrete and insular minorities' who, because of prejudice against them, are unable to protect themselves through the ordinary political processes." (Two and three deal with equal protection.)

In effect, he was saying that there are two types of Due Process claims: if it is a right guaranteed by the ten amendments, then strict scrutiny. Otherwise, rational basis analysis. This led to a dramatic reduction of strict scrutiny analyses in nonenumerated rights claims.

Is the liberty interest protected nonfundamental?

    ii. *Rational Basis Analysis:* Today, economic freedom is no longer considered a fundamental freedom; while it is still protected under the Due Process Clause, the Court uses a rational basis analysis. (Burden of proof on P to show illegitimate governmental interest or irrational relation.)

- *Is there any legitimate goal that the legislature could have been thinking of? (The Court may hypothesize what this legitimate goal is.)*
- *Are the means rationally related to ends in any way?*
- If no to either, then law struck down. (Note: If Court uses rational basis analysis, almost always upheld.)

    iii. Cases using rational basis analysis:

    A. Economic legislation today (will always be upheld)

- *Williamson v. Lee Optical* (1955): Court upheld Oklahoma statute that curtailed ability of opticians to practice profession. "It is enough that there is an evil at hand for correction, and that it might be thought that the particular legislative measure was rational way to correct it."

- *Ferguson v. Skrupa* (1963): Law restricting business of debt adjusting to attorneys did not violate due process because the "Kansas legislature was free to decide for itself that legislation was needed to deal with the business of debt adjusting."

iv. *Is there a tradition or history in our common law that would suggest that the right is a fundamental right?*

A. Right to engage in homosexual behavior

Court uses "history and traditions" approach from *Meyer.*

- *Bowers v. Hardwick* (1986): Georgia criminal sodomy law. No zones, no penumbras. Instead of framing the issue as the "right to privacy," the Court calls it "the homosexuals' right to commit sodomy." Because there is no fundamental right, rational basis scrutiny is required and the law is upheld. The Court says that under a rational basis analysis, it is *legitimate to prohibit behavior on moral grounds. The Court, in defining fundamental rights looks to history, tradition to determine what is implicit in the concept of ordered liberty.* (The Court asks: Is this a fundamental right, based on history and tradition? The answer is sodomy and suicide (*Washington v. Glucksburg*) have always been against the law, therefore they are not fundamental rights).

B. Right to Refuse Unwanted Medical Treatment (Is this right equivalent to choosing the time and manner of one's death; the so-called "right to die"?)

- *Cruzan v. Director* (1990): Missouri Supreme Court refuses to allow withdrawal of feeding tube and respirator from Cruzan. Family sues on the basis that it deprives her of the right to refuse unwanted medical treatment. While the Court acknowledges that Cruzan has a liberty

The Court avoids the question of whether the right to die is fundamental by saying it isn't rooted in history and then uses a "balancing" test. (The Court is sensitive to engaging in the creation of broad extra-constitutional rights, à la *Lochner.***)**

interest in dying with dignity, it refuses to decide whether or not this interest is fundamental and upholds the law on the basis that the state's interest in clear and compelling evidence is greater. (The Court thereby uses a modified rational basis analysis; it calls the interest a liberty interest and balances it against the state's need for clear and compelling evidence. While the holding did not expressly state that the liberty to refuse unwanted medical treatment includes the right to refuse life-sustaining treat-ment, the Court said: "For purposes of this case, we assume that the United States Constitution would grant a competent person a constitution-ally protected right to refuse lifesaving hydration and nutrition.")

C. Right to Assisted Suicide

- *Washington v. Glucksberg* (1997): Washington law banning assisted suicide. Here, the Court looks to history and traditions and says that the right to die is not fundamental.

State owes no affirmative duty, unless it has caused the confinement or custody, i.e., a "special relationship" exists.

v. *Is there a "special relationship" between the state and the actor which results in an affirmative duty, thus creating a fundamental right?*

D. Affirmative Rights

- *Maher:* No right to have state pay for your abortion.
- *Deshaney v. Winnebago County* (1989): Child living at home was severely beaten by father. Held: Even though state services knew child was in danger, it had no affirmative duty to protect him (because he was living at home).
- *Youngberg v. Romero* (1982): State owes a duty of care to inmate involuntarily confined to state mental hospital.

The Due Process Clauses of the 5th and 14th Amendments prohibit the federal government and the states from depriving a person of "life, liberty, or property, without due process of law." (This applies to fundamental and nonfundamental interests.)

8. *Is the liberty interest an interest in procedural due process,* i.e., has the state actor violated the individual's interest in life, liberty, or property using procedures deemed to be unfair (either lacking in notice or the right to be heard)?

   a. *Was there a liberty or property interest?*
      - *Constitutional fundamental liberty interest?*
         - Bill of rights (freedom of speech, etc.), right of privacy
            - *Nonfundamental liberty interest?*
               - Freedom to pursue a trade
               - Statutes, regulations, and policies
               - Common law tradition
            - *Was there a property interest?*
               - Established under state law
               - *Board of Regents v. Roth* (1972): Untenured professor not rehired. Argues it violates his right to due process. Held: He had no property interest under state law in being rehired. Being eligible to be rehired does not mean you are entitled to be rehired.

   b. *Was there a deprivation of that interest? If so, what process was due the individual?*
      - "Bitter with the sweet"
      - *Arnett v. Kennedy* (1974): Dismissal of a federal employee. Held: "Where the grant of a substantive right is inextricably intertwined with the limitations on the procedures which are to be employed in determining that right, a litigant . . . must take the bitter with the sweet."
      - Constitutional Guarantee
         - *Cleveland Bd. of Educ. v. Loudermill* (1985): Overruled Arnett, "The right to due process is conferred not by legislative grace, but by Constitutional guarantee."

- Balancing Test
  - *Mathews v. Eldridge* (1976):
    1. The significance of the private interest that will be affected
    2. The extent to which additional procedural safe-guards would reduce the risk of error and the probable value of other safeguards
    3. What is the government's interest and what will be the administrative burden?

Fourteenth Amendment §1: "No State shall . . . deny to any person within its jurisdiction the equal protection of the laws."

9. *Is the action an equal protection violation?* Strict Scrutiny, Rational Basis, Intermediate Scrutiny
   a. *Does it involve a "suspect classification"?*
      i. Carolene Products Footnote Four: "Prejudice against discrete and insular minorities may be a special condition, which tends to seriously curtail the operation of those political processes ordinarily to be relied upon to protect minorities."
      ii. *Is the classification based on either race or national origin?*
          - *Plessy v. Ferguson* (1896): Court upholds segregated facilities on the basis of "separate but equal" and says that this does not stamp blacks with "badges of inferiority."
          - *Missouri ex rel Gaines* (1938): Black law student. If state doesn't maintain separate facilities, then it can't give him the tuition to go out of state. It must either provide separate facilities or admit him.
          - *Sweatt* (1950): Qualities of UT law school that are impossible to measure, i.e., reputation of faculty, alumni network make "separate but equal" impossible.
          - *Brown v. Board of Educ.* (1954): Segregated schools. Laws that classify on the basis of race or national origin are "odious to free people" and if "they are ever to be upheld, they must be shown to be

> **The evolution of race as a *suspect classification* and the dismantling of *separate but equal* following *Plessy*. Court shifts from rational basis to strict scrutiny.**

necessary to the accomplishment of some permissible state objective, independent of the racial discrimination." However, it was still unclear as to whether this holding was limited to education.

- *Loving v. Virginia* (1967): Clarified race as a suspect classification. Law banning interracial marriages struck down. "At the very least, [equal protection] demands that racial classifications, especially suspect in criminal statutes, be suspect to the most rigid scrutiny."
- *Palmore v. Sidoti* (1964): Custody battle of interracial couple. Court says that race is suspect classification and while "granting custody based upon the best interests of the child" is a compelling governmental interest, it does not allow the court to remove a child from his mother.

Is the law facially discriminatory? Is the law discriminatory as applied? Is the discriminatory impact based on a discriminatory purpose or design?

- *Washington v. Davis* (1976): Hiring criteria for D.C. police department alleged to discriminate against blacks. Held: Even if the impact of the criteria is disproportionate, it is "a basic Equal Protection principle that the invidious quality of a law claimed to be racially discriminatory must ultimately be traced to a racially discriminatory purpose." "An invidious discriminatory purpose may often be presumed from the totality of the relevant facts." (However, this doesn't give much guidance as to how to establish intent.)
- *Arlington Heights* (1977): Discriminatory purpose doesn't necessarily have to be the sole or even dominant purpose. Rather, it is generally enough "that a discriminatory purpose has been a motivating factor in the decision." The Court gives elements of impacts:

1. Clear pattern, unexplainable on grounds other than race
2. Historical background (particularly if it shows a series of actions taken for invidious purposes)
3. Departure from normal procedural sequence
4. Specific sequence of events leading to the challenged decision
5. In a mixed motive case, this creates a rebuttable presumption of discriminatory purpose.

Is a fundamental right at risk? (based on history, tradition, and the first ten amendments) Court tries to limit the fundamental right analysis to the Constitution.

- *Kramer v. Union Free School Dist.* (1969): Person sues because of statute that says that only homeowners or renters can elect school board. This triggers strict scrutiny because voting is a fundamental right.
- *San Antonio ISD v. Rodriguez* (1973): Person sues because of statute that awards school funding based on district income. Issue is whether or not wealth is a suspect class and education is a fundamental interest.

If suspect classification or fundamental right, then strict scrutiny (always struck down).

    a. *Is there a compelling governmental interest?*

      i. Affirmative Action: *Is the legislation intended to advantage a classification, rather than disadvantage?*

- *City of Richmond v. J.A. Croson* (1989): City sets aside 30 percent of its contracts for MBEs. The Court says that the city had not demonstrated a compelling need for its quotas. Further, the Court says that the only compelling need is to redress past wrongs. (This circumscribes affirmative action to a tight fit.)

Court struggles to define proper standard of review for affirmative action cases: strict or intermediate scrutiny.

- *Metro Broadcasting v. FCC* (1990): Here, the Court applies intermediate scrutiny, arguing that a different standard applies to Congress than to the states.
- *Adarand Contractors v. Pena* (1995): Overrules Metro and applies strict scrutiny.

b. *Is there a "tight fit" between the means and the ends? (Note: The Court uses "overinclusiveness" and "underinclusiveness" as indicia of another, underlying purpose for the law. If the fit isn't "tight," it probably means that there is some other underlying reason for the law.)*

i. If not a suspect classification or fundamental right, then either rational basis or intermediate scrutiny.

Rational Basis: Economic Legislation (always upheld)

a. *Is there any conceivable (hypothetical) reason for the challenged classification?*

- *REA v. New York* (1949): New York statute prohibiting advertising for sale on non-owned vehicles. Held: Does not violate equal protection. Court engages in a hypothetical analysis of reasons behind law and upholds on a rational basis.
- *U.S. Railroad Retirement Board v. Fritz* (1974): Congress restructured retiree benefits and grandfathered in certain classes of employees. Held: There are a lot of goals at work here. It is sufficient to hypothesize a goal and determine that there is a rational relationship between that goal and the means the Congress is using to achieve it.

b. *Is there any rational relationship between the means and the ends?*

- Rational Basis with "Bite": Sexual Orientation
- *Romer v. Evans* (1996): Colorado passes amendment outlawing state legislation that makes homosexuality a basis for protection. Court does not call homosexuality a suspect classification (and thus overruling *Bowers*) but overrules the amendment. However, it does use "suspect classification" verbiage. This is either an isolated opinion or suggests that the law regarding homosexual status is in flux.

Intermediate Scrutiny (gender as a "quasi-suspect" classification)

a. In the 70s, much pressure to designate gender as a suspect classification. Frontiero was the high water mark with four justices saying they would do so. *Craig v. Boren* settled on the current approach, an intermediate scrutiny:

i. *Is there an important governmental objective? (must be actual, not hypothetical)*

ii. *Are the means substantially related to the ends?*

- *Goessart v. Cleary* (1946): Michigan woman bartender law. Court upholds with rational basis test.
- *Craig v. Boren* (1976): Different drinking ages for men and women. Court says that it may not be correct that "all discriminations between the sexes ultimately redound to the detriment of females, because they tend to reinforce 'old notions' restricting the roles and opportunities for women." Court uses the intermediate standard for the first time. This standard still stands, although *U.S. v. Virginia* brings it into question.
- *Mississippi University for Women v. Hogan* (1982): Man challenges all-female nursing school. "The fact that a law discriminates against males rather than against females does not exempt it from scrutiny or reduce the standard of review." Court uses "exceedingly persuasive justification" language that is thought to perhaps raise the level of scrutiny. However, the Court actually uses an intermediate standard of review.
- *JEB v. Alabama* (1994): Held that peremptory challenges based on gender are unconstitutional. Court uses "exceedingly persuasive language" again but with an intermediate standard.
- *United States v. Virginia* (1996): Woman challenges VMI males-only policy. Again, the Court uses "exceedingly persuasive" language. The question is whether this case actually raised the standard from intermediate to a heightened standard.

Racial Gerrymandering

      a. *Is this a race case or a gerrymandering case?*

- *Shaw v. Reno* (1993): Court uses the *Washington v. Davis* and *Arlington Heights* analysis: Discrimination purposeful? In a mixed motive case, this creates a rebuttable presumption of discriminatory purpose.
- *Miller v. Johnson* (1995): Overturns Shaw. In the case of electoral districting based upon race, the P has to prove that race was the predominant factor motivating the legislature's decision.

Wealth as a Suspect Class

    10. *What about stare decisis?*

      a. Weigh the pros and cons of overturning a precedent.

    11. *Should the Court be allowed to step in?*

      a. Is the Court legislating; overstepping its bounds?

      b. Legitimacy concern

Sample First-Year Pyramid Outline for Contracts

A **CAVEAT: REMEMEMBER THAT** in law school outlining, the *process* of outlining is infinitely more important than the *output*. This is because the process of creating the outline is also the process by which you learn legal reasoning, as well as the black letter law. This is why you cannot and must not ever solely rely on someone else's outline, including any of those in this book, to prepare for an exam. **The outlines that follow are intended to illustrate the components of the Pyramid Outline Method but are by no means complete. Many of the cases cited in these outlines are fictitious and presented for illustrative purposes only.**

The following is an example of what a Pyramid Outline for your first-year contracts course might look like. Recall that you create your Pyramid Outline by trimming down your Base Outline substantially on a weekly basis. Your Base Outline will incorporate virtually everything you read and write, including cases, class notes, case briefs and summaries, commercial outlines, hornbooks, and unedited cases. Each week, you will boil this down into your Pyramid Outline. Remember: you should keep a copy of the full Base Outline as a reference tool and as a comprehensive record of all information you learn throughout the semester. It is also useful to periodically review the Base Outline as your understanding of the subject evolves. You may find that you have distilled out information that should be reinserted into the Pyramid Outline. Pyramid outlining is the process of digesting and reducing the Base Outline into a more succinct and usable document, helping you begin to assimilate all of the law and legal reasoning you learn during the semester.

As you begin to create your Pyramid Outline, you should focus on organization, broad concepts, and the cases that support these concepts. Your Pyramid Outline will be roughly one-third the length of your Base Outline. For example, the Base Outline from which this Pyramid Outline was constructed was approximately 70 pages in length.

CONTRACTS

I.   OFFER AND ACCEPTANCE IN THE FORMATION OF AN ENFORCEABLE AGREEMENT

    A. Enforceable versus Unenforceable Promises: People make promises to each other every day. The real question (ethical issues aside) is how should the law distinguish between promises that should be binding and enforceable as law and those which the law should not interfere with.

    B. Common Law: "Mirror image" rule. Offer and acceptance must match exactly as a threshold question as to legal enforceability.

    C. Revocation Prior to Acceptance: The offeror creates power of acceptance in offeree; however, offeror can revoke anytime prior to acceptance. An offer manifests intent and certainty of the offeror.

        1. Quotations: Normally are considered an invitation for an offer, rather than an offer.

        2. Advertisements: Same (unless specific language is used which would be construed as an offer).

      a. Offering Circulars: May or may not be offer. (Test is whether a reasonable person would consider writing to be addressed to him individually and if he could act on it.)

D. Indefiniteness: An offer can fail for indefiniteness if it is so vague as to being incapable of being accepted.

    1. Certainty: The terms must be reasonably certain. Terms left open may suggest that intent was not to be bound. E.g., *Billy Bob v. Gomer*: Because future rent was left open, this was an agreement to agree and not enforceable. E.g., *Joe v. Jim*: Seller made an offer, but no quantity was included. Held: Too indefinite. Reasonable for offeror to expect one more step in transaction. E.g., *Atlas v. The World*: Letter of intent signed, subject to definitive agreement. Not enforceable.

E. UCC 2-204. Formation in General: Contract for sale of goods may be made in any manner sufficient to show agreement. Won't fail for indefiniteness, even though terms left open. (Price, delivery, quality may be omitted.) Only required term is quantity term.

F. UCC 2-306. Output, Requirement, and Exclusive Dealings: If quantity measured by output or requirements, this means good faith requirements. Exclusive dealing contracts imply best efforts. E.g., *Alvin v. Darc*: Requirements contract upheld. Quantity based on good faith.

II. WHAT IS CONSIDERATION AND WHY IS IT NECESSARY FOR THE FORMATION OF A LEGALLY ENFORCEABLE AGREEMENT?

The threshold question in distinguishing enforceable and unenforceable promises is always whether parties intended to be bound. A court will find consideration in some fashion, where it believes parties intended to be bound. The legal doctrine of consideration is almost a construct, which the court uses to establish that a promise was legally enforceable.

A. Consideration: A formality for differentiating legally enforceable contracts. Legal detriment that is incurred by promisee, in exchange for a promised benefit from promisor.

E.g., *Uncle v. Willie*: Uncle Gerry promises nephew Willie a great deal of money to stop living La Vida Loca. Held: This was a promise to make a gift.

1. Requirement of Exchange; Type of Exchange: Performance or return promise must be bargained for to constitute consideration. (Note: Under UCC, technically no consideration explicitly required. Only requirement is writing or conduct indicating agreement.)

2. Courts will not analyze adequacy of consideration, but rather only if it existed at the time of formation. In other words, a court will not protect plaintiffs from making a bad deal for themselves. However, gross disparity in consideration may be evidence of other defenses to formation, i.e., fraud, duress, or unconscionability.

B. Donative Promises (promises to make a gift): Unenforceable unless the promisee can show detrimental reliance on the promise.

1. Conditional Donative Promises: "I'll give you a suit, if you'll go around corner to store." CDPs are unenforceable unless there is detrimental reliance by the promisee.

2. Restatement of the Law on Contracts §90 View on Detrimental Reliance: An offer which could be expected to induce reliance is enforceable to prevent injustice.

C. Detrimental Reliance/Promissory Estoppel as a Substitute for Consideration: Is typically evidence of parties' intent (recovery in quasi-contracts, quantum meruit, restitution). Was reliance foreseeable? Did the party rely on the promise? If so, then the promisor should be liable for reliance.

D. Moral Obligation and Past Consideration: Ordinarily, past consideration (this is where the promise, obligation, duty, or task has already been performed) is unenforceable. However, in some cases it is simply just to hold past consideration as enforceable. E.g., *Meredith v. Lauren*: A man saves another's life, who promises him $1,500 a week; afterward, is held to be enforceable. (Promisor was personally benefited. "Material benefit" plus "moral obligation" equal consideration. However, must also prevent injustice.) (Note: A new promise to pay a past debt is enforceable because the new promise is new consideration, especially if the promisor forebears enforcement.)

  1. Common Law: Promise for Benefit Received: Enforceable to the extent necessary to prevent injustice unless gift promise or very disproportionate.
E. Agreements to agree are unenforceable.
  1. Illusory promises are unenforceable. E.g., "Terminate at any time." "If I want to." "As I desire." Not a real promise. (Note: Distinguish from outputs or requirements contracts, where quantities are not fixed, but the parties intend to be bound.)
  2. Letters of Intent: Are enforceable, provided that material terms are included and it is clear that the parties intended to form a basic agreement, subject to further and final terms.

III. HOW DOES A COURT DETERMINE WHETHER THERE WAS MUTUAL ASSENT BETWEEN THE PARTIES SUCH THAT AN ENFORCEABLE CONTRACT WAS FORMED?

Courts use an objective standard. Always start by looking at circumstances and asking whether parties intended to be bound, as manifested by a reasonable person's perspective. (Note: Rationale is that the other party has to be able to rely on a party's manifestations, if it is reasonable to do so.) (Note: If both parties attach the same subjective meaning, then they are bound, regardless of the objective interpretation of the circumstances.)

A. Common Law Effect of Misunderstanding: No contract is formed if the parties attached materially different meanings, unless one party knows of the misunderstanding and tries to take advantage of it. Then the innocent party's meaning enforced. (Note: Acceptance is effective upon dispatch but all other communications effective upon receipt.)

IV. REVOCATION AND LAPSE OF AN OFFER
A. Offered Acceptance Period and Offer Lapse
  1. Common Law: Offeror can revoke any time prior to acceptance.

B. UCC 2-205: Offer which stays open by terms for period of time is not revocable, if signed in writing by offeror (three mo. max).

C. Indirect Revocation: Offeree learns of sale of property while an offer is pending. Held: He can't then accept offer because he knew what was really going on, and it would be unjust to undo the transaction.

D. Offer terminated on date of offeror's death or incapacity. (Unless an option contract, which is transferrable.)

E. Irrevocable Option Contacts: Require consideration; nominal okay.

 1. Option Contract: Purported consideration or reliance.

 2. Option Contract created by part performance or tender.

F. Conditional offers, which are conditioned upon certain occurrences are valid.

G. Common Law Principle of Detrimental Reliance: An offer which should and does induce action is binding if injustice can only be avoided by enforcement of the promise (donative promise). E.g., *James v. Kirk*: General contractor relies on subcontractor's bid in making his own bid. Later, subcontractor withdraws bid. Held: The bid is enforceable.

 1. Non-Writing Enforceable by Virtue of Reliance: A promise which would reasonably be expected to induce forbearance is enforceable. Reasonable, foreseeable reliance, no other remedies.

H. TIME

 1. UCC 2-309: Absence of Specific Time Provisions; Notice of Termination

 2. If contract term is indefinite in duration, then for reasonable time. If terminated, must be reasonable notice.

V. ACCEPTANCE OF AN ENFORCEABLE OFFER AND ISSUES RAISED BY NEW AND/OR DIFFERENT TERMS RAISED IN THE ACCEPTANCE

A. UCC 2-206: An offer shall be construed as inviting acceptance in any reasonable manner including shipment. However, offeree must notify offeror of acceptance within reasonable time.

B. Common Law Mirror Image Rule: Counteroffer is a rejection, cannot subsequently accept offer (however, Restatements distinguishes between mere inquiries and counteroffer). Silence is not acceptance. (However, accepting goods is acceptance.)

C. Common Law: Acceptance by Silence or Exercise of Dominion: Silence valid only of course of dealing or prearranged or acceptance of performance.

D. UCC: Different or Additional Terms
1. UCC 2-207(1): Treats supplier acknowledgment as acceptance of purchaser's offer (terms which prevail are purchaser's, unless seller expressly conditions acceptance on purchaser's assent to its terms).
2. UCC 2-207(2): Additional terms are treated as proposals for contract, accepted unless purchaser rejects or they materially alter contract.
3. UCC 2-207(1): Different terms are either "knocked out" (w/ missing terms supplied by UCC) or minority approach is purchaser's terms prevail ("first shot" rule).
4. UCC 2-207(3): If writings don't establish K and goods shipped and received, then conduct manifests agreement; K is based on terms that do agree (with missing terms supplied by UCC).
5. Common Law: If buyer accepts goods, then last terms apply ("last shot" rule).

VI. MODIFICATION OF AN ENFORCEABLE AGREEMENT
A. Common Law: Preexisting Duty Rule: Promise to do something already obligated to do is not enforceable for lack of consideration. (Prevents and discourages "holdups.") E.g., *Fish Packers v. Fishboy*: Fishermen held company "hostage," thus modification unenforceable.
B. UCC 2-209: An agreement, in writing, to modify is binding, no consideration required. Modification must be in "good faith." (See discussion on honesty in fact and fair dealing.) Parties can make own Statute of Frauds regarding modification, however, party to be charged must have signed.

C. Common Law: Oral modification can act as a waiver, which cannot be retracted if other party has detrimentally relied on the modification.

D. Common Law: Modification of executory contract binding if fair and equitable, given that the circumstances were not anticipated by the parties.

E. If original contract requires writing, then modifications must be in writing.

F. Change of circumstances as basis for modification. E.g., *Guys v. Dolls*: Supplier threatens to breach unless given price increase and additional contract. Held: Economic duress, thus unenforceable.

G. Modifications despite "no modifications unless in writing" clauses: *Moon v. Mullins*: A right can be orally waived for a period of time.

VII. DETERMINING WHETHER A WRITTEN AGREEMENT WAS INTENDED TO BE A COMPLETE AND ENFORCEABLE CONTRACT

A. Determining the Intent of the Parties: There are two common law views:

1. Williston: Restatement I; pure objective standard (regardless of actual intent).

2. Corbin: Restatement 2d §202; look to parties' intent first, then fill in gaps using an objective standard.

B. Parol Evidence Rule: Was writing intended to be final memorialization of party's agreement? Admissibility/exclusion of written and oral evidence regarding contract (question of fact for judge). (Note: Trend is toward liberalization.)

1. Was this a final expression or merely a draft?

2. Was this a complete statement or incomplete? (full integration v. partial integration)

C. Common Law Integrated Agreement: An integrated agreement is a writing or writings constituting a final expression of one or more terms of an agreement. Note: Most contracts today contain an "integration clause" which expressly states that the contract is intended as a full and complete statement of the intent of the parties and that no other documents, etc., may be used to ascertain the parties' intent.

1. Common Law Parol Evidence Rule: Writing that is found to be completely integrated by court, thus rendering any prior communications inadmissible. Thus, it may not be shown to be inaccurate, due to other outside evidence. (Note: Consistent additional terms may be used to prove writing was partial integration, even with merger clause.) If writing found to be (1) not integrated or (2) not final, then differences between the oral agreement and the written agreement show that the agreement sought to be enforced is inaccurate, thus unenforceable.

2. If writing partial integration, then those terms may not be contradicted, but consistent additional terms admissible. E.g., *Barney v. Andy*: Woman buys house under written contract; seller orally agrees to remove tree stump prior to closing. Held: Writing appeared to be a complete integration; however, tree stump arrangement could be collateral agreement. E.g., *Geer v. Mark*: Extrinsic evidence admitted to explain meaning of terms.

3. Question of Law: Judge uses extrinsic evidence to determine whether integrated.

4. Tests to Determine Completeness
   a. Four Corners Rule/Williston: Document is only evidence of whether or not integrated (strong parol evidence rule).
   b. Corbin/UCC 2-202/§213 Parol Evidence Rule: Evaluate all of the evidence ("soft" parol evidence rule). Exceptions: Naturally omitted terms? Could be separate agreement?
   c. UCC 2-202 Parol Evidence: Terms under which confirmatory memoranda agree become part of the contract and may not be contradicted by parole evidence but may be explained or supplemented by course of dealing, usage of trade, or by course of performance.

(Idea is to use circumstances, industry practices, etc., to establish the terms of the contract.)

    d. Merger Clauses: Upheld, unless in adhesion contracts.

D. Standardized Agreements (also called "form" agreements; in the extreme, these are called "contracts of adhesion")

    1. Common Law: Where a party signs a writing and has reason to believe that like writings are regularly used, he adopts writing as an integrated agreement unless the other party has reason to believe that the party wouldn't sign if he understood or knew of particular terms.

        a. Form contracts are always interpreted against drafter.

        b. Court uses an objective standard in its analysis, e.g., "Would a reasonable person have interpreted the term this way?"

VIII. COMMERCIAL WARRANTIES AS ENFORCEABLE CONTRACTS

A. UCC 2-313 Express Warranty: Any fact or promise that relates to the goods creates an express warranty that goods conform to the promise.

B. UCC 2-314 Implied Warranty: If seller is a merchant, goods fit for purpose.

C. Exclusion or Modification of Warranties: Party excluding (typically the seller) must exclude conspicuously. E.g., *Towne v. Kaplan*: Waiver of warranty in adhesion contract involving limited market supply was against public policy. (Note: Today, state and federal statutes also govern the limitation of warranties.)

IX. OMITTED TERMS IN CONTRACTS AND HOW THEY ARE RESOLVED

A. Common Law: Omitted terms are usually decided by the court, based upon the parties' manifested intent.

B. UCC 2-306(1): Output contracts imply good faith and expectable range. A party can't exit for poor profitability and simply because that party made a bad deal.

C. UCC 2-306(2): Exclusive contract implies good faith to use best effort. E.g., dress designer signs exclusive with marketer and tries to get out of contract for lack of consideration. Court implies good faith effort on his part, which results in consideration.

D. UCC: Other terms. See analysis and discussion on the "battle of the forms" issue. Where forms agree, contract is formed. Conflicting terms are discarded. Remaining "gaps" are filled with UCC provisions.

X. THE CONTRACTUAL DUTY OF GOOD FAITH AND FAIR DEALING

A. Common Law Good Faith, e.g., *Willis v. Tillis.* Parties are required to act in good faith and not try to escape their obligations on technicalities.

B. UCC 1-203, 201: Good faith means honesty in fact; Article 2 requires of merchants "reasonable commercial standards of fair dealing" (a higher standard than common law).

XI. PERFORMANCE AND BREACH: HAVE THE PARTIES KEPT THEIR OBLIGATIONS?

A. Common Law: Single completed performance, no payment until substantial completion (unless otherwise agreed). E.g., excavation work for mill building. P wanted payment monthly. Held: "Entire" contract, thus no payment until substantially completed. E.g., employment; no pay until work completed. (Note: Today, all construction contracts typically provide for progress payments, in which payments are made as progress is made in construction.)

B. Constructive Conditions of Exchange: Where two promises are exchanged, two performances are constructed. However, other promises may require an order of performance. E.g., silk business owner contracts to sell his business and refuses to turn it over because P can't furnish adequate security. Held: Implied condition of exchange. No security, no title.

C. Substantial Performance: No payment unless substantial performance; conversely, no withholding if substantially completed (construction, service contracts). However, court will not "construct" this condition if completed performance expressly stated. Further, other party can still offset damages.

D. Perfect Tender (Under UCC, anything less than perfect
   tender is breach, subject to sellers rights.)
   1. UCC 2-601: Goods, which fail in any respect; buyer can
      reject whole, accept whole, accept some and reject rest, or
      entire for being late.
   2. UCC 2-602: Buyer must seasonably notify.
   3. UCC 2-508: Seller may cure if time for performance has
      not yet expired.
   4. UCC 2-608: Buyer who has accepted, thinking seller would
      cure, may revoke seasonably.
   5. UCC 2-714: Buyer may recover damages for nonconform-
      ing goods accepted.
   6. UCC 2-715: Plus incidental and consequential damages.
   7. UCC 1-203: Buyer must act in good faith.
   8. UCC 2-103: Must observe reasonable standard of fair deal-
      ing in the trade.
E. Material and Nonmaterial Breach:
   1. Common Law: Material breach; treated as a non-
      occurrence of a condition. Performance excused (party
      may suspend performance and sue for damages from
      total breach), unless cured or cure expected (then party
      may suspend performance until cured, sue for partial
      breach, i.e., damages for being late). E.g., *Dumy v. Klutz*:
      Contractor runs bulldozer into P's house. P stops paying
      contractor. Held: Contractor breached "material" clause
      for "workmanlike" behavior, thus stopping payment was
      allowed.
   2. Nonmaterial: Performance unexcused.
F. Anticipatory Repudiation: Normally, a party cannot sue until
   the contract is actually breached. However, if it becomes
   clear that a party does not intend to perform its obligations, the other party can sue and possibly terminate its own
   performance.
   1. Common Law: Anticipatory repudiation may be total
      breach, just as failure to perform.
   2. UCC 2-609: Insecurity; right to adequate assurances.

XII. CONDITIONS PRECEDENT TO CONTRACT FORMATION
AND SUBSEQUENT PERFORMANCE
   A. Conditions are generally defensive. They are typically
      asserted by the defendant to show that his duty to perform
      never arose, because the condition was not satisfied. A
      condition either creates or discharges a duty under a
      contract, based on its occurrence or nonoccurrence. A
      promise, on the other hand, is a duty in and of itself, and
      its breach creates damages. E.g., *Farmer v. Dell*: Farmer has
      insurance contract and loses crop. Clause in insurance
      contract says "insurance company must inspect," Farmer
      fails to allow inspection. Held: This was a breach of a
      promise, not a condition precedent to payment. Farmer
      can sue for damages.
   B. Contracts are typically interpreted in favor of a promise,
      rather than a condition.
   C. Constructive Condition: Court will create, in interest of
      fairness, without regard to parties intentions (can include
      concurrent or precedent, to avoid "you go first"), must be
      substantially performed. (Frequently, no duty to pay until
      other side performs.) E.g., in construction contracts, if
      contractor substantially performs, then duty to pay. Can
      sue for remaining performance or deficient performance
      as damages.
   D. Express Conditions: Expressed as term of contract ("provided
      that," "if," "upon the condition that"). Must be fully per-
      formed. E.g., you promise to mow my lawn. I promise to pay
      you. I will not pay you until you mow (express condition).
   E. Implied Conditions: Implied in order to effect performance
      by other party.
   F. Constructive Condition: Failure of a condition means no duty
      has arisen.

XIII. REASONS FOR THE EXCUSE OF CONDITIONS
   A. Waivers: A voluntary relinquishment of a known right.
      1. Estoppel Waiver: Court will impose where reliance.

2. Different than modifications.
3. Election Waiver: Can elect to waive nonmaterial conditions.
4. Cannot waive performance.
5. Cannot be used to impose new conditions.
6. Revocable, unless other party has changed position.
7. Although an agreement specifies no modifications unless in writing, they may be allowed if orally or tacitly waived. E.g., contract to build motel. P's agent orally agrees to pay for extra work. Held: Waived.

B. Tender of Performance
C. Excuse of condition by impossibility. E.g., letter from city engineer required in contract; however, he doesn't do letters. Held: Condition excused due to impossibility.
D. Excuse of condition by forfeiture: Like unconscionability, occurs when a contractor substantially performs, but not to the letter of an express condition. A court will typically excuse the condition rather than total.

XIV. DEFENSES TO ENFORCEMENT OF A CONTRACT— MISTAKE, FRUSTRATION OF PURPOSE, IMPOSSIBILITY
A. Fraud/Misrepresentation: If one party is induced into action, then voidable. If a party was tricked, then no contract. No duty to disclose, unless fiduciary or special position.
1. Restatement §161 Where Nondisclosure Is Equivalent to an Assertion: Nondisclosure of a material fact which party knows other party is mistaken about is equivalent to misrepresentation (bad faith). E.g., *Jones v. Jones*: House seller, when asked about whether foundation had shifted, said it was okay. Held: Under the contract, there was no duty to disclose but once asked, duty to answer honestly. (Note: Most states today have enacted "seller disclosure" laws for the sale of residential real estate.) *Seymor v. Jane*: Sister sold brother land cheaply. Held: Because he handled her financial affairs, he had a fiduciary duty to advise her the price was too low.

B. Common Law When a Misrepresentation Is Fraudulent or Material: A misrepresentation is fraudulent if the maker intends his assertion to induce a party to manifest his assent and the maker so relies.

C. Common Law When Misrepresentation Prevents Formation of a Contract: If a misrepresentation as to the character or essential terms of a proposed contract induces conduct that appears to be a manifestation of assent by one who neither knows nor has reasonable opportunity to know of the character or essential terms of the proposed contract, his conduct is not effective as a manifestation of assent.

D. Common Law When a Misrepresentation Makes a Contract Voidable: If a party's assent is induced by either a fraudulent or material misrepresentation, then the contract is voidable.

E. UCC 1-203: Duty of Good Faith
   1. Ambiguity/Indefiniteness
   2. Williston: Reasonable person standard (nonintegrated), four corners (integrated). If ambiguous, then no contract. However, if one party knew of ambiguity and that other party interpreted one way, then contract is that way. E.g., *Ruffles v. Houscman*: Two ships named Titanic; each party thought referring to other ship.

F. UCC 2-204: Formation in General: Contract won't fail for indefiniteness if parties intended to contract and terms can be filled in.
   1. UCC 2-305: Open Price Terms: The parties if they so intend can conclude a contract for sale even though the price is not settled. In such a case, the price is a reasonable price at the time for delivery.
   2. Duress: Express or implied improper threat that overcomes free will of party.
      a. Subjective Standard: Did person actually feel threatened?
      b. If economic, then an objective standard. Economic duress requires extremely high standard.
         i. Was there a reasonable alternative?
      c. Threat not to engage in business.

    d. Threat to commit criminal act, blackmail.

    e. Threat to terminate an at-will employee for refusal to participate in wrongful conduct. E.g., QA mgr. refuses to falsify data.

3. Undue Influence

4. Breach of fiduciary relationship. P not so lacking capacity, nor duress; this is a middle ground.

5. Incapacity

    a. Minors: Can affirm contract at majority.

    b. Incompetents, drunks: However, a drunk who offers to sell his property will be held to offer if reasonable, from an objective viewpoint.

6. Mistake: Relates to basic assumption of contract, makes it voidable. Typically, misidentification of property by both parties. However, if parties assigned risk, not voidable. E.g., *Sherwood v. Walker*: Both parties thought that the champion horse was barren, which was untrue. Held: No enforceable contract. E.g., "rare" coin sold by a dealer to a dealer; selling dealer thought coin was worthless. Held: Mistake. E.g., contract to dig hole, hits rock. Held: Parties did not assign risk of what happens when rock hit; therefore, contract was void.

    a. Restatements of the Law on Contracts View of Mistake: Mistake by both parties is voidable by adversely affected party, unless he bears risk per contract or court assigns to him for justice.

        i. Generally, harder to escape unilateral mistake w/ exception of clerical bid errors from contractor or where offeree has reason to know of mistake. If other party induced mistake, then potential misrepresentation. Cannot "snap up" an opportunity. E.g., *Boris v. Karloff*: Honest clerical error. District had reason to know.

        ii. One view: Let losses fall where they land.

        iii. In other cases, where one party simply has better info or expertise, then no mistake. The court will not create a situation of fairness if both parties have opportunity for due diligence and one fails to do so.

7. Impossibility/ Frustration of Purpose: (Duty to perform excused.) Court asks: "Did parties assign risk?"
   a. UCC 2-613: Casualty to identified goods, before risk of loss passes, then K avoided.
   b. Must be unexpected occurrence, unassignment of risk expressly or by custom, and impossible to perform (where risks unassigned, courts let risk fall where it may). E.g., *Beth v. Andy*: K to rent hall for symphony performance, which burns down. Held: Object of K destroyed, so performance is impossible. E.g., *Henry v. Kravetz*: K to rent apt. to view coronation, which doesn't happen. Held: Purpose of K frustrated, so performance impossible.
   c. Party may recover for enrichment prior to destruction of improvements.
8. Commercial Impracticability: Rarely awarded because the parties can always find a way to fulfill their obligations.
   a. UCC 2-615: Excuse by Failure of Presupposed Conditions: Impracticability due to contingency unanticipated and goes to a basic assumption about K.
9. UCC 2-302: Unconscionability: Prevention of oppression and unfair surprises, one-sided as to be unconscionable (unfair bargaining power) question of law for the court. Fine print (terms unknown to one party). *Srygley v. Wells*: Cross collateralization clause.
   a. Common Law
      i. Question of Law: Employment contracts/covenant no to compete. Enforceable only if employee learned trade secrets or has knowledge of customers. Reasonable; only enforceable if they do not impose disproportionate hardship oppression and unfair surprise (unfair bargaining process or lopsided terms not unconscionable if knowingly and voluntarily assumed one-sided). E.g., *Waters v. Neal*: Woman buys furniture under contract w/ cross collateralization clause. Held to be unenforceable.
10. Statute of Frauds: Common law. (Note: This comes up anytime someone tries to enforce an oral agreement.

Should always consider whether a contract must be in writing to be enforceable.) (Note: Makes K voidable, not void.) E.g., *Gilbert's v. Aspen*: Agreement to buy and sell pork was on a transaction to transaction basis; hence, no writing required. Further, terminable at will. (Note: Party may still be able to sue for restitution.)

    a. Real Property: Liens, option contracts (promise to pay a broker not required).

    b. Promises in consideration of marriage (not mutual promises to marry).

    c. Contracts that can't be performed within one year of the day of making. (However, if any possibility that can be performed within one year, then no requirement.)

    d. Writing must contain:
       i. Signatures of parties to be charged
       ii. Subject matter of the contract
       iii. Essential terms and conditions

XV. THIRD PARTY BENEFICIARIES
    A. Restatements I: Creditor and donee beneficiaries may recover; incidental beneficiaries may not.
      1. Test for incidental beneficiary is whether donor intended to benefit. If not, then incidental beneficiary.
    B. Restatements 2d (what was the intent of parties?)
    C. Express agreement
    D. Benefit "runs" to beneficiary, then not incidental

XVI. ASSIGNMENT AND DELEGATION OF RIGHTS AND OBLIGATIONS UNDER A CONTRACT
    A. Assignment of Rights: All rights assignable, unless they would materially change duty of obligor or the risks. E.g., personal service contracts, requirements contracts, insurance policies, credit.
    B. Delegation of duties. Duties may or may not be assignable.

XVII. DAMAGES (Philosophy: money damages wholly adequate, "promotes efficiency," unless equitable relief ordered.)

A. Expectation: Contract price, benefit of bargain, consequential damages (foreseeable only), plus incidentals. However, if cost to complete is disproportionate, then market value. Also, some courts will allow subjective value. E.g., botched hand surgery: value of hand if done right, less value of actual hand. Grain seller who breaches to benefit of buyer: expectation damages "0."

   1. Several ways to look at expectation damages:
      a. Value expected plus expenditures made. E.g., contractor builds house partially, buyer breaches. Expectation damages equal expected profit plus $ spent.
      b. Contract price, less cost avoided. If contractor breaches, then cost to complete work.
   2. Sale of goods: buyer breach.

B. Market Damages
   1. UCC 2-708: Lost profits. E.g., boat buyer breaches, seller resells. Could have sold two, so lost profits.
   2. UCC 2-706: Resale or 2-709: Action for the price if unable. Sale of goods: seller breach.
   3. UCC2-602: Seasonable notification.
   4. UCC 2-712: Cover without unreasonable delay.
   5. Difference between price at contract and current market.

C. Reliance: Expenditures in reliance on contract. Used if expectation damages cannot be proven, e.g., future profits too speculative. Puts nonbreaching party in pre-promise position. Includes preparation for performance. E.g., botched surgery; reliance to P is cost of surgery, plus pain and suffering from "repair" surgery.

D. Restitution: Value gained. Compels D to restore benefit realized that P conferred.

E. Breaching Plaintiff
   1. UCC 2-714(2): Value of goods as warranted less value of goods received. E.g., employee breaches K. Can recover value of work performed.
   2. Common Law: Breaching party entitled to benefit conferred less loss caused by own breach. E.g., a buyer of land breaches, sues to recover down payment. Can recover if

can prove seller not damaged. E.g., contractor breaches because of dispute on crane rental. Can recover value of service rendered.

3. Buyer pays in advance, seller doesn't deliver; simpler to just get $ back.

F. Liquidated Damages (predetermined by terms of contract)

1. Must be reasonable estimate at time contract is formed. Damages difficult to estimate. If arbitrary, then a penalty and unenforceable. E.g., city sets damages (performance bond) for late completion which are very high, when actual cost to city is nominal.

G. An agreement to limit damages is enforceable. E.g., alarm company limits damages to $500.

H. Specific performance (equitable remedy). UCC 2-716: specific performance or replevin.

1. Money damages are inadequate.
2. Unique goods involved.
3. Buyer unable to cover for nonperformance.
4. Typically not awarded in service contracts.
5. Contracts for the sale of real estate.

I. Limitations on Damages

1. Consequential Damages. E.g., *Tommy v. Julie.* Damages limited to foreseeable; (1) reasonable at time of contract formation or (2) within contemplation of parties.

2. Damages Must Have Degree of Certainty: E.g., future profits are too speculative to be determined and awarded.

3. Mitigation: Nonbreaching party cannot recover losses that he could have avoided.

4. Employment Contracts: Duty to seek other employment, doesn't have to be lesser work. E.g., movie star doesn't have to take on bad movie, especially given that he had acted in big-budget "A" flicks previously and had a reputation to uphold.

5. Construction Contracts: Builder can't continue work even though client clearly indicated that deal is over. E.g., bridge builder keeps on even though city hall says "no deal."

6. Diminution in value (may not be claimed where breach is willful) versus cost to complete performance.
    a. E.g., tenant agrees to restore grade, breaches. Held: Although value of land was sig. less, tenant must pay cost to regrade.

Sample Capstone Outline for Contracts

YOUR CAPSTONE OUTLINE IS the most brief synopsis of the course and will be generally no longer than a few pages. You should begin to develop your Capstone Outline about two to three weeks prior to the exam. At this point, you will truly begin to make the material you have developed over the semester your own. The objective is to develop a document that is a memory trigger for the vast amount of information you have assimilated through the Pyramid Outline Method.

Your Pyramid Outline has reduced your Base Outline (which contains all of your reading, class notes, commercial outline information, and other reading) by about two-thirds. Your Capstone Outline will reduce your Pyramid Outline down to two or three pages.

Upon completion of your Capstone Outline, you should be relatively close to having the entire course material committed to memory. Having the essence of the subject distilled and memorized will be of tremendous value as you read the exam fact pattern, spot issues, and analyze the issues.

CONTRACTS

I.   FORMATION OF AN ENFORCEABLE AGREEMENT,
      CONSIDERATION, AND BARGAINED-FOR EXCHANGE
      A. Common Law Consideration: Legal detriment incurred
          by promisee in exchange for promised benefit; adequacy
          irrelevant. Manifestation of mutual assent determined under
          objective standard.
      B. UCC 2-204: Contract made in any manner showing agree-
          ment; no consideration required, only a writing signed by
          both parties.
      C. UCC 2-201: Statute of Frauds: Contract must be memorial-
          ized in writing to be enforceable.
          1. UCC goods: $500 or more
          2. Sale of real property
          3. Agreements in consideration of marriage
          4. Contracts that can't be performed within one year

II.   ELEMENTS OF AN OFFER
      A. Common Law: "Mirror image" rule.
      B. Common Law: Offer fails for indefiniteness, i.e., advertise-
          ments are construed as invitations for an offer.
      C. Revocation: Common law—any time prior to acceptance.
          1. UCC 2-205: Offer which stays open by terms for period of
              time is not revocable.

III. ACCEPTANCE OF AN OFFER
      A. Common Law Mirror Image Rule: Counteroffer is a rejec-
          tion, cannot subsequently accept offer.
      B. UCC 2-206: An offer shall be construed as inviting acceptance
          in any reasonable manner including shipment. Silence is not
          acceptance (however, accepting goods is).
      C. Common Law Acceptance by Silence or Exercise of Domin-
          ion: Silence valid only in course of dealing or prearranged or
          acceptance of performance.
      D. UCC: Different or Additional Terms
          1. 2-207(1): Treats supplier acknowledgment as acceptance
              of purchaser's offer.

2. 2-207(2): Additional terms are treated as proposals for K, accepted unless purchaser rejects or they materially alter K.
3. Common Law: If buyer accepts goods, then last terms apply (last shot rule).

IV.   MODIFICATION OF CONTRACTS
A. Common Law: Preexisting duty rule.
B. UCC 2-209: An agreement, in writing, to modify is binding, no consideration required.

V.   CONTRACT INTERPRETATION AND THE MISSING TERMS PROBLEM
A. Common Law: Intent of parties
B. Parol Evidence Rule: Admissibility/exclusion of written and oral evidence regarding contract. Was this a final expression or merely a draft?
    1. Restatements §209: Integrated Agreement: An integrated agreement is a writing or writings constituting a final expression of one or more terms of an agreement.
C. UCC 2-306(1): Output K implies good faith and expectable range. Exclusive K implies good faith to use best effort.

VI.   COMMERCIAL WARRANTIES IN CONTRACTS
A. UCC 2-313 Express Warranty: Any fact or promise that relates to the goods creates an express warranty that goods conform to the promise.
B. UCC 2-314 Implied Warranty: If seller is a merchant, goods fit for purpose.
C. Exclusion or Modification of Warranties: Must be conspicuous.

VII.   PERFORMANCE AND BREACH (OBLIGATION OF GOOD FAITH AND FAIR DEALING)
A. Common Law Order of Performances: No payment until substantial completion.
B. Common Law Substantial Performance: No payment unless substantial performance; conversely, no withholding if substantially completed.

    C. Common Law Perfect Tender Rule: Anything less than perfect tender is breach.

       1. UCC 2-601: Goods, which fail in any respect; buyer can reject whole, accept whole, accept some, and reject rest.

       2. UCC 2-602: Buyer must seasonably notify.

       3. UCC 2-508: Seller may cure if time for performance not expired.

       4. UCC 2-608: Buyer who has accepted, thinking seller would cure, may revoke.

       5. UCC 2-714: Buyer may recover damages for nonconforming goods accepted.

       6. UCC 2-715: Plus incidental and consequential damages.

       7. UCC 1-203: Buyer must act in good faith.

       8. UCC 2-103: Must observe reasonable standard of fair dealing.

    D. Material and Nonmaterial Breach

       1. Restatements §235: Material; performance excused (party may suspend performance and sue for damages from total breach), party may suspend performance until cured.

       2. Nonmaterial: Performance unexcused.

       3. Anticipatory Repudiation: May be treated as total breach.

       4. UCC 2-609: Insecurity; right to adequate assurances.

VIII.   CONDITIONS TO PERFORMANCE

    A. Express Conditions: Expressed as term of contract. Must be fully performed.

    B. Implied Conditions

    C. Excuse of Condition by Impossibility

    D. Excuse of Condition by Forfeiture

IX.   DEFENSES TO CONTRACT FORMATION

    A. Common Law Misrepresentation: A misrepresentation is fraudulent if the maker intends his assertion to induce a party to manifest his assent.

    B. UCC 2-204: Formation in General and Indefiniteness: Contract won't fail for indefiniteness if parties intended to contract and terms can be filled in.

C. Common Law Duress: Express or implied improper threat.

D. Common Law Undue Influence

E. Incapacity: Minors: Can affirm or void at majority.

F. Mistake: Relates to basic assumption, makes K voidable.

G. Impossibility/Frustration of Purpose (duty to perform excused)

H. Unconscionability

X. THIRD PARTY BENEFICIARIES

A. Common law creditor and donee beneficiaries may recover; incidental beneficiaries may not.

XI. ASSIGNMENT AND DELEGATION

A. Assignment of Rights: All rights assignable, unless they would materially change duty of obligor or the risks.

B. Delegation of Duties: Duties may or may not be assignable, depending upon their materiality.

XII. DAMAGES

A. Expectation: Contract price, benefit of bargain, consequential damages (foreseeable only), plus incidentals hand.

B. Reliance: Expenditures in reliance on contract.

C. Restitution: Value gained.

D. Liquidated Damages: Must be reasonable estimate at time of K.

E. Specific Performance: Money damages inadequate.

F. Limitations on Damages

1. Consequential Damages

2. Certainty

3. Duty to Mitigate

Appendix D

Sample First-Year Pyramid Outline for Criminal Law

THIS OUTLINE IS INCLUDED to show the contrasting principles between the Model Penal Code (MPC) and the common law. Similar to the tension between the common law and the Uniform Commercial Code in contract law (as illustrated in Appendix A), this outline may also help you understand how these competing principles affect criminal law. This presents perfect opportunities for analysis on law school exams using the "on the one hand/on the other hand" principle described previously in this book. Additionally, most first-year subjects deal with majority/minority common law principles, presenting further opportunity for discussion.

The most important thing to remember, as you prepare your outlines, is that the body of law contains these competing principles, which should both be discussed on your exam answers. Do not assume, for example, that because the MPC has become law in most states, that an exam fact pattern assumes this reality. Instead, an A exam assumes almost nothing and explains both principles in its analysis of a legal issue presented. Always remember to show your analysis!

CRIMINAL LAW

The analysis of a criminal action is similar to that of a tort civil action. Generally, an offending act is required, as well as the requisite intent formation on the part of the actor. The question, however, is whether the actor's act rises to such a level that society has deemed it to be offensive enough to be punishable by the state. In tort theory, the only question is whether the plaintiff should recover monetarily from the defendant.

I.   THEORIES OF SOCIETAL PUNISHMENT AND THEIR EFFECT ON CRIMINAL LAW
  A. Retribution Theory
      1. Requires free choice: otherwise why punish?
      2. Requires responsible actor: can't punish those who don't appreciate consequences of their actions.
      3. "Just" punishment varies with harm caused, state of mind of actor; "grading." (How much is "just" punishment?)
  B. Societal Utility Theory
      1. Deterrence Theory
         a. Assumes rational actor.
         b. Assumes that penalty is known and something actor would like to avoid.
         c. Counter: does it really work?
      2. Incapacitation of the Criminal Theory
         a. Based on predictions of dangerousness.
      3. Rehabilitation of the Criminal Theory
         a. Based on predictions of behavioral improvement.

II.   BURDENS OF PROOF AND PRODUCTION IN A CRIMINAL ACTION
  A. Burden of Production: The prosecution has burden to file document with essential elements of crime and basic facts supporting it, in order to overcome a directed verdict.

B. Defendant has burden of producing evidence to support affirmative defense.

C. Burden of Proof Quantum: Enough evidence that each element can be proven beyond a reasonable doubt.

III. USE OF PRESUMPTIONS IN A CRIMINAL PROSECUTION

A. Presumptions are rules which a court uses to allow a jury to make inferences based upon facts.

IV. ELEMENTS OF A CRIME

A. The *Actus Reus* Requirement

1. Common law and the MPC generally require three ingredients of a crime: (1) A voluntary (volitional movement of the body) (2) act (merely a muscular contraction), (or omission: failure to perform a voluntary act that one has a legal duty to perform), (3) that causes (4) social harm.

2. Omission: Criminal liability only where there is a duty to act.

a. Some states have enacted Good Samaritan statutes, which establish statutory duty to rescue, etc.

b. Creation of risk by D, contractual relationship, D isolates.

c. Voluntary assumption of duty creates duty to use reasonable care and to continue once begun.

d. Status relationship (in some cases, spouse, parents, doctor, etc.). The question in omission cases is always: "Where do you draw the line?"

i. *Frickle v. Fracke.* Marital relationship creates a duty of care between spouses. (Note: Courts are mixed on this, and whether there is a duty is very fact dependent.)

3. Society will not punish thoughts alone; there must be action.

4. "Status crimes" violate Eighth Amendment prohibition against cruel and unusual punishment. These are crimes for being someone or something.

5. The Essential Requirement of a Voluntary Act by the Defendant
   a. For criminal liability, the conduct must be voluntary.
   b. *Drunkman v. State:* Drunk man not guilty of public drunkenness because police put him in public.
   c. Excludes: Physically coerced movement, reflex movements, muscular contractions produced by disease, unconsciousness, somnambulism, hypoglycemia, etc.
   d. Involuntary Act in a Voluntary Course of Conduct: Knowing you are epileptic, foregoing medicine, and driving anyway.
B. Analysis of the Causation Element in a Criminal Prosecution
   1. "But for" cause: The crime would not have occurred "but for" the defendant's act.
   2. Proximate cause: The defendant's actions were such that he should be held criminally liable, even though there were intervening events in the causation chain.
C. The *Mens Rea* Requirement
   Two Meanings:
   1. Broad Meaning: Culpable mental state—literally "a guilty mind."
   2. Elemental Meaning: The mental requirement for each element of the offense.
      a. Specific Intent: Definition of the offense (1) includes an intent to do some future *act* or *cause* some further *result* beyond the conduct or result that constitutes the *actus reus* of the offense or (2) provides that the actor must be aware of a statutory attendant *circumstance.* (An offense that does not contain either of these features is termed "general intent.") E.g., burglary: "breaking and entering of the dwelling of another in the nighttime with intent to commit a felony"; the *actus reus* is merely breaking and entering, while the *mens rea* pertains to the future act, hence it is a specific intent crime. On the other hand, battery is intentional application of unlawful force upon another. This is general intent because the actor isn't applying force necessarily for

any reason. (Note: There must be a *mens rea* for the *conduct, circumstance,* and *result.*)

b. General Intent: Anything not specific intent; often describes negligence and possibly recklessness. Only requirement is that D intended to commit the act. General intent may be inferred from the fact that D engaged in proscribed conduct (one who voluntarily does an act is presumed to have intended that act; however, if judge instructs jury that the law presumes that a person intends the ordinary consequences of his voluntary acts, this may be held to violate his right to due process). (Note: If a statute is vague or silent regarding intent, a court will default to general intent; negligence as minimum *mens rea* requirement.)

c. Compare Motive (reason for committing crime): Not essential to establish liability. Contrary to popular television myth, a prosecutor need not establish a motive in order to convict. Instead, a motive can be useful to show intent.

d. Criminal Negligence: Done without an awareness of the facts, but done with gross lack of care. (Note: This is a higher standard than for civil negligence.)

e. Transferred Intent: Where the contemplated harm is criminal and there is great similarity between the harm and the result that actually occurs, D will be treated legally as though he had contemplated the result that occurred.

D. Concurrence of *Actus Reus* and *Mens Rea*

1. D must have requisite intent at the moment he performed the act. (E.g., D breaks into dwelling for purpose of shelter. Once inside, decides to steal jewels. Not burglary because the intent to commit a felony was formed after D was inside.)

2. Concurrence between *mens rea* and result: if crime requires proof of a result, prosecutor must prove that it was as a result of the *mens rea.*

E. MPC § 202: Takes an "elemental" approach and provides that
(w/ exception of "violations") a person may not
be convicted of an offense unless "he acted purposely,
knowingly, recklessly, or negligently, as the law may require,
with respect to each material element of the offense." (The
prosecution must prove that D committed the *actus reus* and
each ingredient of the offense with the mental culpability
defined in the statute.)

1. Purposely (with desire): If the element involves the nature
of his conduct or a result thereof, it is his *conscious object*
to engage in conduct or obtain result, and if the element
involves the attendant circumstances, he is aware of the
existence of the circumstances or he believes or hopes
that they exist.

2. Knowingly (with awareness of a certainty): If the element involves the nature of his conduct or the attendant
circumstances, he is aware that his conduct is of that
nature or that such circumstances exist, and if the element involves a result of his conduct, he is aware that it is
practically certain that his conduct will cause such a result.

3. Recklessly (with awareness of a high risk): A person acts
recklessly with respect to a material element of an offense
when he consciously disregards a substantial and unjustifiable risk that the material element exists or will result
from his conduct. The risk must be of such a nature and
degree that, considering the nature and purpose of the
actor's conduct and the circumstances known to him, its
disregard involves a gross deviation from the standard of
conduct that a law-abiding person would observe in the
actor's situation.

4. Negligently (existence of high risk, should have awareness): A person acts negligently with respect to a material
element of an offense when he should be aware of a
substantial and unjustifiable risk that the material element exists or will result from his conduct. The risk must
be of such a nature and degree that the actor's failure
to perceive it, considering the nature and purpose of his

conduct and the circumstances known to him, involves a gross deviation from the standard of care that a reasonable person would observe in the actor's situation.

5. Offense Silent as to *Mens Rea*: § 2.02(3) establishes *recklessness* as minimum for every element of the offense.

6. Hierarchy: §2.02(5): If negligence is required, then purposely, knowingly, or recklessly will suffice, etc.

F. Strict Liability (exception to *mens rea* requirement)

1. Common Law Presumption: No liability unless:

   a. Express Provision: In statute (Note: The criminal law's tradition of requiring *mens rea* and the likelihood that the legislature would have followed require that one arguing for strict liability has burden of proving that it was legislature's intent.)

      i. New statutory offense

      ii. Doesn't involve infringement on personal rights

      iii. Relatively light penalty

   b. Factors suggesting not legislative intent to impose strict liability:

      i. Crime closely resembles traditional common law offense.

      ii. Serious risk of convicting entirely innocent persons.

      iii. Constitutional considerations.

   c. Public Welfare Offenses: Traffic offenses, food & drug, sale of alcohol to a minor, firearms.

   d. Independent Moral Wrongs: An independent moral wrong would have been committed even if facts were as D believed them to be, i.e., statutory rape, bigamy.

2. Some courts have construed statutes lacking *mens rea* as having dispensed with it; thus, strict liability (controversial). However, some courts determine based upon size of penalty (the smaller the penalty, the more likely strict liability).

3. Constitutional Concerns

   a. No notice

   b. Grossly disproportional punishment

V.   DEFENSES
   A. Mistake of Fact (Negates *mens rea*; thus, not a true defense
      doctrine, like insanity; however, can prevent liability if it
      shows D lacked requisite *mens rea*.)
      1. Specific Intent Crimes: Fact question—whether D honestly
         knew required circumstances. (Honest mistake about
         circumstance = no awareness, no knowledge = not guilty.)
         (Some statutes require honest and reasonable mistake.)
      2. General Intent Crimes: Was the mistake reasonable?
        a. Honest and reasonable mistake = no negligence = not
           guilty.
        b. Honest but unreasonable mistake = negligence, could
           be guilty.
      3. Strict Liability: Mistake no defense.
   B. Ignorance or Mistake of Law
      1. Under the common law, "ignorance of the law was no
         excuse." ("Everyone is presumed to know the law." How-
         ever, counter is that today, the law is much more compli-
         cated; there are more *malum prohibitum* crimes.)
      2. Rationale: Sacrificing the individual for the public good.
      3. Exceptions
        a. Reasonable reliance on official statements of the law
           (however, conflict as to what constitutes "official state-
           ments"; in some cases, nothing less than state supreme
           court).
        b. Fair notice lacking (*Lambert*; D's right to due process
           was violated; however, most courts haven't followed).
        c. Knowledge express element in the crime: very rare.
        d. Food stamp offenses: Person must "knowingly" acquire
           food stamps in "any manner not authorized by the
           statute" in order to be guilty. Prosecution must prove
           that D knew enough about the statute to understand
           that his acquisition was against the statute.
      4. Problems with Maxim: Punishment without awareness is
         ineffective as a deterrent. Further, it is viewed as unfair.
         However, if you allowed ignorance as a defense, everyone
         would argue that they didn't know.

5. Analysis under MPC 2.02(9): "Neither knowledge nor recklessness or negligence as to whether conduct constitutes an offense or as to the existence, meaning or application of the law determining the elements of an offense is an element of such offense, unless the definition of the offense or the Code so provides."

C. Mistake of Noncriminal Law (or "different law" mistake)

1. Common Law

   a. Specific Intent Crimes: Mistake of noncriminal law, e.g., property law may negate specific intent. E.g., common law larceny is the "taking and carrying away the personal property of another with intent to deprive the owner of the property permanently." Woman takes her car from mechanic's garage, unaware of the lien, and mistakenly believing she had a right to take her car.

   b. General Intent Crimes: Not allowed because actor "should have known."

   c. Analysis under MPC § 2.04(1): Treats mistake of fact and noncriminal law the same. If it negates *mens rea* (specific intent), then no liability. (Note: Does not require reasonableness.)

D. Intoxication

1. Common Law

   a. General Intent Crimes: No defense, because D should have known.

   b. Specific Intent Crimes: Three Approaches
      i. No defense
      ii. Defense if negates specific intent
      iii. Defense if negates specific intent and D has burden of persuasion

   c. Analysis under MPC 2.08(2): Not a defense if *mens rea* is reckless.
      i. 2.08(4): May be a defense if not self-induced or pathological and negates appreciation of criminality or disables actor's ability to conform to law.

VI. THE CRIME OF ATTEMPT
   A. Inchoate: Activity after the formation of *mens rea* but short of attainment of the criminal goal.
   B. Until the MPC, most states punished but did not define attempt: "a criminal attempt occurs when a person, with the intent to commit an offense, performs any act that constitutes a substantial step toward the commission of that offense."
   C. Many crimes today were formerly attempt crimes: assault (attempted battery), burglary, etc. Courts are split on whether attempted assault is a criminal offense.
   D. Attempt is a specific intent crime, even though target offense may only require general intent.
   E. An attempt to commit a felony is graded as a felony but typically treated as a lesser offense. A person may not be convicted of both the attempt and the target offense; attempt merges with the target offense.
   F. *Mens Rea* Required
      1. The actor must intentionally commit the *actus reus* of an attempt.
      2. She must commit the *actus reus* with the specific intention of committing the substantive offense. (As a result, impossible to commit an attempt negligently or recklessly.)
      3. Result Crimes: Crimes defined in terms of a result must be committed with the specific purpose of causing the result. (Therefore, a person who causes the result may be convicted of the target offense, although result is unintentional; whereas they would not be convicted of attempt; e.g., blindfolded person who shoots gun in room may be guilty of murder because of recklessness but not guilty of attempt if unsuccessful.)
      4. Attempted Felony Murder: Nearly all states have held that this is not a cognizable crime. This is because of the specific intent requirement of attempt.
      5. Strict Liability
   G. *Actus Reus*
      1. Very difficult to draw the line between perpetration and preparation.

2. Tests
   a. "Last Act" Test (old common law approach): Actor performed all acts she believed necessary to commit target offense, except crime does not result.
   b. "Physical Proximity" Test: Did actor's acts come so close to commission of target offense that there was a reasonable likelihood of success but for intervention of police?
   c. "Equivocality" Test: Attempt occurs when a person's conduct, standing alone, unambiguously manifests her criminal intent.
3. Analysis under MPC § 5.01 (significantly broadens liability for attempt)
   a. Purposely engages in conduct which would constitute crime if circumstances were as he believed them to be.
   b. Substantial step:
      i. Lying in wait, searching for victim, following victim
      ii. Enticing victim
      iii. Reconnoitering
      iv. Unlawful entry
      v. Possession of materials to be used in crime
H. Defenses (Note: These are not "true" defenses, like infancy, insanity, diminished capacity, and intoxication. Rather, these are bars to conviction if the prosecutor cannot prove beyond a reasonable doubt.)
   1. Impossibility
      a. Legal Impossibility *Is* a Defense to Attempt: Wouldn't be a crime if completed because it isn't against law, e.g., defendant attempts to sell "bootleg liquor" after Prohibition is repealed. (Legal impossibility is a defense under MPC and common law.)
      b. Factual Impossibility *Is Not* a Defense to Attempt: Wouldn't be a crime if completed because facts aren't as D believes, e.g., a pickpocket puts her hand in an empty pocket.
      c. Analysis under MPC § 5.01: Viewed from circumstances as D believed. § 5.01(1), § 5.05(2) permits grade to be reduced if conduct is so inherently unlikely to result

in a crime (toy pistol). A person is guilty of an attempt when, with intent to commit a crime, he engages in conduct that tends to effect the commission of such crime. It is no defense that, under the circumstances, the crime was factual or "if such crime could have been committed had the circumstances been as such person believed them to be."

    d. Analysis

        i. Was there no completed crime because facts were not as D believed? Go with what D believed for attempt. (E.g., D buys corn starch, thinking it is cocaine. D is guilty of attempt but not guilty of buying cocaine.)

        ii. Was there no completed crime because criminal law was not as D believed it to be? Go with what law really is. (E.g., D sells a real Picasso, thinking it is fake. D is guilty of attempted theft by deception.)

  2. Abandonment

    a. Common Law (Majority): Abandonment no defense.

    b. MPC and Minority: Abandonment is defense but only when complete and voluntary renunciation of criminal purpose.

VII. THE CRIME OF BEING AN ACCESSORY TO A CRIME

  A. Common Law (common law classifications were important for procedural purposes)

    1. Liability extends to anyone who has encouraged, assisted, or hindered apprehension.

    2. Accessories before/after the fact (lesser penalty): key distinction. (eliminated in MPC)

    3. Conviction of principal no longer required for accessory conviction.

    4. Innocent Agent: If primary dupes innocent agent into committing crime, he can be held liable as a primary.

    5. *Actus Reus*

      a. If omission is basis of accomplice liability, must have had duty to act.

      b. Mere presence is not enough, unless presence combined with failure to act = encouragement by assent (*Russell*).

      c. P need not be aware of A's assistance (*Tally*).

      d. Question is how much conduct is enough to constitute "aiding or encouraging" the primary actor.

B. *Mens Rea* (intent to aid and intent for the crime)

      a. Conduct Elements of D's Offense: It is not enough that A knows D will engage in conduct; A must wish D to engage in conduct., e.g., selling stolen silverware; "purposive attitude toward" principal's conduct.

      b. *Mens rea* for result required: Same level as D.

      c. Circumstance: Same level as D.

      d. Intent to aid P and aid has impact on actual perpetrator. (Note: Under MPC, attempt to aid is all that is required.)

C. Accessory After the Fact

      a. Commission of completed felony

      b. Knowledge of felony

      c. Aid to felon

D. Analysis under MPC §2.06(3)(a): A person is liable as an accomplice if:

      1. Purpose: With the purpose of promoting or facilitating the commission (help in planning or commission) of the offense, he:

        a. Solicits such other person to commit it.

        b. Aids or agrees or attempts to aid such other person in planning or committing it.

        c. Having a legal duty to prevent the commission of the offense, fails to make proper effort to do so.

      2. Result:(§ 2.06 (4)): Same as P.

      3. Circumstance: Same as P (however, not explicit in code).

      4. Attempted aid prohibited (unlike CL).

E. Defenses

      1. Common Law

        a. Withdrawal: Must be effective and timely.

        b. Inciter: Communication of renunciation sufficient.

        c. Abettor: Must countermand prior aid.

2. Analysis under MPC § 2.06(6)(c)
   a. Wholly depriving prior assistance of its effectiveness
   b. Providing timely warning to law enforcement
   c. Making proper effort to prevent commission of crime
3. Protected Classes: A person who is a member of the class the object offense is intended to protect cannot be convicted as an accessory (13 yr. old girl cannot be an accomplice to statutory rape).

VIII. ANALYSIS OF SPECIFIC CRIMES
A. Homicide
   1. Common Law Murder (keys are premeditation and deliberation)
      a. Intent to kill or knowledge that death would result (premeditation). (Intent is subjective: Prosecutor must prove that D formed intent to kill. This is inferred from conduct.)
      b. Intent to inflict grievous bodily harm (premeditation).
      c. "Depraved heart" or reckless indifference (non-premeditation).
      d. Death occurs during commission of a felony (non-premeditation).
      e. No degrees of common law murder (this was statutory).
   2. Common Law Manslaughter
      a. Voluntary: Sudden heat of passion engendered by adequate provocation. (Objective standard: would provocation render any reasonably prudent person incapable of cool reflection on an act that would otherwise be considered murder?) (However, there is a trend to subjectivize the standard.)
         i. Legally adequate provocation sufficient to mitigate intentional murder to manslaughter:
            • D assaulted by V.
            • D witnesses V assaulting relative/friend.
            • D witnesses unlawful arrest.
            • "Heat of passion."
            • No cooling time.

- Sufficient to provoke reasonable person to a state of passion/high emotion.
- D witnesses spouse in flagrente delicto.
- Never "mere words," gestures, harm to property.

   b. Involuntary: Reckless or grossly negligent behavior that didn't rise to level of murder. (E.g., baby develops tooth infection and dies; parents prosecuted.)

   c. Misdemeanor Manslaughter: Death occurs during commission of nonfelony.

3. What distinguishes manslaughter from extremely reckless murder?

   a. Obvious likelihood of death.

   b. Likelihood: high probability of death.

   c. Obvious that D was aware of risk.

   d. Vicious/depraved: no justification for disregard of risk.

4. Analysis of MPC § 210

   a. § 210.1: Homicide: Purposely, knowingly, recklessly, or negligently causes the death of another human.

   b. § 210.2: Murder: Purposely, knowingly, recklessly.

   c. §210.3: Manslaughter (replaces "provocation"): A homicide which would otherwise be murder is:

      i. Committed under the influence of extreme emotional or mental disturbance for which there is reasonable excuse from actor's situation under circumstances as he believes them to be (reasonable is subjective). (Note: Most states have rejected subjective standard and use objective standard.)

      ii. Committed recklessly

   d. §210.4: Negligent Homicide: Committed negligently

5. Felony Murder

   a. Traditional Common Law Rule: A person who commits any felony and all accomplices in that felony are guilty of murder if a death occurs during the commission or attempted commission of the felony (this is a form of strict liability, no inquiry into D's culpability).

   b. Only certain enumerated felonies, otherwise:

  i. Must be "inherently dangerous."(E.g., a felon carrying a gun is inherently dangerous.)
- Majority: abstract (can this be done safely?)
- Minority: looks at actual felony (was it dangerous?)

  ii. Enumerated first degree, unenumerated usually second degree.

  iii. Must not "merge": lower forms of homicide, i.e., manslaughter. (Otherwise, all killing would become felony murder under the "felony murder" rule.)

  iv. Felony (called "predicate felony") must be proximate cause of death.

  v. Downside: can have extremely harsh results for accidents and unintentional killings.

  vi. Limits based on who the criminal actor is
- Majority Rule: Agency approach (*Antick*)—killing must be committed by D or co-felon acting in furtherance of felony.
- Minority Rule: Proximate cause approach (*Canola*)—D is guilty of all foreseeable killings proximately caused by felonious activity.

  vii. Analysis of MPC § 210.2(1)(b)
- Has changed felony murder rule to a presumption:
  - Presumption of recklessness or extreme indifference to the value of human life
  - Presumed if killing occurs during commission of robbery, rape, deviant sexual intercourse, arson, burglary, kidnapping, or felonious escape

B. Rape
 1. Common Law
  a. General intent for each element: sexual penetration, by force, without consent.
  b. Sexual penetration by force or threat of force.

    i. Some courts required "earnest resistance" as proof of force (common law).

    ii. Some courts use fear as proof of force, thus no need to show resistance.

    iii. Threat by D causing reasonable fear of imminent bodily harm.

    iv. Extreme evolution of "force." Today, definitions of force are being expanded to include implicit threats of injury and threats of future injury. MTS: Rape is sexual assault without consent, the only force required is sexual penetration without affirmative and freely given permission (New Jersey).

    v. Without consent of V
- If D honestly and reasonably believed, mistakenly, that V had consented, may prevent conviction.
- Rape shield laws: many states have enacted laws preventing introduction of evidence of prior sexual conduct as evidence of probability of consent.
- Under common law, man could not be convicted of raping his wife.
- Because rape is a general intent crime, intoxication is no defense.

2. Analysis of MPC § 213: Force required.
3. Statutory Rape: Strict liability.
4. Analysis of MPC § 213 (1)(d): Imposes strict liability for statutory rape (< 10 yrs. old). However, "corruption of a minor" (213.(6)(1) "woman less than 16 yrs. old and man at least 4 yrs. older," places burden on D to prove that he "reasonably believed V to be above the critical age."

IX.   JUSTIFICATION AND EXCUSE (DIFFERENCE WAS SIGNIFICANT AT COMMON LAW BECAUSE JUSTIFIED ACTOR WAS ACQUITTED, WHILE EXCUSED ACTOR WAS STILL LIABLE, SUBJECT ONLY TO PARDON FROM CROWN)

A. True Defense: If proved, results in acquittal of D, although prosecutor has proved every element beyond a reasonable doubt. (Significance is that constitutionally, the legislature may allocate the burden of production and persuasion, regarding true defenses. Conversely, the prosecution bears the burden of disproving "D's failure of proof claim.")

B. Necessity: Basic common law principle of "choice among evils."

   1. Justification Defense (Note: This is a codification of CL defense of necessity): Conduct which would otherwise be criminal but which is socially acceptable, under the circumstances, and does not deserve criminal liability.

      a. D must establish:

         i. Clear and imminent harm.

         ii. No legal alternative.

         iii. Legislature had not precluded.

         iv. Defense not available if charged with murder.

C. Analysis of MPC § 3.02(1): Justification Generally: Choice of Evils (broader than CL: rejects imminence requirement)

   1. Harm or evil sought to prevent is greater than harm caused by preventing.

   2. Not precluded by law or statute.

   3. Actor didn't bring situation upon himself.

D. Defense against Aggression

   1. Self-Defense: Deadly force may be used if:

      a. D reasonably believes (CL—objective standard) that the use of deadly force is necessary (retreat may be required) to prevent deadly force (likely to cause death or serious bodily injury) by the aggressor.

      b. Imminent death or serious bodily harm.

      c. D is not the aggressor.

         i. D can lose aggressor status if V uses unreasonable force in response.

         ii. D retreats.

E. Analysis of MPC § 3.04: Use of Force in Self-Protection

   1. Immediately necessary

   2. Against unlawful force

a. Death

b. Serious bodily harm

c. Kidnapping

d. Sexual intercourse compelled by force or threats

3. Retreat unavailable

4. Actor believes:

a. Immediately necessary (Note: Some courts are relaxing imminency requirement and allow threat of future, inescapable danger.)

F. Effect of Mistake on Claims of Self-Defense

1. Requirement is honest and reasonable, even if hindsight reveals belief incorrect.

G. "Retreat" Rule: Some jurisdictions require D to retreat, if can be done safely.

1. Exception: Generally, no duty to retreat in one's home ("Castle" rule).

2. Excuse Defense: Focus on the actor, e.g., insanity. While justification tries to show that the act was not wrongful, excuse focuses on the actor and tries to show that he is not morally culpable for his conduct.

Appendix E

First-Year Issues Checklist: Contracts

I SUGGEST THAT, FROM THE very beginning of the semester, you continually think about the issues that may be presented in an exam based upon the law that you are learning. Keep in mind that every case you read is based upon an issue of fact or law that is in dispute between the parties. How the court resolves the issue of law (for example, by adopting the majority position) or the issue of fact will often provide a clue as to the kinds of issues that your casebook editors and professor find important.

Developing an issues checklist will help you in two ways. First of all, the checklist will serve as a good memory prompter as you prepare for exams and as you eventually read through exam fact patterns. More importantly, however, the thought process that you will develop by continuously thinking about your issues list will help you to learn to anticipate potential issues and arguments, a key attribute of the successful law student and lawyer.

CONTRACTS CHECKLIST

1. Is there an enforceable agreement?
    A. Which is the applicable law—UCC or common law?
    B. Did the parties manifest mutual assent?
        1. Offer: Must be definite, revocable prior to acceptance.
            a. UCC 2-204: Requires qty. term.
            b. Quotes not offers.
            c. Option K: Rest 45: Part performance, purported consideration, not sham.
            d. UCC: If signed, not revocable (up to three mos.).
        2. Acceptance: "Mirror image rule," counter is rejection. Silence not acceptance, taking goods is. UCC 2-206: Any reasonable manner, 2-207 conduct.
    C. Is there consideration?
        1. Is this really a donative promise/detrimental reliance/ promissory estoppel?
            a. Rest 90: Expect /does induce reliance (consideration sub).
        2. Is this really past consideration?
            a. Rest 86: Paid if material benefit conferred, but not for "gift."
2. Is writing required for the contract to be enforceable?
    A. Statute of Frauds, 2-201: K's > 1yr., sale of land, goods ≥ \$500, oral agreement confirmed, not objected within ten days.
    B. Does the parol evidence rule come into plan? Did the parties intend the contract to be a final memo-rialization? Fully integrated? If not, then partial? (Additional consistent terms allowed.)
    C. Confirmatory Memoranda: "Last shot" UCC 2-207: Additional terms, proposal unless material; different terms "gap."
3. Can the contract be modified?
    A. Preexisting Duty: Needs new consideration (but can rescind).
    B. Rest 139: If "fair and equitable."
    C. UCC: No new consideration, in writing if SoF.

4. Can contract be defeated through defenses?
   A. Ambiguity
   B. Impossibility
   C. Frustration of Purpose
   D. Commercial Impracticability
   E. Unconscionability
   F. Duress
   G. Misrepresentation
   H. Mistake
   I. Capacity
   J. Conditions
   K. Good Faith
   L. Public Policy
5. How can I prove my position in the event of a contract dispute?
   A. Parol Evidence
   B. Perfect Tender
   C. Substantial Performance
   D. Constructive Conditions
   E. Course of Performance, Dealing, Usage of Trade
6. What if the other side appears to be contemplating or has threatened breach? anticipatory repudiation?
7. Is there a battle of the forms issue/duty to read?
8. How do I measure damages in the event of a breach?
   A. Expectation
   B. Reliance
   C. Restitution
   D. Liquidated Damages—Forseeability
9. Other remedies
   A. Specific Performance
10. Does the nonbreacher's duty to mitigate come into play?

Appendix F

First-Year Issues Checklist: Criminal Law

CRIMINAL LAW CHECKLIST

The prosecution must prove each element of the offense, as well as the purpose and circumstance (and any accompanying *mens rea*) where specified. (Therefore, if he does not meet this burden of proof, D is not liable.)

GENERAL ISSUES
1. What acts must the defendant have performed to be guilty? (*actus reus*)
2. What attendant circumstances must have existed for the acts to constitute a crime? Was D required to be aware of circumstances?
3. What state of mind must D have to be guilty? (*mens rea*)
   A. *Mens rea* for act: specific intent?
   B. Conscious and volitional act?
   C. No *mens rea*: strict liability?

4. Must there have been a concurrence of the *actus reus* and *mens rea*? (Must the act have been attributable to the state of mind required?)
5. Is there any particular result that must be shown?
6. Was D required to desire result?
7. Was D liable as an accomplice?

I. HOMICIDE
A. Murder
1. Did D act with a state of mind that is sufficient to establish malice aforethought?
2. Did D act with intent to kill?
3. Was killing premeditated? (frequently first degree)
4. Did D act with intent to cause serious bodily injury?
5. Did D act with awareness of high risk that death or serious bodily injury would result? (recklessness) ("depraved heart" second degree)
6. Was death caused during commission of a felony?
7. Was killing caused during commission of enumerated felonies? (frequently first degree) Otherwise, was killing inherently dangerous?
B. Manslaughter
1. If murder, was there adequate provocation?
2. Was there no "cooling off" period?
3. Did D act w/o malice aforethought but was negligent?
4. Was killing during commission of nonfelony unlawful act?
5. Was there but for causation?
6. Was there proximate causation?
C. Rape (general intent)
1. Resistance required?
2. Proof of force? Reasonable fear?
3. Lack of consent?
D. Attempt (specific intent)
1. Act required? (Was this mere "preparation" or was it attempt?)
2. Proximity Test: How close did D get to committing crime?
3. *Mens rea* required? (Attempt is a specific intent crime.)

E. Complicity
  1. Intent to assist?
  2. Intent that the primary party complete the offense?
F. Defenses to Completed Offenses
  1. Mistake of fact?
  2. Mistake of law? No defense.
  3. Mistake of noncriminal law?
  4. Intoxication?
      i.   Self-induced? No defense.
      ii. General intent crime? May be a defense.
  5. Duress?
  6. Insanity?
  7. Necessity?

Appendix G

Sample Legal Memorandum

THE FOLLOWING IS AN example of a typical law school memorandum exercise. The student is typically provided with a case file, which may include factual information and case law, which may or may not be applicable. The idea is to simulate a real-world project that a new associate might be assigned for a client. In law practice, generally a senior associate or partner will assign the work; hence, the memorandum is written for the purpose of providing objective information to the senior associate or partner, who would in turn use this information for the purpose of advising a client. (Please note: This memorandum is for illustrative purposes only. It is intended to show you the basic format of a legal memorandum and the reasoning process employed, which is commonly assigned to first-year law students. The law and citations contained herein are fictitious. Additionally, only the memorandum is provided; other accompanying documents that would ordinarily accompany a legal memorandum, such as a Fact Statement, are not included.)

MEMORANDUM

TO:	Senior Partner
FROM:	Associate
DATE:	November 15, 2010
RE:	Analysis of Client Liability for Purchase Price under Sales Agreement Dated May 1, 2009

I. QUESTION PRESENTED

Whether, under Michigan's adoption of the Uniform Commercial Code, the risk of loss of 30 hogs passed to our client, Betty Bond. They were destroyed after Dr. Joseph Brown had tendered delivery to Ms. Bond, but before she had taken physical possession of the hogs.

II. BRIEF ANSWER

Most likely, the risk of loss did not pass to our client. Under the Michigan adoption of the Uniform Commercial Code (the "Code"), the seller may recover the purchase price of "goods lost . . . after the risk of their loss has passed to the buyer." *Hogman v. Trough,* 230 A.B. 2d 311 (Mich. Civ. App. 1950). If the seller is a merchant then the risk of loss passes only when the buyer receives the goods. *Id.* at 312. Otherwise, the risk of loss passes when delivery of the goods is tendered. *Id.*

A merchant is a person who 1) holds himself out 2) as having knowledge or skill 3) particular to the practices involved in the transaction or 4) goods involved in the transaction. *Wayne v. Grayson,* 284 A.B. 2d 423 (Mich. Civ. App. 1958). In this case, Dr. Brown held himself out as having expertise in the birthing and raising of hogs. As a result, a court would most likely find that Dr. Brown retained the risk of loss of the goods.

III. FACTS

Betty Bond, the client, raises hogs and ostriches on her ranch in Lake Orion, Michigan. (Facts at 1.) Ms. Bond desired to expand her hog stock. (Facts at 6.) Because of the difficulty in birthing and raising hogs, Ms. Bond wanted to buy hogs, which were already a few months old. (Facts at 3.)

On July 4, 2008, she contacted Dr. Joseph Brown, a retired veterinarian who had operated a thriving practice in Muskegon, Michigan, and still owned a farm in the area. (Facts at 12.) Ms. Bond asked whether he would be interested in birthing 30 hogs, raising them until they were age three to six months, and selling them to her. (Facts at 12.) Ms. Bond also offered to sell Dr. Brown the equipment and supplies necessary to birth and raise the hogs. (Facts at 1.)

Ms. Bond and Dr. Brown subsequently signed a sales agreement. (Facts at 14.) Ms. Bond agreed to buy 30 hogs, each between three and six months old, at the prevailing market price. (Facts at 14.) Dr. Brown agreed to raise the hogs and tender delivery by October 15, 2009. (Facts at 14.) "Tender" was defined in the sales agreement as: 1) Dr. Brown making them available to Ms. Bond for immediate receipt at his ranch and 2) notifying Ms. Bond that they were available. (Facts at 14.) The sales agreement specified that the goods would be "deemed received when Buyer takes physical possession of them." (Facts at 10.) Ms. Bond paid $5,000 toward the purchase price and agreed to pay the balance within two days after Dr. Brown tendered delivery of the goods. (Facts at 14.) The agreement did not assign the risk of loss to either party and was silent in this regard. (Facts at 14.)

Dr. Brown bought the equipment and supplies from Ms. Bond, as well as some of the required eggs. (Facts at 9.) He renamed his ranch the "Jumpin' Jehosophat Hog Farm." (Facts at 9.) Dr. Brown successfully raised 30 hogs, each between three and six months old. (Facts at 9.)

On October 11, 2009, Dr. Brown notified Ms. Bond that the hogs were available for immediate receipt at his ranch, thus tendering delivery. The parties agreed that she would pick them up the next day. (Facts at 5.) Ms. Bond arrived at the Jumpin' Jehosophat Hog Farm the next day, ready to pick up the hogs. (Facts at 6.) However, before Ms. Bond could take physical possession of the hogs, a severe storm developed. (Facts at 7.) The storm killed the hogs. (Facts at 8.) Ms. Bond refuses to pay Dr. Brown because she never received the hogs. (Facts at 7.) Neither party had insurance to cover the loss. (Facts at 19.)

IV. ANALYSIS

A person is a merchant if: (1) By his occupation, he holds himself out as having knowledge or skill peculiar to the practices involved in the transaction or (2) by his occupation, he holds himself out as having knowledge or skill peculiar to the goods involved in the transaction. *Wayne v. Grayson*, 284 A.B. 2d 423 (Mich. Civ. App. 1958).

A.   Dr. Brown Held Himself Out as a "Merchant," as Defined under the Michigan Code

As a veterinarian and businessman, Dr. Brown "held himself out" as having knowledge of the business practices involved in the sales agreement, thus satisfying this definition of "merchant." In *Grayson*, the Michigan Supreme Court held that a person "holds himself out as having knowledge or skill" relative to the transaction in dispute solely through his occupation, using an objective standard. 284 A.B. 2d 423 (Mich. Civ. App. 1958). If a reasonable person would expect a person in the party's occupation to have knowledge or skill, relative to the practices involved in the business transaction, then the party is considered to have held himself out as having that knowledge or skill. *Id.*

In *Grayson*, the defendant was a wheat farmer who sold his crop once a year. *Id.* at 424. The defendant entered into an oral sales agreement to sell wheat to the plaintiff with a total value of about $18,000. *Id.* The court found that the defendant was a "merchant" as defined in the Michigan enactment of the Uniform Commercial Code. *Grayson* at 458 citing MCA § 2-207. As a result, the trial court found that the plaintiff's confirmation of the oral agreement resulted in an enforceable agreement. *Id.* at 459.

On appeal, the Michigan Supreme Court held that a reasonable person would expect an experienced wheat farmer to have "knowledge or skill," relative to the business of raising and selling wheat. *Grayson v. Wayne*, 285 A.B. 2d 336 (Mich. 1959). A person's actual knowledge or skill or any representations he may have made about them are irrelevant to the court's definition of merchant; instead, the question is how a reasonable person would view that person. *Id.* The defendant, by his occupation, held himself out as having "knowledge of nonspecialized business practices" and was therefore a "merchant." *Id.*

Similarly, in this case, Dr. Brown was a retired veterinarian and businessperson. He had operated a thriving solo companion animal practice for 30 years. (Facts at 16.) He also had business arrangements that generated income from his farm. (Facts at 16.) A reasonable person would view Dr. Brown as a "merchant." *Wayne* at 337. It was reasonable for Ms. Bond to infer that a person with Dr. Brown's knowledge and skill relative to business arrangements would adequately insure against the risk of loss.

Dr. Brown may argue that he was inexperienced in hog farming and therefore not a "merchant" as defined under the Code. Like the defendant in *Baxter*, who bought green chop for the first time, this was the first time he had attempted to raise hogs. *Baxter v. Ridden*, 275 A.B. 2d 336 (Mich. 1968). However, based upon all the facts and circumstances, a reasonable person would expect Dr. Brown to have knowledge and skill pertaining to hog farming. Dr. Brown, although a novice hog breeder, had significant business experience. He had operated a thriving solo veterinary practice for over 30 years and owned a commercial farm. (Facts at 17.) Further, the size of the transaction, and the fact that he renamed his farm Jumpin' Jehosophat Hog Farm, indicate that Dr. Brown viewed this as a serious business proposition. (Facts at 110.)

B.   Because Dr. Brown Was a Merchant, the Risk of Loss of the Hogs Did Not Pass to Ms. Bond

Under the Michigan adoption of the Code, the seller may recover the purchase price of "goods lost . . . after the risk of their loss has passed to the buyer." *Banner v. Ferigno*, 230 A.B. 2d 311 (Mich. Civ. App. 1950). As discussed in the prior section, if the seller is a "merchant" then the risk of loss passes only when the buyer receives the goods. *Id.* at 312. Otherwise, the risk of loss passes when delivery of the goods is tendered. *Id.*

In this case, Dr. Brown merely tendered delivery of the goods to our client. (Facts at 16.) The parties agreed that she would pick them up the next day. (Facts at 5.) Ms. Bond arrived at the Jumpin' Jehosphat Hog Farm the next day, ready to pick up the hogs. (Facts at 6.) However, before Ms. Bond could take physical possession of the hogs, a severe storm developed, which killed them. (Facts at 7–8.) Because Dr. Brown would be considered a "merchant," pursuant to the Code, the risk of loss did not pass to our client because she never received the hogs.

V.   CONCLUSION

Most likely, the risk of loss did not pass to our client, and she is therefore not liable for the hog loss. Under the Code, a seller may only recover the purchase price of "goods lost . . . after the risk of their loss has passed to the buyer." *Hogman v. Trough*, 230 A.B. 2d 311 (Mich. Civ. App. 1950). If the seller is a "merchant" then the risk of loss passes only when the buyer receives the goods. *Id.* at 312. A person is a "merchant" under the Code if he: (1) holds himself out (2) as having knowledge or skill (3) particular to the practices involved in the transaction or (4) goods involved in the transaction. *Wayne v. Grayson*, 284 A.B. 2d 423 (Mich. Civ. App. 1958). In this case, Dr. Brown held himself out as having expertise in the birthing and raising of hogs. As a result, a court would most likely find that Dr. Brown retained the risk of loss and therefore must absorb the tragic and unfortunate loss of the hogs in question.

Page numbers in *italics* refer to tables and figures.